THE ELEVENTH PILLAR

New York State and the Federal Constitution

Published under the direction of the American Historical Association from the income of the Albert J. Beveridge Memorial Fund.

For their zeal and beneficence in creating this fund the Association is indebted to many citizens of Indiana who desired to honor in this way the memory of a statesman and historian.

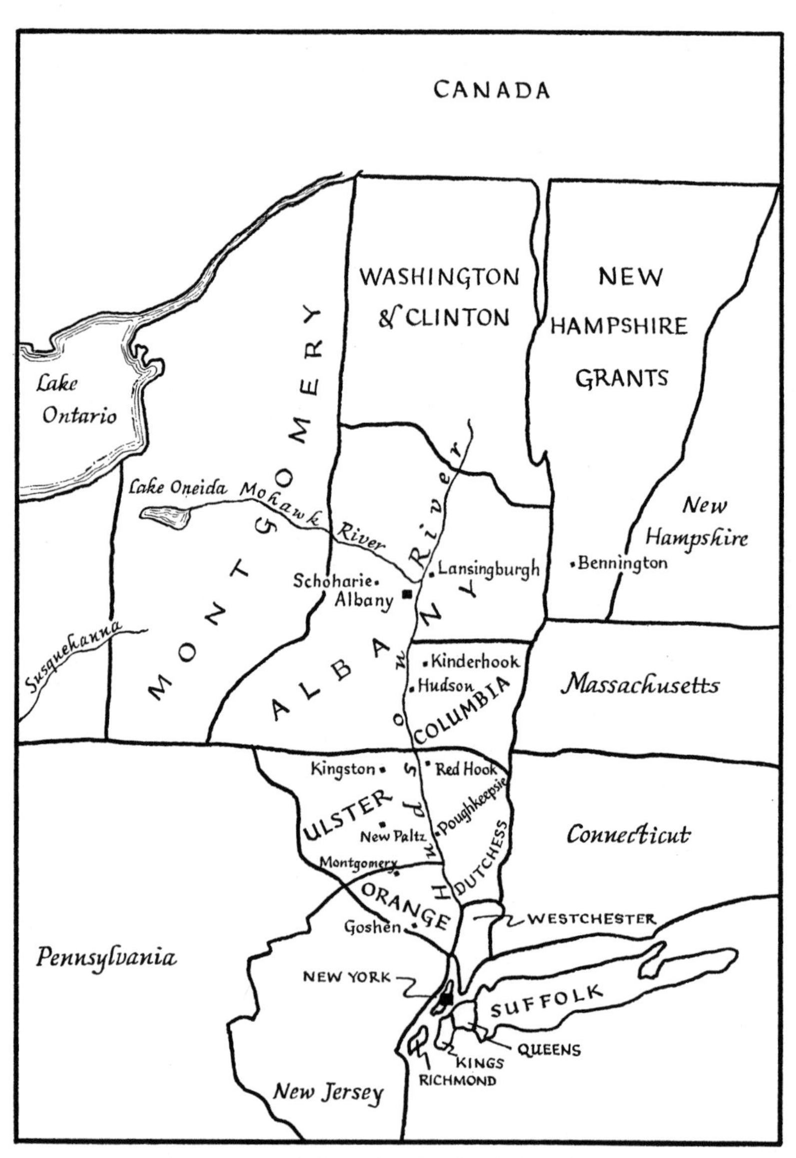

New York State in the Confederation

The Eleventh Pillar

New York State and the Federal Constitution

By Linda Grant De Pauw

PUBLISHED FOR THE

American Historical Association

CORNELL UNIVERSITY PRESS

ITHACA, NEW YORK

CORNELL UNIVERSITY PRESS

First published 1966

Library of Congress Catalog Card Number: 66-22657

PRINTED AND BOUND IN THE UNITED STATES OF AMERICA

BY VAIL-BALLOU PRESS, INC.

To John

Preface

NEW YORK was the last state to ratify the federal Constitution before the new government went into operation, and in no state was ratification carried by a narrower margin. An entirely satisfactory explanation of how unconditional ratification was secured in the face of New York's solid Antifederalism has never been given. A substantial majority of the state's voters were Antifederalists, and the delegates that New Yorkers sent to the ratifying convention at Poughkeepsie opposed ratification without previous amendments by a majority of better than two to one. The final vote in favor of ratification at the Poughkeepsie Convention is the most conspicuous example of the Federalists' astonishing ability to succeed even when success appeared impossible. Confirmed opposition to the Constitution existed in almost every part of the Confederation, and, as a contemporary remarked, the Federalists "seemed throughout the course of the whole Transactions, to have been on the Brink of Failure." [1]

A study of ratification in New York State contributes to an understanding of the remarkable Federalist success on the national as well as on the local level. The ratification campaign in

[1] Joshua Atherton to John Lamb, 23 February 1789, John Lamb Papers, New-York Historical Society.

New York lasted for more than seven months—the longest campaign in any ratifying state—and the Antifederalists were better organized there than anywhere else in the Confederation. Consequently, New York presents the best opportunity for studying the Antifederalists close up, for identifying their political aims, and for evaluating the means by which they sought to achieve them.

No historian has attempted an extended and comprehensive study of New York's ratification of the Constitution, and only three books—E. Wilder Spaulding's *New York in the Critical Period* (New York, 1932), Clarence E. Miner's *The Ratification of the Federal Constitution by the State of New York* (New York, 1921), and Staughton Lynd's *Anti-Federalism in Dutchess County, New York* (Chicago, 1962)—devote any considerable space to the subject. Spaulding's book covers the entire decade preceding ratification. It is a very useful volume, but fewer than one hundred pages are devoted to the ratification contest. Spaulding was strongly influenced by Charles Beard's *An Economic Interpretation of the Constitution* (New York, 1913), a work which he respected to such a degree as to copy from it an error in addition.[2] Miner also wrote under Beard's influence, and his study is valuable chiefly for its examination of the propaganda campaign in New York City. Lynd's concise study is deliberately restricted to a single county.

For many years it has been impossible to begin a study of the ratification period without explaining its relation to the work of Charles Beard. "But after all is said and done," wrote Louis Hartz in 1955, "Beard somehow stays alive, and the reason for this is that, as in the case of Marx, you merely demonstrate your subservience to a thinker when you spend your time attempting to disprove him."[3] I believe it is time for Beard to leave the

[2] Spaulding, *New York in the Critical Period*, p. 203.

[3] Louis Hartz, *The Liberal Tradition in America* (New York, 1955), p. 28.

spotlight in studies of the Constitution. He has held it for a good many years, which is, perhaps, not altogether to the benefit of the play.

Beard's thesis, as set out in his *An Economic Interpretation of the Constitution*, first published in 1913, was that Federalists could be distinguished from Antifederalists according to whether their property holdings were chiefly personalty or realty. Federalists, according to Beard, were holders of public securities while Antifederalists were landowners. For almost fifty years Beard's view of the formation and ratification of the Constitution dominated the historiography of the subject. His theory seemed so "right" that even the most careful historians overlooked the insubstantial nature of his research and carried his conclusions into their books.

In recent years the picture has changed. The year after Louis Hartz made the statement quoted above, Robert E. Brown published a slim volume entitled *Charles Beard and the Constitution: A Critical Analysis of "An Economic Interpretation of the Constitution"* (Princeton, 1956). Brown questioned the thoroughness of Beard's research and the validity of his methodology. Two years later, in 1958, Forrest McDonald published an impressively thick work entitled *We the People: The Economic Origins of the Constitution* (Chicago, 1958). The book, heavy with footnotes, tables, and detailed factual summaries of property holdings, struck the casual reader as a work of exhaustive scholarship that finally disposed of the Beard hypothesis. Unfortunately, McDonald's entire treatment of ratification in New York State, and, one suspects, in other states as well,[4] is marked by unreasonable carelessness both in the collection and interpretation of his data. While this negligence might be overlooked in his narrative pages, which, after all, are not essential to his criti-

[4] Jackson Turner Main and Forrest McDonald, "Charles A. Beard and the Constitution: A Critical Review of Forrest McDonald's *We the People*," *William and Mary Quarterly*, third series, XVII (1960), 86–100.

cism of Beard, the errors, omissions, and distortions in his summary of the economic interests of the delegates at Poughkeepsie are harder to excuse.[5]

It is regrettable that McDonald's distorted presentation of the evidence prevents *We the People* from delivering the final word in the Beard controversy. The intensive research that testing Beard on his own terms requires is far too tedious to be done twice. Fortunately, there should be no need to repeat the laborious hunt through questionably reliable sources, tabulating holdings of personalty and realty, since the Beard thesis may be successfully challenged on other grounds,[6] and there is reason to conclude that his method is sterile and the holdings of delegates altogether irrelevant to the fundamental questions of Constitutional history. No one in recent years has come forward to defend an unmodified Beardian interpretation of the Constitution, although Jackson Turner Main's work, *The Antifederalists:*

[5] Jackson Turner Main has identified a few of McDonald's inaccuracies, and the table he constructs for New York is substantially correct (*ibid.*, 99, 100). No useful purpose would be served by listing all the errors in McDonald's summary. I shall merely describe one characteristic distortion. On page 308 of *We the People*, John Williams of Washington County is described as " 'lord of vast estates' with many tenants." In his footnote, McDonald cites Spaulding's volume, *New York in the Critical Period.* The phrase quoted reads in context: "He [Williams] was lord of vast estates in his as yet sparsely settled county." In another place Spaulding repeats that "Williams' holdings were but sparsely settled in 1788" (pp. 239, 74n.). Not only is McDonald's remark about "many tenants" wholly unsupported by the materials he cites, it is explicitly contradicted. Washington County was rugged frontier country. Only Kings and Richmond had smaller populations in 1790 (United States Bureau of the Census, *Heads of Families at the First Census of the United States Taken in the Year 1790: New York* [Washington, 1908], pp. 9, 10). Williams's estates could not possibly have been so heavily populated as the rich holdings of Dutchess, Columbia, and Albany manor lords, and to describe them in the same terms is grossly misleading.

[6] Beard is particularly vulnerable to methodological criticism. See, for instance, Lee Benson, *Turner and Beard: American Historical Writing Reconsidered* (Glencoe, Ill., 1960).

Critics of the Constitution, 1781–1788 (Chapel Hill, N.C., 1961), which associates Antifederalism with the agricultural interests, particularly with the small farmer, shows some sympathy with Beard.

The present study is an attempt to turn the history of ratification from the lines set down by Beard by shifting the focus. It does not bow to Beard's dominance by "attempting to disprove him." It is concerned neither to support, modify, nor join in the attack on the *Economic Interpretation.* Beard himself admitted that his thesis did not fully explain the situation in New York,[7] and Main confesses that New York is an apparent exception to his socioeconomic analysis.[8] Staughton Lynd suggests an interpretation of Antifederalism in Dutchess County that identifies opposition to the Hudson manor lords as the basic element in Antifederalism. But he, too, is forced to admit that such an analysis cannot be fully supported.[9] The difficulty all three historians have faced is that the sort of evidence on which any socioeconomic interpretation must be based is especially scanty and contradictory in New York. That state, therefore, seemed a good place to try out a new approach to the subject, which would not ignore social and economic aspects where these seemed relevant, but in which the primary concern would be with what the men of 1787–1788 wanted to achieve politically and how they went about getting it rather than with their social status or material possessions. Refocusing on the political issue as it appeared to the men of the time proves to have unexpected and illuminating results. It reveals that Antifederalism, in New York State at least, was compatible with a strong attachment to the Union and a sincere desire to augment the power of the central government, and that the final vote at the Poughkeepsie Convention was probably as much a victory for the Antifederalists as for the Federalists.

[7] Beard, *Economic Interpretation,* p. 246.

[8] Main, *Antifederalists,* p. 280.

[9] Lynd, *Anti-Federalism in Dutchess County,* pp. 85, 88.

I wish to thank the Dolfinger-McMahon Foundation and the Woodrow Wilson Foundation for the grants I enjoyed while working on this study and to acknowledge the courtesies of the libraries that assisted me: the New York Public Library, the New-York Historical Society, the Library of Congress, Columbia University Library, and the libraries of Swarthmore College and the Johns Hopkins University. I am deeply grateful to those who read and criticized the manuscript in one or all of its forms: Dr. James A. Field, Jr., and Dr. Frederick B. Tolles of Swarthmore College; Dr. F. Wilson Smith of the University of California at Davis; Dr. Charles A. Barker of the Johns Hopkins University; the members of the Albert J. Beveridge Award Committee; my former colleague, Dr. Joseph H. Harrison, Jr.; my father, Phillip Grant; and my husband, John W. De Pauw. And finally, my sincerest thanks to Edward A. Klein, whose offer of assistance in typing the original manuscript of this book made it possible to enter it in the 1964 Beveridge Award competition.

LINDA GRANT DE PAUW

Falls Church, Virginia
February 1966

Contents

Map

Tables

PART I

New York and the Union

I

A Federal Disposition

ON the morning of 25 November 1783, the British lowered their flag from Fort George at the foot of Manhattan Island and, after spitefully cutting the halyards from the flagstaff and greasing the post to prevent the raising of "the glorious stripes," sailed away from New York City.[1] In the afternoon the governor of New York, General George Clinton, entertained George Washington and other dignitaries at dinner in Fraunces's Tavern. After they had dined, toasts were drunk, and as the wine was poured for the twelfth time, the governor lifted his glass and called out, "May a close union of the States guard the Temple they have erected to liberty." [2] In peace as in war, prudence and patriotism would bind New York State to the Confederation.

Isolated from the other states, eighteenth-century New York was hopelessly weak and vulnerable. Extending from the Atlantic to the Great Lakes and from Lake George to the Delaware River, the state was an immense wilderness cutting through the

[1] Extract of a letter from New York City, 26 November 1783, Hugh Hastings, ed., *Public Papers of George Clinton, First Governor of New York, 1777–1795, 1801–1804* (New York, 1899–1914), VIII, 297.

[2] *Ibid.*, 299, 300.

core of the Confederation, dividing the South from the New England states, and New England from the West. Although the state covered 29,000,000 acres, an estimate made in 1784 judged that only one million acres had been improved.[3]

The Adirondacks dominated the northernmost part of the state, an area of rugged forests where much of the land was so forbidding that even the Indians avoided it. In the west, beyond the headwaters of the Mohawk River, lay the hunting grounds of the Six Nations. Indian lands embraced all of the present state west of Lake Oneida, and their inhabitants ferociously resisted the extension of civilized settlement. During the Confederation period, only about 20,000 venturesome individuals made homes on the desolate frontier that ran north along the shores of Lake George and Lake Champlain for one hundred and fifty miles to Canada and west about one hundred miles along the Mohawk River valley.[4] Almost the whole of New York's population lived in the Hudson valley or on the three islands, Manhattan, Long Island, and Richmond, that pushed into the Atlantic where the Hudson River met the sea. Geographically the islands were more closely united to the neighboring states of Connecticut and New Jersey than to New York.

New York's five tiny island counties, approaching the mainland of the state only at a narrow point and highly vulnerable to sea attack, were the most densely populated part of New York State. The census of 1790 gave New York City a population of 33,131. More people lived in the City than could be found in all of Montgomery County, which covered almost half the state. Indeed, the city and county of New York had a larger population than any other single county in the state except for Albany

[3] E. Wilder Spaulding, *New York in the Critical Period, 1783–1789* (New York, 1932), p. 5.

[4] Ruth L. Higgins, *Expansion in New York* (Columbus, Ohio, 1931), p. 138; Thomas Cochran, *New York in the Confederation: An Economic Study* (Philadelphia, 1932), p. 3; Alfred Fabian Young, "The Democratic-Republican Movement in New York State, 1788–1797" (unpublished Ph.D. dissertation, Northwestern University, 1958), p. 4.

and Dutchess. Except in the island counties, New York's population was remarkably sparse. The total number of persons living in the state at the time of the first federal census was 340,120. Virginia, Pennsylvania, North Carolina, and Massachusetts had substantially larger populations, and New Yorkers outnumbered Marylanders by fewer than 25,000.[5] New York's relatively small population was partially due to the hostility of the Indians, but the primary cause of her stunted growth was the manorial land system.

When the first settlements were made in the Hudson River valley, the land was granted to Dutch aristocrats in enormous tracts. Ordinary men were expected to settle as tenants on the estates owned by the patroons. Some men did so, but the majority of immigrants, who cherished their independence, made their homes in the colonies that offered the freeholds. Pennsylvania and the New England states grew at the expense of New York, while the settlers who accepted the terms of New York's land system came to loathe the burdensome, degrading condition of tenancy and to hate the manor lord. Throughout the eighteenth and on into the nineteenth century, antirent agitation smoldered in the Hudson valley and at least once in every generation flared into bloody revolt.[6]

The power of the manor lords was concentrated on the eastern shore midway up the Hudson in Albany and Columbia

[5] United States Bureau of the Census, *Heads of Families at the First Census of the United States Taken in the Year 1790: New York* (Washington, 1908), pp. 9, 10. Although it is possible to find population statistics for the 1780's, they are notoriously unreliable. For example, a 1786 census of New York City reported a population of 23,614 (I. N. Phelps Stokes, *The Iconography of Manhattan Island, 1492–1909* [New York, 1915–1928], V, 1207), yet it is not likely that the City actually grew by almost 50 per cent in three years. It is safest to rely on the reports of the first federal census, which were reasonably accurate.

[6] Spaulding, *New York in the Critical Period*, pp. 45, 77–80; Irving Mark, *Agrarian Conflicts in Colonial New York, 1711–1775* (New York, 1940), *passim.*

counties and extended along the eastern shore of the lower Hudson in Dutchess and Westchester counties. The Livingstons, the Schuylers, and the Van Rensselaers were the greatest of the manor lords, and between them the three families held a quarter of New York's tenanted land. Still, despite the importance of the manorial system in the eastern river counties, only 20,000 New York families were tenants, and they composed a minority of the population even in Albany and Columbia counties. Furthermore, the manor system was almost unknown in the southern counties.[7]

Suffolk County, at the eastern end of Long Island, was settled on the New England system. The settlement was made, not by a patroon, but by a congregation which received the land grant as a body and distributed farms to its members. The rest of Long Island, Richmond, and Manhattan, as well as the western bank of the lower Hudson (Ulster and Orange counties), were settled under the Dutch method known as "Freedoms and Exemptions," a system granting a modest land parcel of 200 acres to the colonist who brought five adult settlers with him to America.[8] While there were a small number of manors of the Hudson valley type in southern New York before the Revolution, they disappeared after the war. There were large land holdings in the southern counties, and these were sometimes called "manors," but since they had no tenants they are not strictly comparable to the holdings of the Hudson manor lords.[9]

The southern counties were the richest part of New York State as well as the most densely populated. In the years before the Revolution, the five island counties bore three-fifths of the colonial tax burden.[10] During the Confederation period nine out of ten New Yorkers made their living from the soil. The principal crops were cereals, especially wheat, and there was also

[7] Young, "Democratic-Republican Movement," p. 8.
[8] Spaulding, *New York in the Critical Period*, pp. 56, 57.
[9] *Ibid.*, p. 56n.
[10] Cochran, *New York in the Confederation*, p. 49.

money to be made in lumbering and the fur trade. In Dutchess County horse breeding was the fastest growing industry in the decade following the Revolution.[11] Yet even in the 1780's the greatest income came to the state through the port of New York, and the wealth of the City was based not on agriculture, but on commerce.

New Yorkers did little manufacturing in the Confederation years, but New York merchants and shipowners enjoyed a sizable export trade from the upstate farms and from the neighboring states of New Jersey and Connecticut. Wheat, flour, livestock, and lumber went through the City to the West Indies to be traded for sugar, and to the South where cotton and indigo were purchased.[12] Necessities and luxuries from Europe came into New York harbor where merchants accepted orders from Connecticut, New Jersey, and Hudson valley farmers as well as from the City people.

The City people were by far the most cosmopolitan and sophisticated citizens of the state. They had easy access to books and newspapers, opportunity for daily conversation in taverns and coffee houses, and frequent contact with men from other states and other countries, and they naturally developed a view of life different from that of the country folk up the river. The only other city in New York State was Albany, a two to five days' journey up the Hudson,[13] with a population scarcely more than a tenth that of New York City. A few villages, none even a third the size of Albany, were scattered along the Hudson between Albany and New York. The metropolis, which was the

[11] Spaulding, *New York in the Critical Period*, p. 6; Henry Noble MacCracken, *Old Dutchess Forever! The Story of an American County* (New York, 1956), pp. 425, 426.

[12] Spaulding, *New York in the Critical Period*, p. 6.

[13] In 1807 a traveler noted that the river passage from New York to Albany usually took from two to five days (Joel Munsell, ed., *The Annals of Albany* [Albany, 1850–1859], II, 243). In 1784 a stage company advertised a run from New York to Albany in two days, but the time was increased to three days a few months later "for the ease of the passengers" (*ibid.*, 202).

largest city in America in 1790, was all the more imposing in such surroundings. No wonder "A Citizen" felt he spoke what all admitted to be true when he wrote to the *Daily Advertiser* in 1788 that "the Island of New-York contains a sufficient quantity of ground for a much larger city than will ever be built upon it,"[14] although at that time the City covered only four square miles,[15] much of it enclosed farmland. The entire population would have fit easily into Yankee Stadium—with room left over for the populations of Philadelphia and Boston as well.[16] Streets were frequently unpaved and always badly lighted. There was no police force, an army of pigs did most of the street cleaning,[17] and the sewerage system consisted of the 2,000[18] slaves owned by New Yorkers, "a long line of whom might be seen late at night walking to the river, each with a tub on his head."[19] Nevertheless, even in the 1780's, New Yorkers looked on the men from upstate as "hicks," or, as they would put it, "a set of ignorant Dutchmen."[20]

New York State's trials during the Revolution began with the capture of New York City by the British in 1776. For the rest of the war New York suffered from the amputation of her wealthiest counties. In 1777, the year of the Burgoyne expedition, the entire state was devastated except for a small area around Albany. In 1778, the Indians attacked, and the whole of Montgom-

[14] *Daily Advertiser* (New York), 9 January 1788.

[15] John Bach McMaster, *A History of the People of the United States from the Revolution to the Civil War* (New York, 1885), I, 497.

[16] Philadelphia, the Confederation's second largest city, had a population of 28,522 in 1790. Boston, the third largest city, had a population of 18,320 (*Heads of Families*, p. 7).

[17] Technological unemployment had not yet overtaken these pigs when Charles Dickens visited New York City fifty years later (Charles Dickens, *American Notes* [Greenwich, Conn., 1961], pp. 105, 106).

[18] *Heads of Families*, p. 9.

[19] Thomas E. V. Smith, *The City of New York in the Year of Washington's Inauguration* (New York, 1889), p. 9.

[20] Samuel Blanchley Webb to Joseph Barrell, 1 July 1788, W. C. Ford, ed., *Correspondence and Journals of Samuel Blanchley Webb* (New York, 1893–1894), III, 108.

ery County south of the Mohawk was laid waste. While the settlements around the Mohawk were rebuilt after the war, the damage to the region on the upper Susquehanna River was so severe that it remained desolate for many years. In 1779, the British and the Indians were quiet, but the Hessian fly came to plague New York farmers and an exceedingly poor harvest added to the state's troubles. Finally, in 1780, Montgomery County was ravaged again, and the British captured all but one of the northern fur forts.[21]

That New York found herself on the winning side three years later was due to the support received from the other confederated states. Every New Yorker knew that without the Union, they would never have seen British redcoats haul down the Union Jack that flew over Fort George. With the most valuable part of the state occupied and the remainder subject to devastating attacks, aid from the other colonies had been a patent necessity. Simple self-preservation dictated devotion to the Union during the war, and Governor Clinton was frequently in a position to boast of his state's federalism. "This State I flatter myself," he wrote to the president of Congress in 1781, "has for its Spirit & Exertions in the War stood equal in point of Reputation with any other in the Union."[22] George Washington was equally appreciative of the efforts made by the patriots of the Hudson valley. "New York is among the few that has felt the necessity of energy," the Commander-in-Chief wrote to Clinton in June of 1780, "and considering its situation has done everything that could be expected of it."[23]

"Everything that could be expected" did not include meeting in full the requisitions of the Continental Congress, which some historians have taken as the proper test of patriotism during the

[21] Higgins, *Expansion in New York*, p. 100; Cochran, *New York in the Confederation*, p. 49.

[22] George Clinton to John Hanson, 24 November 1781, Hastings, ed., *Public Papers of George Clinton*, VIII, 520, 521.

[23] John C. Fitzpatrick, ed., *The Writings of George Washington*, (Washington, 1931–1944), XIX, 84.

war. No state met its requisitions in full. To do so was impossible. Before the Revolution, the entire cost of government in the thirteen colonies was probably less than $300,000 a year.[24] The failure of the states to meet Congressional requisitions for sums ten times greater than they were accustomed to raise in peacetime should not be construed as willful neglect of Congress. New York failed to supply Congress with the full amounts required from her not because her legislature was unwilling to vote taxes or to pass on the sums collected to Congress, but simply because county tax collectors were unable to raise the cash.[25] At the end of the war, taxes in every New York county were at least three years in arrears.[26] When it is remembered that the state treasury was almost empty for the whole of the war, and that Governor Clinton had to open his own purse to pay for "Measures adopted for the immediate Defence and Safety of the State," [27] the financial support the state gave to the Confederation during the Revolution appears properly impressive. When peace returned and the collection of taxes improved, New York paid a larger percentage of her Congressional requisitions than did any other state.[28]

New York's devotion to the Confederation during the Revolution is too obvious to be disputed. But her attachment to the Union after the British had withdrawn from the south and the devastated parts of the state were rapidly rebuilding has been questioned.[29] Did New York require Congressional support to solve her peacetime problems, or did she find Congress a needless hindrance? An examination of three areas in which New York sought Congressional assistance in the Confederation period in-

[24] Charles J. Bullock, *Finances of the United States, 1775–1789* (Madison, Wis., 1895), p. 151.

[25] Cochran, *New York in the Confederation,* p. 55.

[26] *Ibid.,* pp. 156, 157.

[27] New York State, *Messages from the Governors,* Charles Z. Lincoln, ed. (Albany, 1909), II, 162.

[28] Cochran, *New York in the Confederation,* pp. 151, 158, 192.

[29] Most notably by Forrest McDonald, *We the People: The Economic Origins of the Constitution* (Chicago, 1958), pp. 290–292.

dicates that the state hoped for extensive support from the central government and, although she was continually disappointed in her expectations, Congress was not criticized for interfering but rather for lacking energy.

The Vermont dispute was more than two decades old when the Revolution began.[30] In 1749, the governor of New Hampshire made a township grant at Bennington, twenty miles east of the Hudson River. New York protested that the land lay within her boundaries, and the protest was upheld by the king in council. But it took fifteen years before the king rendered his decision, and in the meantime the New Hampshire governor had made more than one hundred grants in New York territory between the Hudson and the Connecticut River. When New York tried to dispossess the settlers who held New Hampshire titles, the men of Vermont resisted, and when the Revolution began the New Hampshire Grants declared themselves an independent state. At this point New York State appealed to Congress for aid in curbing the revolt.

For almost seven years New York continued to petition Congress to take decisive action against Vermont, but the Vermonters refused to be suppressed. They extended their territorial claims still farther into New York State and also into New Hampshire so that New Hampshire, too, was brought into the dispute. The Vermonters intensified the problem for Congress by entering into negotiations with the British in 1781. When, at the end of 1782, Congress finally passed a strong resolution denouncing Vermont and threatening "effectual measures to enforce a compliance" with an order to make restitution for the territory usurped, the Vermonters calmly replied that they were not afraid of the Continental army, and Congress was silenced. New York continued urgent appeals for action until early in

[30] Detailed accounts of this extraordinarily complicated affair may be found in Cochran, *New York in the Confederation*, pp. 85–93; Alfred B. Street, *The Council of Revision of the State of New York* (New York, 1859), pp. 95–105; Edmund C. Burnett, *The Continental Congress* (New York, 1941), pp. 540–546; Allan Nevins, *The American States During and After the Revolution* (New York, 1927), pp. 579–583.

1784, and then gave up hope in Congress,[31] leaving the position of the New Hampshire Grants unsettled until 1790.

The New York Legislature's final attempt to force Congress to action is worth examining in detail since one historian views it as an "ultimatum" to Congress, threatening secession from the Union.[32] On 2 February 1784, the New York Senate passed a resolution of instructions to its delegation in Congress. As often before, the delegates were directed "to press Congress for a Decision" in the matter of the New Hampshire Grants. They were told to represent "in the most pointed Terms" the injustice suffered by New York and the dangers involved in further procrastination. They were to point out that Vermont had actually raised an army and was employing it against men who acknowledged themselves citizens of New York. And finally, the delegates should "if necessary, be most explicit on the Subject," and inform the men in Congress that unless some sort of decision was made within two months after Congress had assembled a quorum, the State of New York would entertain no further hopes of ever obtaining a decision, and "with whatever deep Regret, will be compelled to consider herself as left to pursue her own Councils, destitute of the Protection of the United States, to whose Judgement they have cheerfully submitted, and on whose Justice they have hitherto relied." [33]

[31] After February 1784, there are only a few unimportant references to Vermont in the Duane Papers or the Clinton Papers, and equally few references in the *Journals of the Continental Congress* (Cochran, *New York in the Confederation*, p. 92n.; Street, *Council of Revision*, p. 105).

[32] McDonald, *We the People*, p. 291. McDonald identified the context of his quotations improperly; they relate to the Vermont dispute, not to the attempts to force the British to evacuate the northern forts. The citations given by McDonald are also incorrect. No resolutions containing the words he quotes are recorded for 2 March 1784 in the *Journal of the Senate of the State of New York* (New York, 1784) or for 22 April 1784 in the *Journal of the Assembly of the State of New York* (New York, 1784).

[33] *Journal of the Senate*, 2 February 1784; *Journal of the Assembly*, 2 March 1784.

Was this a threat to leave the Union? It does not seem so. It was a simple declaration that if, after seven years, Congress still refused to make a ruling on the Vermont issue, it was pointless for New York to continue pressing for one. Congress apparently expected the state to deal with the problem herself. It is significant that when Congress continued to ignore Vermont, New York's reaction was not to send an army of her own against the men of the Green Mountains, but to cease all agitation, including petitions to Congress, until a peaceful compromise was worked out in 1790. It is also noteworthy that these remarks were to be made to Congress only if the delegates found it "necessary," and there is no evidence that they were ever delivered.[34] Moreover, the author of the resolution was James Duane,[35] a nationalist who later became a Federalist, and the resolution appears to have passed both houses of the New York Legislature without opposition although, presumably, such nationalists as Alexander Hamilton's father-in-law, Philip Schuyler, would have voiced an objection if an ultimatum of secession had been intended.

Failing to settle the Vermont dispute, Congress failed again when called on to settle a less serious territorial disagreement between New York and Massachusetts. In 1784, Massachusetts renewed an old claim to a parcel of land between the western end of Lake Ontario and the limit of New York settlement near the eastern end of the lake.[36] Since no land grants had ever been made in the area and since the land was occupied by the Six Nations who had no intention of surrendering their ownership, the

[34] There is no reference to this resolution of instructions in Worthington C. Ford and Gaillard Hunt, eds., *Journals of the Continental Congress* (Washington, 1904–1937), or in Edmund C. Burnett, ed., *Letters of Members of the Continental Congress* (Washington, 1921–1936).

[35] *Journal of the Senate*, 26 January 1784, 2 February 1784.

[36] Summaries of the dispute may be found in Cochran, *New York in the Confederation*, pp. 93–96, and in Edward P. Alexander, *A Revolutionary Conservative: James Duane of New York* (New York, 1938), pp. 172–176.

dispute between the two states was scarcely more than academic. Still, Massachusetts wished the legal title to the territory clarified and appealed to Congress.

Article IX of the Articles of Confederation provided that "the United States in Congress assembled" should be the final arbiter of all territorial disagreements between states. When a dispute arose, Congress was to call on both parties to appoint commissioners who would in turn agree on a panel of judges to decide the case. For almost two years New York and Massachusetts commissioners made up lists of judges, but the men they chose refused to serve. They could not agree on a convenient place for the court to meet, they said. Evidently the Congressional method for settling territorial disputes was not going to work.

Finally, in April 1786, the legislature of New York State empowered its agents to settle the dispute with Massachusetts outside a federal court. The Massachusetts General Court agreed to the expedient. Agents from the two states met at Hartford, Connecticut, and promptly agreed to a compromise settlement of the disagreement. The face-to-face negotiation of differences was unconstitutional, and some historians have cited the side-stepping of the prescribed Congressional procedure as evidence of a contempt for the Confederation in New York State.[37] Contemporaries, however, did not take that view. John Adams cited the settlement of the Massachusetts–New York controversy as proof that "the Union has great weight in the minds of the people" and was recognized as "an object of such magnitude that great sacrifices ought to be made to its preservation." [38]

When Congress failed to solve the Vermont problem, New York learned to live with the situation, and when Congress failed to settle the disagreement with Massachusetts, the states succeeded in making their own arrangements. But when the

[37] For example, Spaulding, *New York in the Critical Period*, pp. 181, 182.

[38] John Adams to John Jay, 8 May 1787, quoted in Charles Warren, *The Making of the Constitution* (Boston, 1928), p. 54.

weakness of Congress made it impossible to expel the British from the New York forts, the state's exasperation was sharpened by the realization that what the United States in Congress assembled could not do, New York State could never do alone. The state's experience during the Revolution left her with no illusions about her ability to take on the British single-handed.[39]

Eight forts dominated the fur trade country around the Great Lakes. Seven of them were ceded to the United States at the conclusion of the Revolution, and five of the seven, Niagara, Oswego, Oswegatchie, Point au Fer, and Dutchman's Point, were located in New York State. Article II of the Treaty of Paris pledged Great Britain to evacuate the American posts "with all convenient speed," but the British did not find it convenient to leave until the negotiation of Jay's Treaty eleven years later. The occupation was a source of discomfort to New York for two reasons. First was concern for "our Furr Trade," [40] which had been a lucrative business for Albany before the British at Oswego closed the route to the Indian country by way of Lake Ontario via the Mohawk River and Lake Oneida. Second was the fear that the British might evacuate the posts suddenly, before the United States was prepared to take control. The forts would then "be seized by savages inimical to these United States, whereby the inhabitants of the frontiers may be exposed to great danger and distress." [41]

Throughout the Confederation period, Congress was unable to force the British to give up the posts or to make provision for garrisoning the forts in case of a precipitate withdrawal by the

[39] Although Forrest McDonald states (*We the People*, p. 291) that many New Yorkers believed as early as 1784 that the state could "go it alone" on the fort dispute, he presents no convincing evidence for the assertion, and it is hard to see how any man who had spent the years from 1776 to 1783 in New York State could have entertained such an absurd belief. George Clinton certainly did not (Lincoln, ed., *Messages from the Governors*, II, 253).

[40] *Journal of the Senate*, 28 January 1784.

[41] *Journals of the Continental Congress*, XXVII, 308.

British troops. Despite constant prodding by New York, there was only one practical proposal for sending an American garrison to the Western forts, and this was rejected by New York since Congress intended to use Massachusetts troops and the land occupied by the forts was still a subject of dispute with Massachusetts.[42]

Thus in all three cases where New York sought aid from Congress in the decade following the war, Congress failed to act. Still, Congress remained New York's best hope, and frustration with the weakness of the central government encouraged movements to strengthen Congress. There was never a suggestion that New York might be better off without the Union. However unsatisfactory New York might find the Congress, she could not afford disunion.

Although New York recovered rapidly from the damage suffered during the Revolution, and although she began to enjoy considerable material prosperity during the Confederation decade, geography, if nothing else, made it impossible for her to consider acting independently of the Union in her relations with other states or foreign nations. The richest part of New York State lay exposed in the Atlantic and the river valleys were open to land invasion from Canada. Had New York separated herself from the Union her safety would have been threatened not only by Great Britain but by the other American states. The states forming the economic hinterland of the New York City port—New Jersey, Connecticut, and Massachusetts—resented being taxed through the New York custom house. New Yorkers were aware that if the ties of the Confederation were broken, the

[42] Burnett, *Continental Congress*, p. 608; Samuel Flagg Bemis, *Jay's Treaty: A Study in Commerce and Diplomacy* (rev. ed; New Haven, Conn., 1962), pp. 3, 4; A. L. Burt, *The United States, Great Britain, and British North America from the Revolution to the Establishment of Peace after the War of 1812* (New Haven, Conn., 1940), p. 82; Curtis P. Nettels, *The Emergence of a National Economy, 1775–1815* (New York, 1962), p. 53; Wayne Edson Stevens, *The Northwest Fur Trade, 1763–1800* (Urbana, Ill., 1928), pp. 44, 54, 66, 67.

neighboring states would soon come "to wish that there was no such state as New York." And they knew equally well that "the wish once formed, and no confederation existing, the thing is done." [43] Even within the Confederation, New York was not well-loved by her neighbors. Early in 1786 a member of Congress observed that "there is nothing but the restraining hand of Congress, (weak as it is), that prevents N. Jersey and Connecticut from entering the lists very seriously with N. York and bloodshed would very quickly be the consiquence [*sic*]." [44]

In the years following the Revolution, the State of New York held fast to the Union, not merely in patriotic remembrance of what was owed to the aid of the other states during the war, but because even in peacetime New York could not do without it. Federalism—that is, devotion to the Confederation—was recognized as a political necessity by all New Yorkers, however much they might differ on other matters.

[43] Philip Schuyler to Henry Van Schaack, 13 March 1787, Henry C. Van Schaack, ed., *Memoirs of Henry Van Schaack Embracing Sections of his Correspondence* (Chicago, 1892), p. 152.

[44] Nathaniel Gorham to James Warren, 6 March 1786, Burnett, ed., *Letters of Members of the Continental Congress*, VIII, 318.

II

An Antifederal Reputation

WHEN the British evacuated New York City and the Revolution ended for New York State, George Clinton was governor. The capable, popular general won a plurality of votes both for governor and for lieutenant governor in 1777 when New York held its first state election, and he was re-elected to the first office in the state without opposition every three years throughout the Confederation period.

Property and social status were the usual prerequisites for high office in the eighteenth century, and in 1777 George Clinton was not remarkable for either. His defeat of General Philip Schuyler of Albany in the first gubernatorial election surprised the manor lord. "General Clinton I am informed has a majority of votes for the Chair," Schuyler wrote. "If so he has played his cards better than was expected." [1] Schuyler, who was one of the great men of the state, pointed out that Clinton's "family and connections do not entitle him to so distinguished a predominance," [2] but despite that handicap, Clinton had been supported

[1] Philip Schuyler to John Jay, 30 June 1777, H. P. Johnston, ed., *The Correspondence and Public Papers of John Jay* (New York, 1891), I, 144.

[2] Philip Schuyler to John Jay, 14 July 1777, *ibid.*, 147.

by some of the Livingstons,[3] and even General Schuyler was easily reconciled to his success.[4] Schuyler wrote to John Jay that Clinton was "virtuous and loves his country, has abilities and is brave," [5] and to Clinton himself, he wrote a hearty letter of congratulation in which he promised to "embrace every opportunity to make you sit as easy in the chair of government as the times will admit. Your virtue, the love of my country, and that friendship which I have always and with great truth professed, are all so many inducements to it." [6] In addition to winning the favor of the gentry, Clinton had the enthusiastic support of the army rank and file.[7]

While George Clinton did not belong to the traditional governing class,[8] he had personal leadership qualities to an outstanding degree. Physically Clinton was a giant, tall and powerfully built, a six-footer in a day when few men attained that height. His appearance was impressively virile, and he has been called "the most masculine" New Yorker of the Revolutionary era.[9] In 1777 he was thirty-seven, in the prime of his manhood. He had, in addition, an exceptional military record and had probably contributed more to the war than any other general officer in the state. Although General Schuyler's record rivaled that of Clin-

[3] E. Wilder Spaulding, *His Excellency George Clinton, Critic of the Constitution* (New York, 1938), p. 92.

[4] Baynard Tuckerman, *Life of General Philip Schuyler, 1773–1804* (New York, 1903), p. 251.

[5] Philip Schuyler to John Jay, 14 July 1777, Johnston, ed., *Correspondence of John Jay*, I, 147.

[6] Quoted in Tuckerman, *Life of Schuyler*, p. 252.

[7] Spaulding, *His Excellency George Clinton*, p. 92.

[8] Far back in Clinton's ancestry there was blue blood. Branches of his family tree can be traced to John of Gaunt and most of the Plantagenets. He was a distant cousin of the other George Clinton, governor of the New York colony from 1743 to 1753. But Clinton's father was an Ulster County farmer and it was the marriage of George's brother, James, to a De Witt and his own marriage to a Tappen that first gave status to the New York Clintons (Spaulding, *His Excellency George Clinton*, pp. 1–8, 10, 11, 30, 31).

[9] E. F. De Lancy, quoted in *ibid.*, p. 91.

ton, Schuyler was a haughty, overbearing individual whom his men suspected of Tory sympathies. Schuyler's chaplain wrote in 1775 that "full one-third of my time is taken up in trying to make them [the soldiers] see that we have no warrant for suspicions of him and every reason for the greatest confidence." [10] No one ever questioned General Clinton's loyalty, and it was said that he "had rather roast in hell to all eternity than consent to a dependence on Great Britain or shew mercy to a damned tory." [11]

Intellectually Clinton was an ordinary man. Hamilton wrote of him with a contempt that the young genius could easily afford, that "it is certain that without being destitute of understanding, his passions are much warmer, than his judgment is enlightened." [12] Clinton had little formal education, and his biographer observes that "it was only in his later years that he learned to write correct English and to spell passing well, and he was never an eager reader." [13] He seldom spoke in public,[14] and when he did venture a few remarks his style was blunt and unornamented for an age with a taste for elegant oratory. Yet New Yorkers did not require brilliance in their leader. They were content to be ruled by a man with an ordinary, good head on his shoulders, a man identified with "plain, practical, sound, wholesome common sense," who attracted people of every class by his manner: "plain but dignified, his conversation easy, shrewd, sensible and commonly about matters of fact," [15] and who had a

[10] Rev. Cotton Mather Smith to his wife, July 1775, quoted in Tuckerman, *Life of Schuyler*, p. 108.

[11] Thomas Jones, *A History of New York During the Revolutionary War* (New York, 1879), II, 329.

[12] Alexander Hamilton to Robert Morris, 13 August 1782, Harold C. Syrett, ed., and Jacob E. Cooke, assoc. ed., *The Papers of Alexander Hamilton* (New York, 1961–), III, 137.

[13] Spaulding, *His Excellency George Clinton*, p. 11.

[14] *Ibid.*, p. 97; John Rutledge to John Jay, 29 June 1776, Edmund C. Burnett, ed., *Letters of Members of the Continental Congress* (Washington, 1921–1936), I, 517.

[15] Gulian C. Verplanck, "Reminiscences of New York," *The Talisman*, I (1829), 345, 346.

reputation for simplicity, honesty, virtue, and a sincere devotion to his state.

The governor of New York was the most powerful executive officer in the United States. He was the only governor not elected by members of the legislature, and he consequently enjoyed a measure of independent authority. His constitutional prerogatives included influence over legislation and appointment of state officers. The governor and the members of the New York Supreme Court composed a Council of Revision, which had a veto over all legislation and could be overridden only by a two-thirds vote. The governor and a group of four senators, chosen by the Senate itself, formed a Council of Appointment, which chose all the appointed officials for the state. Clearly the governor held a considerable measure of power so long as he avoided disagreements with the Council of Revision and the Council of Appointment, and George Clinton was never troubled by such disagreements.

New Yorkers would not have tolerated so much authority in the executive had they not been well satisfied with the governor. In the early days after independence, New Yorkers shared with the men of other states an intense suspicion of all executive power. Experience with colonial governors had convinced them of an apparent connection between executive power and arrogant autocracy. When independence was declared, many of the new states abolished the executive office entirely or at least made it subservient to the legislature.[16] In startling contrast, the New York Constitution made the governor an effective head of state and retained an upper house based on a restricted franchise as well. John Jay, the chief author of the New York Constitution, wrote no more than the truth when he said that "another turn of the winch would have cracked the cord." [17]

New Yorkers' satisfaction with George Clinton's perform-

[16] Lynton K. Caldwell, "George Clinton—Democratic Administrator," *New York History*, XLIX (1951), 134, 135.

[17] Quoted in Carl Lotus Becker, *The History of Political Parties in the Province of New York, 1760–1776* (Madison, Wis., 1909), p. 276.

ance as governor was due to his efficiency in carrying out his administrative duties and to his scrupulous observance of all constitutional restrictions on his authority. Clinton's popularity was universal, not limited to men of one class or one section. Historians usually picture Clinton as "the idol of the common folk, of the little Whig farmer and mechanic," [18] and describe his appeal as "primarily to middle-class farmers." [19] The governor was, indeed, popular with the masses, but the men who repeatedly elected him to the governorship were not primarily mechanics or little Whig farmers; they were the hundred-pound-freeholders, the only men entitled to vote for governor in New York, who composed a select group numbering fewer than 20,000 in 1790.[20] The governor's competence and circumspection appealed to everyone, not least of all to the rich.

The propertied men of the state had every reason to be satisfied with Governor Clinton. There was no wildly depreciating paper currency in New York, and there was no Shays. George Clinton was a conservative governor. While Hamilton complained of "an excess of popularity" in the government of New York, declaring that "the inquiry constantly is what will *please* not what will *benefit* the people," he felt that Clinton, personally, had forfeited his popularity by "the vigorous execution of some necessary laws that bore hard upon the people." [21] Clinton was not courting popularity when he urged the legislature to provide for the effective collection of taxes in 1781,[22] or when he moved the state militia against a party of Shays's rebels who

[18] E. Wilder Spaulding, *New York in the Critical Period, 1783–1789* (New York, 1932), p. 97.

[19] Jackson Turner Main, *The Antifederalists: Critics of the Constitution, 1781–1788* (Chapel Hill, N.C., 1961), p. 48.

[20] "A Census of Electors and Inhabitants of the State of New York," 11 January 1791, Broadside Collection, SY 1791–26, New-York Historical Society.

[21] Alexander Hamilton to Robert Morris, 13 August 1782, Syrett, ed., *Papers of Alexander Hamilton,* III, 135, 137.

[22] New York State, *Messages from the Governors,* Charles Z. Lincoln, ed. (Albany, 1909), II, 147.

had fled from Massachusetts and concentrated at Lebanon, New York, early in 1787.[23] The governor was not catering to the poor when he asked for "effectual measures" for the relief of public creditors in his 1786 message to the Legislature.[24]

But while Clinton did not hesitate to exercise his authority to protect property and maintain order in the state, he was sensitive to his position as first republican governor of New York and felt special scruples against doing anything that might invite comparison with the high-handed actions of royal governors. He hesitated to move one tittle beyond the constitution and agonized over the most trivial exercises of discretionary power. In January 1786, for instance, Clinton found himself caught between two sections of the New York constitution. The Legislature had adjourned without setting a time and place for meeting again, and the constitution directed that they must meet at least once a year. Under the circumstances there was nothing to do but for the governor to convene the Legislature, but the constitution forbade the executive to call a meeting of the Legislature except on "extraordinary occasions." Clinton was acutely embarassed. He finally decided to issue the necessary proclamation but began his opening message to the assembled legislators with a profuse apology for having exercised "an authority, in itself questionable, to give the Legislature an opportunity of 'meeting at least once in every year for the dispatch of business,' as the constitution expressly directs." [25] The Senate replied that "the scruples your Excellency entertained respecting your authority to convene the Legislature by 'Proclamation,' at the present juncture, is a new proof of your attention to our excellent constitution." They promised the governor that they would try to prevent "the repetition of so unpleasing a dilemma as that to

[23] Hugh Hastings, ed., *Public Papers of George Clinton, First Governor of New York, 1777–1795, 1801–1804* (New York, 1899–1914), I, 184; Alfred B. Street, *The Council of Revision of the State of New York* (New York, 1927), p. 107.

[24] Lincoln, ed., *Messages from the Governors,* II, 253.

[25] *Ibid.,* 251.

which you were reduced," and they assured Clinton that "the reasons which operated with you for taking that step are cogent, and to us satisfactory, and, we doubt not, will be so to your and to our constituents." [26] Clinton was particularly gratified by this message.[27]

As long as he held office, Clinton punctiliously observed the independence of the legislature. In his addresses to the Senate and Assembly he indicated areas where he felt action was necessary, but he did not propose particular remedies, and even when he was not acting in an official capacity, he was restrained in expressing his personal feelings on legislation. Clinton's biographer is unable to say with certainty where the governor stood on the question of paper money,[28] and when the highly controversial federal impost bill was up for consideration, anonymous newspaper essayists could only guess at Clinton's postion: "It is whispered that he also is in secret an anti-impost man." [29]

Historians frequently speak of a "Clintonian party" in New York during the Confederation period. "Long before the Constitution became an issue," writes Jackson Turner Main, "candidates for office were running as Clintonians or anti-Clintonians on well-understood, though informal, unwritten platforms and were voting in the legislature with remarkable consistency." [30] Forrest McDonald goes even further, speaking of Clinton's "followers" as early as 1777 and talking of a "Clintonian program" in the legislature and a "Clinton organization." [31] To describe the politics of the 1780's in such terms is anachronistic. There were, in fact, no "Clintonians" in the Confederation period. The word itself was never used by contemporaries, and it was not

[26] *Journal of the Senate of the State of New York* (New York, 1786), 19 January 1786.

[27] *Ibid.*, 20 January 1786.

[28] Spaulding, *New York in the Critical Period*, pp. 145, 146.

[29] "Leo," *Daily Advertiser* (New York), 27 February 1787.

[30] Main, *Antifederalists,* p. 234.

[31] Forrest McDonald, *We the People: The Economic Origins of the Constitution* (Chicago, 1958), pp. 290–293.

until 1788 that Hamilton suspected Clinton of wishing "to establish Clintonism on the basis of Antifederalism." [32] Hamilton noted in 1782 that Philip Schuyler had "more weight in the Legislature than the Governor," [33] and three years later he complained that the state was governed by "a couple of New England adventurers—Ford and Adgate." [34] No one thought of accusing Clinton of leading a party or of attempting to use his influence to determine votes in the legislature during the Confederation period, and the suggestion was never made until the vicious gubernatorial campaign of 1789 when Federalists were charging Clinton with every dishonorable action they could think of.[35]

Clinton was by choice an administrator rather than a political leader.[36] He was never particularly interested in "the tedious, humdrum business of legislation," [37] and his lack of interest in legislative affairs is entirely understandable. The business of the legislature during the Confederation period was rarely dramatic. There were few issues that could arouse strong feelings, and the newspapers did not carry legislative debates until 1787.[38] Most of the legislators' time was occupied with such matters as "An Act to restrain Hawkers and Pedlers within this State," "An Act to prevent Damages by Swine, in the Counties of Orange and Ulster," and "An Act to encourage the destroying of Wolves and Panthers." Such bills, with a sprinkling of more significant subjects such as treatment of the Tories or relations with Congress, composed the bulk of business for the New York Legislature during the first ten years of its existence.

[32] Alexander Hamilton to James Madison, 2 July 1788, Syrett, ed., *Papers of Alexander Hamilton*, V, 141.

[33] Alexander Hamilton to Robert Morris, 13 August 1782, *ibid.*, III, 138.

[34] Alexander Hamilton to Robert Livingston, 25 April 1785, *ibid.*, 609.

[35] "To the Electors of the State of New York," 7 April 1789, and H. G. Letter VIII, 28 February 1789, *ibid.*, V, 320, 278.

[36] Caldwell, "George Clinton—Democratic Administrator," pp. 135, 136.

[37] Spaulding, *His Excellency George Clinton*, p. 86.

[38] *Daily Advertiser*, 15 January 1787.

In the absence of significant issues, political parties were slow to develop and did not appear in New York before the campaign for the federal Constitution. There was no sharp factional division in the New York Legislature even at the end of the Confederation period,[39] and elections were generally uncontested. When men got to the legislature they did not answer to a party leader, but voted on every question separately, as they saw fit. Series of resolutions that are obviously intended to further a particular policy desired by certain leading members show men switching sides from one resolution to the next as they judge the

[39] There have been two attempts to trace factional division in the 1780's on the basis of legislative voting records and to define it sectionally. E. Wilder Spaulding (*New York in the Critical Period*, pp. 102, 103) identified New York, Richmond, Suffolk, Albany, Columbia, and Montgomery counties as generally "Federalist," with Ulster, Orange, Dutchess, Westchester, and Washington counties generally "Antifederalist." Kings and Queens, Spaulding said, were "Federalist" but leaning "more and more toward Antifederalism." Forrest McDonald (*We the People*, p. 299) challenges Spaulding: "Only in the City, and in Westchester, Richmond (Staten Island), and Kings counties did the anti-Clinton coalition achieve any consistent success, though Albany, Schuyler's home county, occasionally sent anti-Clintonians to the legislature. Every other county in the state supported Clinton, his measures, and his legislative candidates with majorities ranging from substantial to overwhelming." According to McDonald, his analysis is "based largely" on a tabulation of "all votes cast from 1776 [*sic*] to 1789 in both houses of the legislature on all issues, for the purpose of determining on what percentage of the issues each member voted with each other member." Unfortunately he does not explain why or on what grounds he modified the results of the tabulation. Furthermore the value of McDonald's method of analysis is questionable. The *Journal of the Assembly of the State of New York* (New York and Albany, 1777–1790) and the *Journal of the Senate of the State of New York* (New York and Albany, 1777–1790) record the proceedings of those bodies from September, 1777, but the yeas and nays were not recorded regularly, and the questions for which the division of the vote is given are frequently trivial. The membership of both houses underwent substantial changes at every election, and although some men held seats for the entire period, others, who later became prominent as Federalists or Antifederalists, were never in the legislature or were present only for brief periods. And there is not, in any case, sufficient evidence to identify either "Clinton candidates" or "Clinton measures." Spaulding's method of

individual merits differently.[40] William Nisbet Chambers has coined the phrase "faction politics" to describe the pre-party phase of American politics. "Such politics," he writes, "depended heavily on personalities and personal ties, and was subject to abrupt, kaleidoscopic change." [41] Personalities rather than principles dominated the political alliances of New York in the 1780's. The politics of George Clinton's New York bore closer resemblance to the contemporary English old-Whig "connexions" than they did to the party machine of his nephew De Witt Clinton. Political alignments remained unstable for some years after the adoption of the federal Constitution. Robert Yates, for example, was a leading Antifederalist in 1788. The following year he was the Federalist candidate for governor, and six years later he ran for governor as a Republican. Such easy movement across party lines was common in early New York politics, as it could not have been under a rigidly organized party system.[42]

The factional alignments that developed in New York during the Confederation formed slowly and are difficult to trace. The first clash of factions appears to have occured in the Albany County legislative election of 1785. The extreme anti-Tory legislation that had been passed in 1784, much of which was vetoed by Clinton's Council of Revision, had included measures confiscating Tory property. The confiscatory measures aroused patriot property owners, and, believing the incumbent Albany

---

analyzing the vote on issues acknowledged to be of particular importance yields a more reliable picture of what sectional alignment existed, but while his description of the division is suggestive, it is not sharp enough to justify defining the factionalism of the late eighties in sectional terms.

[40] For instance, four resolutions relating to the federal impost, *Journal of the Senate*, 27 April 1786; three resolutions relating to the federal impost, *Journal of the Assembly*, 15 February 1787; three resolutions relating to the Philadelphia Convention, *Journal of the Senate*, 28 February 1787.

[41] William Nisbet Chambers, *Political Parties in a New Nation* (New York, 1963), p. 26.

[42] *Ibid.*, pp. 15, 20; Howard Lee McBain, *De Witt Clinton and the Origin of the Spoils System in New York* (New York, 1907), p. 44.

representatives to have principles of "the *levelling kind*," [43] the leading men of Albany united to place their own candidates in the New York Assembly. A combination consisting of the Schuyler family (including Schuyler's son-in-law, Alexander Hamilton) with the Van Rensselaer family, the Livingston family, and other "Gentlemen of property" in Albany County succeeded in carrying the election.[44] The next year the Schuyler coalition again used its influence to put candidates of its choice into the legislature and extended its political correspondence to other counties.[45] As they saw it, the "principal people" had formed their alliance in self-defense,[46] but the formation of one faction naturally encouraged the growth of a counter-faction, for, as Clinton later expressed it, when "all the great and opulent families were united in one Confederacy," he intended to "keep a constant eye to the members of this Combination, and he thought the People should be on their Guard against their active Efforts." [47]

The anti-Schuyler faction was led in the New York Senate by a canny, petulant individual named Abraham Yates.[48] Yates began life as a shoemaker in Albany. He went into politics in the early fifties, serving on the common council for Albany City and as county sheriff. The Revolution furthered his career, giv-

[43] Alexander Hamilton to Robert Livingston [25 April 1785], Syrett, ed., *Papers of Alexander Hamilton*, III, 609, 610.

[44] Robert Livingston to Alexander Hamilton, 13 June 1785, *ibid.*, 615.

[45] Spaulding, *New York in the Critical Period*, pp. 110, 111.

[46] Alexander Hamilton to Robert Livingston [25 April 1785], Syrett, ed., *Papers of Alexander Hamilton*, III, 609, 610.

[47] Memorandum by Rufus King, "Subject of a Conversation with Gov. Clinton," 12 June 1789, Charles A. King, *Life and Correspondence of Rufus King* (New York, 1894), I, 356.

[48] The faction had no formal organization, but Clinton was thought to be friendly to it. Yates was identified as its leader by its enemies and he was aware of being so identified ("Leo," *Daily Advertiser*, 27 February 1787; "Timon," *ibid.*, 22 January 1787; Abraham Yates to Abraham G. Lansing, 14 March 1788, Abraham Yates, Jr., Papers, New York Public Library).

ing him the opportunity to serve as chairman of the Committee of the City and County of Albany and as chairman of the Committee that drafted the constitution for New York State in 1777. When the war was over, he got an appointment as New York loan officer for the Continental Congress and won a seat in the state Senate.[49]

Abraham Yates was known for his "influence among the vulgar";[50] the "Gentlemen" of the state detested him. "Mr. Yates," wrote Alexander Hamilton, "is a man whose ignorance and perverseness are only surpassed by his pertinacity and conceit."[51] Thomas Tillotson, brother-in-law of Chancellor Robert R. Livingston, called Yates an "old booby,"[52] and the patrician Philip Schuyler, who had had some difficulty visualizing George Clinton as governor, was considerably more affronted when the shoemaker from Albany aspired to high office: "Abraham Yates," he wrote with heavy sarcasm, "I mean the Honorable Abraham Yates Esq. one of the Senate of this State, a member of the Council of Appointment—one of the Committee of the City and County of Albany, Recorder of the City of Albany—and Postmaster General, late Cobler of Laws and Old Shoes, is to be put in Nomination for Lieut. Governor."[53] On his side, Yates made no secret of his hatred for the "high-flyers."[54]

[49] Allen Johnson and Dumas Malone, eds., *Dictionary of American Biography* (New York, 1928–1937), XX, 597–598.

[50] "Timon," *Daily Advertiser*, 22 January 1787.

[51] Alexander Hamilton to Robert Morris, 13 August 1783, Syrett, ed., *Papers of Alexander Hamilton*, III, 139.

[52] Quoted in Staughton Lynd, "Abraham Yates's History of the Movement for the United States Constitution," *William and Mary Quarterly*, third series, XX (1963), 225.

[53] Quoted in *ibid.*

[54] Abraham Yates to Jeremiah Van Rensselaer and Henry Acthandt [*sic*], 29 August 1787, Burnett, ed., *Letters of Members of the Continental Congress*, VIII, 641; Alexander Hamilton to Robert Morris, 13 August 1783, Syrett, ed., *Papers of Alexander Hamilton*, III, 139.

Yates was a blunt, peevish person, who described himself as "a Suspitious Man." [55] He felt, not without some reason, that the powerful men of the state were his enemies and the enemies of all men of his class. When the New York Legislature convened, Abraham Yates was always the first man present,[56] and he spent the sessions warily eyeing the high-flyers and voting nay whenever he suspected a sinister motive behind their support of a measure. Both in the New York Senate and in the Continental Congress, the frequency with which Abraham Yates ostentatiously cast the single negative vote and then asked for a formal division on a measure that would otherwise have passed unanimously, is astonishing. The habit annoyed his colleagues. After Yates cast the one dissenting vote against the Northwest Ordinance in 1787, Nathan Dane remarked when sending a copy of the Ordinance to a friend, "All agreed to the inclosed plan except A. Yates. He appeared in this case, as in most others, not to understand the subject at all." [57] Yates's lack of understanding was not due to stupidity, for he was a clever man, nor to lack of study, for "in his own crabbed way he read as widely as Madison or Adams," [58] but Yates's intellect was burdened with an abnormal load of suspicion so that he saw diabolic plotting behind the most innocuous resolutions, and whenever he was not fully convinced of a measure's innocence he thought it most prudent to assume the worst and vote nay.

Yates's suspicion was first directed against nationalism in 1782. In that year he began to warn of possible dangers in excessive federal centralization. His attention was drawn to the threat when Robert Morris, "the Financier," created a new post of

[55] Abraham Yates to Jeremiah Van Rensselaer and Henry Acthandt [*sic*], 29 August 1787, Burnett, ed., *Letters of Members of the Continental Congress,* VIII, 641.

[56] Alexander Hamilton to Robert Morris, 13 August 1783, Syrett, ed., *Papers of Alexander Hamilton,* III, 139.

[57] Nathan Dane to Rufus King, 16 July 1787, Burnett, ed., *Letters of Members of the Continental Congress,* VIII, 622.

[58] Lynd, "Abraham Yates's History," p. 4.

state receiver of taxes and placed Alexander Hamilton in the office for the State of New York. Yates, who was the New York loan officer, was bypassed.[59] From that time on, Yates kept a special watch on Hamilton, alert to the chance that the young high-flyer's activities directed toward strengthening the central government might be calculated, for some selfish end, to give it more power than was either necessary or safe. Gradually, Yates's suspicions spread to his friends, and by the time the federal Constitution became an issue, James Madison could write of New York, "This State has long had the character of being antifederal. Most of the respectable characters are zealous on the right side. The party in power is suspected on good grounds to be on the wrong one." [60] George Washington had written wistfully some months earlier, "It is somewhat singular that a State (New York) which used to be foremost in all foederal measures, should now turn her face against them in almost every instance." [61] The development of New York's antifederal reputation was due principally, if not exclusively, to the state's action on the federal impost in 1786.

Imposts—that is, customs duties and excise taxes—were the most important sources of colonial revenue and remained essential in Confederation economies. Direct taxes, particularly if they were to be paid in hard money, struck a population unaccustomed to taxation with an impolitic openness, and they were always difficult to collect.[62] Since the principal source of New York's wealth was commerce, import duties were naturally the chief source of state revenue during the postwar period. In the

[59] Broadus Mitchell, *Alexander Hamilton* (New York, 1957, 1962), I, 265, 266; "Adolphus," *Daily Advertiser*, 19 April 1786.

[60] James Madison to Edmund Pendleton, 28 October 1787, Gaillard Hunt, ed., *Writings of James Madison Comprising His Public Papers and His Private Correspondence* (New York, 1900–1910), V, 46.

[61] George Washington to James Madison, 31 March 1787, John C. Fitzpatrick, ed., *The Writings of George Washington* (Washington, 1931–1944), XXIX, 191.

[62] E. James Ferguson, *The Power of the Purse* (Chapel Hill, N.C., 1961), p. 7.

four years following the British evacuation of the New York port, the state collected approximately $480,000 from the impost, more than half the total receipts of the treasury.[63]

The impost paid at the New York port was not a tax exclusively on New Yorkers; it also took money from the pockets of the men in neighboring states who received their imported goods through the City port. A gentleman writing from New York in 1788 believed that "half the goods consumed in Connecticut, or rather three-fourths of them, all the goods consumed in Vermont, and no small part of those consumed in the western part of Massachusetts, are bought in New York and pay an impost of five per cent. for the use of this State." [64] In the same year, Oliver Ellsworth insisted that Connecticut paid more than $50,000 to New York State each year.[65] It was a source of jealousy that New York should have all the benefit from the impost. It was felt, particularly, that Congress should have the power to collect a tax at the port of New York so that the requisitions on the other states might be reduced. In 1786 the New Jersey House of Delegates resolved "in a moody fit" that they would comply with no more federal requisitions until Congress was given the impost.[66]

Early in 1780 a motion permitting Congress to collect a duty of 1 per cent on all American imports and exports was defeated in Congress.[67] On 3 February 1781, Congress agreed to recommend a duty of 5 per cent to create a fund for paying the national debt. Governor Clinton transmitted this Congressional request to the New York Legislature, observing that "from the

[63] Thomas Cochran, *New York in the Confederation: An Economic Study* (Philadelphia, 1932), p. 167n.

[64] Quoted in Allan Nevins, *The American States During and After the Revolution* (New York, 1927), p. 560.

[65] *Ibid.*

[66] William Grayson to James Madison, 22 March 1786, Burnett, ed., *Letters of Members of the Continental Congress*, VIII, 332.

[67] Worthington C. Ford and Gaillard Hunt, eds., *Journals of the Continental Congress* (Washington, 1904–1937), XVI, 261.

importance of the measures recommended by these resolutions, I doubt not they will engage your earliest attention." [68] New York's federal disposition was manifested in a prompt and full compliance with the Congressional recommendation. The resolution passed by the legislature noted that the duties collected in New York would be managed "under such penalties and regulations, and by such officers, as Congress should from time to time make, order, and appoint." [69]

Other states were less cooperative. Throughout 1781 Robert Morris fired indignant epistles at the delinquent legislatures, but at the end of 1782 the impost still had not been accepted unanimously. The impost proposals were not intended as amendments to the Articles of Confederation, but unanimity was required nevertheless, since the states that did grant the impost did so only on the condition that all the other states would grant it. For this reason, the action of the Rhode Island legislature toward the end of 1782, unanimously refusing to grant the 5 per cent impost, "pretty thoroughly blasted" [70] the hope of Congress's obtaining any revenue from it.

Congress spent the first four months of 1783 seeking a new ground for its revenue measure, and on 18 April 1783 a revised recommendation was sent to the states: the impost of 5 per cent would be used only to pay interest and principal on the national debt and the grant would expire automatically in twenty-five years; the states would appoint the collectors, although Congress would have the power to regulate their activities and to remove them. The only state to vote against this resolution in Congress was Rhode Island. New York's vote was divided. Interestingly enough, it was Alexander Hamilton who voted with Rhode Island in this instance, and William Floyd, an Antifederalist in

[68] Lincoln, ed., *Messages from the Governors,* II, 120.

[69] DeAlva Stanwood Alexander, *A Political History of the State of New York* (New York, 1906), I, 24.

[70] James Madison to Edmund Randolph, 19 November 1782, Burnett, ed., *Letters of Members of the Continental Congress,* VIII, 545.

1788, who voted with the majority in favor of the impost.[71] Hamilton explained to Governor Clinton that he believed the April 1783 proposal would "have little more chance of success than a better one; and that if agreed to by all the states, it will in a great measure fail in the execution." In other words, Hamilton did not believe the act strong enough. Nevertheless, he told Clinton that he hoped "our state will consent to the plan proposed; because it is in her interest at all events to promote the payment of the public debt on Continental funds (independent of the general considerations of Union & propriety)." [72]

Meanwhile, in New York, the legislature still favored granting the impost, although there had been some parliamentary dickering over details. On 1 March 1783 a bill bearing the ponderous title, "An Act to repeal an Act, entitled, 'An Act to repeal an Act, entitled, an Act authorizing the United States in Congress assembled, to levy a Duty on foreign Merchandize, imported into this State; and for other Purposes therein mentioned' " was introduced in the state Senate, and passed with but a single negative vote. The long title was confusing; Abraham Yates demanded a division and recorded his nay.[73]

The Congressional impost recommendation of 1783 made unhurried progress through the various state legislatures. By the spring of 1786, every state but New York had acted and given more-or-less unconditional approval. "There is at present a greater prospect of the impost than has been ever known," William Grayson wrote to Madison in March 1786. "Georgia and Rhode Island have come into the measure,[74] and it remains only with N. York to give her consent to make it productive." Grayson noted that the legislature of New York was presently deliberating on the impost, "but," he said, "I doubt extremely whether

[71] *Journals of the Continental Congress,* XXIV, 257–260.

[72] Alexander Hamilton to George Clinton, 14 May 1783, Syrett, ed., *Papers of Alexander Hamilton,* III, 354, 355.

[73] *Journal of the Senate,* 1 March 1783.

[74] Georgia had never acted on the Congressional impost of 1781, and Rhode Island had rejected it.

the result will be favorable." [75] There was good reason to doubt the issue, for Abraham Yates, writing in the newspapers under the pseudonymns "Sydney," "Rough Hewer," and "Rough Hewer, Jr.," had now thrown the full weight of his considerable political talent against the passage of the 1783 impost in the form recommended by Congress.

"*The Legislature which shall give the last fiat to this recommendation of congress*," wrote Yates in March 1785, "*will sign the death warrant of American Liberty!*" [76] Yates did not object to voting money to Congress. "All agree," he said, "that money must be raised . . . the *power to raise the money* is the only bone in contention." [77] For more than a year Yates beat on this drum, orating before his friends in the Senate and reiterating the theme in the press. The Congressional request for the impost, he cried, was not an innocent program to raise necessary federal funds, but a nefarious plot to destroy American liberties by joining the power of the purse and the power of the sword in "a *mighty continental legislative*, in time (and God only knows how soon) to merge and swallow up the legislatives of the particular states." [78] Yates's fears now seem excessive, but it would be wrong to dismiss them as insincere or as foolish delusions, for there were certainly some among the advocates of the impost who did not cherish the federal system of independent states,[79] and the best political thought of the time agreed that republicanism could not endure in a large consolidated state.

The fear of Congressional power, which developed in New York under Yates's careful nursing, was directly at variance

[75] William Grayson to James Madison, 22 March 1786, Burnett, ed., *Letters of Members of the Continental Congress*, VIII, 333.

[76] [Abraham Yates], *Political Papers, Addressed to the Advocates for a Congressional Revenue, in the State of New-York* (New York, 1786), p. 13.

[77] *Ibid.*, p. 4.

[78] *Ibid.*, p. 19.

[79] Henry Knox to Rufus King, 15 July 1788, quoted in Charles Warren, *The Making of the Constitution* (Boston, 1928), p. 308.

with the economic interest of New Yorkers. New York State had been accepting federal obligations in payment of state taxes and so had acquired a significant percentage of the national debt. New York consequently had a special interest in bolstering the general revenues. Hostility to the impost in New York State had an exclusively political, not an economic motivation. It rested on fear of centralization.[80]

New York did not reject the Congressional impost request. Instead, the legislature attempted to grant Congress the impost revenues without surrendering more power than was unavoidable. The impost act that was passed by the New York Legislature in the spring of 1786 granted the duties requested by Congress, incorporating in the resolution the same schedule of articles and rates as appeared in the Congressional resolution of 18 April 1783. Congress was not permitted, however, to have exclusive control over the collectors; the state would appoint them and stipulate the method of collection. Congress could prosecute negligent collectors in the New York State Supreme Court or Court of Exchequer, and if the officer was convicted another would be appointed. In addition, New York insisted that its paper money should be accepted in payment of the impost, although the state agreed to make up the loss to Congress if the paper should fall below its face value in gold.[81]

The legislature believed that its impost act would be acceptable to Congress if money and not power was the true object. Yet the New Yorkers had failed to consider the imperfect forms that the impost grants of other states had taken. A number of states had stipulated that they would not permit Congress to collect duties until Congress had a similar power in all the states. Since New York's method of state collection would not meet the

[80] Alexander Hamilton to George Clinton, 14 May 1783, Syrett, ed., *Papers of Alexander Hamilton,* III, 354, 355; Cochran, *New York in the Confederation,* p. 159; Main, *Antifederalists,* p. 75.

[81] *Journal of the Assembly,* 13 April 1786, 15 April 1786, 1 May 1786, 4 May 1786; *Journal of the Senate,* 27 April 1786.

condition set by those states, it would prevent the collection of any money whatever. It seemed reasonable to expect that once these facts were explained to the New York Legislature, they would amend their resolution accordingly. "I think there can be little doubt," wrote Rufus King, "but that the next assembly of New York will fully accede to the system, and thereby authorize the commencement of a plan of revenue substantial and productive." [82]

Unfortunately, Congress decided not to wait for the next regular meeting of the legislature. On 11 August 1786 Congress resolved "that it be earnestly recommended to the Executive of the State of New York, immediately to convene the legislature of the said state, to take into consideration the recommendation of the 18 of April 1783, for the purpose of granting the System of impost to the United States, in such conformity with the Acts and grants of the other states, as, on her part, to enable the United States in Congresss assembled, to carry the same into immediate effect." [83] This resolution was singularly ill-advised, as those who were familiar with New York and with Governor George Clinton immediately realized.

James Monroe of Virginia wrote to Clinton shortly after the resolution had been passed, explaining that his delegation had been opposed to rejecting New York's impost act. He realized, he said, that such a rejection "wo'd unnecessarily irritate the state." He thought that Congress ought to have drafted an ordinance for putting the impost into effect "which sho'd shew to the legislature it was not a system of oppression, but in conformity with the laws and constitution of the state itself," thus persuading New York to grant the impost in a form that would make it acceptable to the other states. It was certain, Monroe said, that the impost could never be collected on the basis of the

[82] Rufus King to John Adams, 5 May 1786, Burnett, ed., *Letters of Members of the Continental Congress,* VIII, 355.

[83] *Journals of the Continental Congress,* XXXI, 513.

act passed by New York, "yet in making this known to the state or in proposing any alteration of it I co'd wish it might be in a manner that might give offence to none, especially to those who contributed most to bring it about and are the best friends of the revolution." [84]

Alexander Hamilton also realized that the Congressional resolution could hardly fail to have pernicious consequences. The governor might refuse to call an extraordinary session of the legislature, which would "derogate from the respect due to Congress," or he might call the legislature, which would make the troublesome trip to New York City during the harvest season most reluctantly and would consider the Congressional resolution while in a sour humor.[85] Either way, the form of the impost grant would not be changed and bad feeling would develop between New York and the United States in Congress assembled. Events followed the first path; Clinton refused to call a special session.

Clinton made an extremely polite reply to the Congressional resolution: "I beg leave to assure your excellency," he began his letter to the president of Congress, "that I entertain the highest deference and respect for the authority of Congress," but it was not in his power to oblige Congress by calling the legislature into session before the time fixed by law. He had no power to call special sessions "except on extraordinary occasions; and as the present business proposed for their consideration has already been repeatedly laid before them, and so recently as at their last session received their determination, it cannot come within that description." He did not feel it was his place to express any opinion about the resolution passed by the New York Legislature. Clinton concluded by declaring that he was "unhappy to be formally called on by Congress, in an instance in which I cannot

[84] James Monroe to George Clinton, 16 August 1786, Burnett, ed., *Letters of Members of the Continental Congress,* VIII, 431.

[85] "Address to the Legislature," 19 January 1787, Syrett. ed., *Papers of Alexander Hamilton,* IV, 4.

yield a compliance without breaking through one of those checks which the wisdom of our constitution has provided against the abuse of office." [86]

Clinton had held his temper, but the New York representatives in Congress seethed with righteous anger. They found it scarcely tolerable that their state, which had always been noted for its federal disposition, had sacrificed so much in the war, and had been so attentive to Congressional requisitions since the peace, should be peremptorily directed to reconsider an official action. It was even more offensive that she should be directed to reconsider immediately when the regular meeting of the legislature was only four months away. The New York delegation thought the sudden concern of Congress for its revenues was very improperly placed, and Melancton Smith [87] introduced a motion that committees be sent to the legislatures of Connecticut, New Jersey, and North Carolina, which still had not passed acts providing for the previous year's requisitions, in order "to explain to them more fully the embarassed state of the public finances, to urge upon them the necessity of a full and immediate compliance with the said requisition." And, in addition, Smith suggested that special addresses be sent to New Hampshire and Maryland, which had not complied with their requisitions in full, "enforcing the necessity of a full and immediate compliance therewith." The embarassed delegates voted to postpone.[88]

Still, Congress was not willing to relax the pressure on New York. The committee to which Clinton's letter was referred reported three resolutions explaining in detail why Congress considered New York's resolution inadequate, insisting that since

[86] 16 August 1786, Lincoln, ed., *Messages from the Governors*, II, 279.

[87] Smith's contemporaries spelled his first name in a variety of ways, including "Melankthon," "Melancthon," and "Melanchthon." His parents may have used the last form (J. W. Poucher, "Melanchthon Smith," *Year Book of the Dutchess County Historical Society* [1925], 40). Smith himself, however, always used the form "Melancton," as may be seen from his autograph letters.

[88] *Journals of the Continental Congress*, XXXI, 515–516.

only New York's approval was needed to put the impost into operation, the occasion was "extraordinary" as the word was used in the New York constitution, and repeating the demand that Clinton convene the legislature.[89]

Clinton studied the congressional resolutions, but he could not agree with their interpretation of his duty under the state constitution. His scruples on the point of employing the power to call special sessions were particularly strong,[90] nor did he see anything in Congress's request that would suffer from a delay of a few months. He replied to Congress in a letter still polite, but now faintly reproachful, declaring that he could not "discover a single matter stated in the Report on which the present Resolutions are founded, but such as were fully within the knowledge of the Legislature before, and at the time when they adjourned their last meeting." As to his duty as governor, he conceived "it would be criminal to yield up my judgment from motives of complaissance." [91]

Melancton Smith had predicted to his colleagues in Congress that a repetition of the request to Clinton "would be improper as it would involve an interference of Congress on a question respecting the construction of the Constitution of that State upon which Congress have by the Constitution no right to decide," that it would lead to an open dispute between Congress and the governor, and "disgust the Legislature" of New York.[92] The New York Legislature was, indeed, most decidedly disgusted.

When the legislature convened at its appointed time in January 1787, Governor Clinton submitted the correspondence that had passed between himself and Congress during the summer.[93] Both houses made a point of expressing strong approval of the

[89] *Journals of the Continental Congress,* XXXI, 558–561.

[90] See above, pp. 23–24.

[91] Quoted in Cochran, *New York in the Confederation,* p. 176.

[92] *Journals of the Continental Congress,* XXXI, 556n.

[93] Lincoln, ed., *Messages from the Governors,* II, 264.

governor's conduct when they replied to his opening message.[94] The significance of that action did not escape members of Congress, one of the honorable gentlemen noting that by their addresses the legislators had "step'd as twere out of their way to give Congress a Slap in the face." [95] When the bill to reconsider the impost came up before the Assembly in February, Alexander Hamilton took the floor in favor of a grant acceptable to Congress.[96] He spoke for an hour and twenty minutes.[97] When he sat down the vote was taken immediately, without debate,[98] and revision of the impost failed by a substantial majority. The Assembly was still willing to grant the money to Congress, but it absolutely refused to yield control of the collectors.[99] Men who had previously stood with Hamilton in support of Congressional control of the impost and other strong measures to increase the

[94] *Journal of the Senate*, 17 January 1787; *Journal of the Assembly*, 20 January 1787.

[95] Stephen Mix Mitchell to Jeremiah Wadsworth, 24 January 1787, Burnett, ed., *Letters of Members of the Continental Congress*, VIII, 531.

[96] Syrett, ed., *Papers of Alexander Hamilton*, IV, 71–92.

[97] Philip Schuyler to John Lansing, Jr., 20 February 1787, John Lansing, Jr., Papers, New-York Historical Society; *New-York Journal*, 22 February 1787. McDonald describes this address as a "day-long speech" which left Hamilton "doubled up in pain from physical exertion" (*We the People*, p. 285n.). This is an amusing misreading of the source. The article McDonald cites from the *Daily Advertiser*, 27 February 1787, refers to the "Goliath" of the anti-impost group, Abraham Yates, as "doubled up" while listening to Hamilton's oration. Yates had always found Schuyler's son-in-law hard to stomach.

[98] McDonald, citing "Leo" in the *Daily Advertiser*, 27 February 1787, declares that failure to debate important issues was a "customary parliamentary practice" with the "Clintonians" (*We the People*, pp. 286, 287, 287n.). Actually, and as "Leo" describes it, allowing an important issue to go to a vote without debate was an unusual occurrence. The impost incident, as described by "Leo," was, in the strict legal sense, an exception proving the existence of a contrary rule. The silence of the anti-impost group was remarkable and particularly offensive for being so unexpected (Philip Schuyler to John Lansing, Jr., 20 February 1787, John Lansing, Jr., Papers, New-York Historical Society).

[99] *Journal of the Assembly*, 15 February 1787.

power of Congress, now voted against him without so much as offering an explanation for their change of opinion. It was apparently a studied insult.[100]

Outside the legislature a division in public opinion became noticeable. Before the summer of 1786, there had been very little opposition to the impost expressed in the newspapers, and most of the anti-impost [101] articles had been written by Abraham Yates. Gradually, in the fall of 1786, Yates began to find supporters, and although articles from his hand ceased appearing, the impost continued to be debated.[102]

One of the first to come forward to argue against "the specious arguments that have been used . . . to prove the urgent necessity of enlarging the powers of Congress," was a writer using the signature "Philo-Patria." This writer placed an article in the *New-York Journal* at the end of September 1786 and observed that he "was lead to these reflections, on hearing the conduct and policy of the legislature of this state reprobated, for not adopting the recommendation of Congress (of the 18th of April 1783) in its fullest latitude." He resented "the clamour which has been artfully raised against this state" and pointed out that "not one in the union, made greater exertions throughout the war; and, that since the peace, none has either more fully complied with requisitions founded on the confederation, or discovered a better disposition to grant such other aids as the public exegencies require." [103] Another writer in the same paper also connected indignation at the slurs on the federal reputation of

[100] Philip Schuyler to John Lansing, Jr., 20 February 1787, John Lansing, Jr., Papers, New-York Historical Society; Syrett, ed., *Papers of Alexander Hamilton*, IV, 80.

[101] The term "anti-impost" is somewhat misleading, since the "anti-impost" men usually agreed that the proceeds of a customs tax should be given to Congress. For convenience the term is used to indicate those who opposed the impost in the form recommended by Congress.

[102] The impost continued to have numerous vocal supporters, especially in New York City, but it is the birth of a comparatively large and vocal opposition that is of interest.

[103] *New-York Journal*, 28 September 1786.

his state with an opposition to the impost based on the Yates argument: "It is *money*, and not *power*, that ought to be the object," insisted "A Republican," "the former will pay our *debts* —the latter might destroy our *liberties*." [104]

Thus, by the beginning of 1787, the year that was to see the meeting of a federal constitutional convention, New Yorkers had started to take sides on the issue of federal power. The adjectives "anti-federalist" and "federalist" were used as epithets as men discussed the impost, although they were not used to denote parties until after the Constitution became a subject of political controversy and the basis of political division in September 1787. Meanwhile, the failure of the impost, which had seemed so near success,[105] brought the Confederation to a new point of crisis. "None will have the hardiness to deny that the federal government trembles to its basis and threatens ruin by its fall," wrote an essayist in the *Daily Advertiser* in February. "Among wise, and great, and good men throughout the continent, the only question is, can it be propped? or Phoenix like must a new one rise from its ashes?" [106]

[104] *New-York Journal*, 12 October 1786; 19 October 1786.

[105] The rejection by New York was not the sole cause of the impost's failure, but the importance of New York's concurrence was overestimated even by contemporaries (Ferguson, *Power of the Purse*, p. 239).

[106] *Daily Advertiser*, 13 February 1787.

III

A More Perfect Union

NEW YORK was the first state to propose a general convention to revise the Articles of Confederation. On Saturday, 20 July 1782, a resolution passed in the New York Senate unanimously, unopposed even by Abraham Yates. The resolution observed that "the radical Source of most of our Embarassments, is the Want of sufficient Power in Congress," that the defects of the Articles of Confederation "ought to be without Loss of Time repaired," and that to achieve revision it would be desirable to call "a general Convention of the States, specially authorised to revise and amend the Confederation." [1] Hamilton and Schuyler had been advocating such a convention for some time,[2] but Congress never acted on New York's proposal.

Rather than a general convention, local meetings between two

[1] *Journal of the Senate of the State of New York* (Albany, 1782), 21 July 1782. The Assembly concurred on the following day.

[2] Alexander Hamilton to James Duane, 3 September 1780, Harold C. Syrett, ed., and Jacob E. Cooke, assoc. ed., *The Papers of Alexander Hamilton* (New York, 1961–), II, 400–418; Philip Schuyler to George Washington, 21 January 1781, Jared Sparks, ed., *Correspondence of the American Revolution; being Letters of Eminent Men to George Washington* (Boston, 1853), III, 213. Hamilton is generally assumed to have been the author of the New York resolution for a general convention, but there is no conclusive evidence of the fact (Syrett, ed., *Papers of Alexander Hamilton,* III, 110n.).

or more states had been frequently called to deal with some specific commercial or economic problem. Congress did not approve of such conventions, which, as one member put it, had "the appearance of young Congresses," [3] but they were frequently necessary when a problem arose that Congress seemed unable to handle. New York participated in half a dozen.[4] But as the years passed, a general dislike of the divisive sectional conventions added to a history of Congressional failure to obtain commercial and taxing powers from the states nourished a desire for a convention of all the states devoted exclusively to the problem of constitutional reform.

The meeting that culminated in the Constitutional Convention at Philadelphia began like many others. In 1785 Virginia and Maryland sent commissioners to Alexandria to discuss problems relating to the Potomac River, their mutual boundary. The convention moved to George Washington's home at Mount Vernon, and after the immediate questions had been settled, the commissioners moved to a discussion of the broader issues of customs duties and the regulation of commerce in general. The Mount Vernon Convention reported to the legislatures of Maryland and Virginia. The former considered the report and then proposed that invitations be sent to Pennsylvania and Delaware inviting those states to join with Virginia and Maryland to formulate a common commercial policy. Virginia's legislature went even further, proposing that all of the Confederation states send delegates to a general trade convention to meet in Annapolis in September 1786.[5]

The trade convention proposed by Virginia was not likely to

[3] Gaillard Hunt, ed., *Writings of James Madison, Comprising His Public Papers and His Private Correspondence* (New York, 1900–1910), I, 438.

[4] Curtis P. Nettels, *The Emergence of a National Economy, 1775–1815* (New York, 1961), p. 28; Charles Warren, *The Making of the Constitution* (Boston, 1928), p. 9; George Bancroft, "A Hartford Convention in 1780," *Magazine of American History*, VIII, part 2 (1882), 690.

[5] Max Farrand, *The Fathers of the Constitution* (New Haven, Conn., 1921), p. 100.

appeal to those who were concerned for the authority of Congress. As Daniel Carroll put it, "the measure appeared . . . to have a tendency to weaken the authority of Congress, on which the *Union,* & consequently the Liberty and safety of all the States depend." He believed that "all matters of a general tendency, shou'd be in the representative Body of the whole, or under its authority." [6] But a number of nationalists believed it would be possible to turn the trade convention to some good by making it "subservient to a plenipotentiary Convention for amending the Confederation," [7] devoting the meeting to preparations for a second general meeting rather than to a discussion of commerce.

New York State accepted Virginia's invitation to appoint delegates to the Annapolis Convention. On 5 May 1786 the legislature named Alexander Hamilton, R. R. Livingston, James Duane, Egbert Benson, Leonard Gansevoort, and Robert C. Livingston, and provided that any three of them could cast the state's vote at Annapolis.[8] About three weeks after the appointments had been made, Alexander Hamilton wrote to Chancellor R. R. Livingston: "We have talked over the Question. Who of the Commissioners are to go to the Southward? And it seems to be decided that you and myself are to be of the number and that a *third* must be either Mr. R. C. Livingston or Mr. Gansevort, as they may arrange it between themselves." [9] But Chancellor Livingston refused to go. Both he and James Duane were, according to Rufus King, "very little concerned in the politics of the present times," [10] and no one was surprised when Duane pleaded

[6] Daniel Carroll to James Madison, 13 March 1786, United States Bureau of Rolls and Library, *Documentary History of the Constitution of the United States* (Washington, 1894–1903), IV, 6.

[7] James Madison to Thomas Jefferson, 12 August 1786, *ibid.*, 21.

[8] *Journal of the Assembly of the State of New York* (New York, 1786), 5 May 1786.

[9] Alexander Hamilton to R. R. Livingston, 23 May 1786, Syrett, ed., *Papers of Alexander Hamilton,* III, 671.

[10] Rufus King to Jonathan Jackson, 3 September 1786, Massachusetts Historical Society *Proceedings,* XLIX, 89.

illness as an excuse for his disinclination to make the journey to Maryland. Robert C. Livingston explained that business would prevent him from prompt attendance at the Convention, and Leonard Gansevoort simply declined the appointment. By the last week in August Egbert Benson was hesitating,[11] and only Alexander Hamilton had firmly stated his intention to go south.

In the end, Egbert Benson and Alexander Hamilton left New York City for Annapolis on 1 September 1786.[12] Since the legislature had stipulated that a minimum of three delegates must be present to cast the vote of the state in the convention, the New Yorkers must have realized that their presence would not further the establishment of commercial agreements. Yet they set out on the journey eagerly enough. Neither man was particularly interested in the trade convention,[13] but both saw the meeting at Annapolis as an opportunity "for obtaining a Convention to revise the whole of the Articles of Confederation as a Mode or System of Government." [14]

When the Annapolis Convention began its deliberations, only three states were present officially. Virginia, Delaware, and New Jersey had sent full delegations, one man arrived from Pennsylvania, and New York was represented by Benson and Hamilton.[15] Attendance might well have improved had the Convention been willing to wait. Travel along the rutty roads of the old Confederation was not a business one could plan according to

[11] Memorandum of Egbert Benson, 31 December 1816, quoted in Alfred B. Street, *The Council of Revision of the State of New York* (Albany, 1859), p. 183n.

[12] Egbert Benson and Alexander Hamilton to John Lansing, 1 September 1786, John Lansing, Jr., Papers, New-York Historical Society.

[13] Statement by Robert Troup, quoted in Allan Nevins, *The American States During and After the Revolution, 1775–1789* (New York, 1924), p. 284.

[14] Memorandum by Egbert Benson, 31 December 1816, quoted in Street, *Council of Revision*, p. 183n.

[15] James Madison to Thomas Jefferson, 12 August 1786, *Documentary History*, IV, 21.

time tables, nor was it possible to inform those who were waiting when bad weather, sickness, or a lame horse forced a delay. Promptness was not to be expected of delegates under such circumstances, and official bodies were accustomed to long waits before quorums assembled. The scanty attendance at Annapolis worked to the interest of those who wished to avoid the discussion of commercial matters and use the convention to issue a call for a second convention with broader powers. One observer believed that some of the delegates appointed to Annapolis had purposely dawdled on their way to the meeting in order to provide those already present with a pretext for adjourning.[16] Another blamed the convention for refusing to wait long enough for the missing delegates to make their appearance.[17] At any rate, the Annapolis Convention began its meetings on 11 September 1786, and decided the same day that it would "be inexpedient for this Convention, in which so few States are represented, to proceed in the business committed to them." [18] By 14 September, they were ready to adjourn.

The report of the Annapolis Convention was the work of Alexander Hamilton.[19] It was directed to the legislatures of Virginia, Delaware, Pennsylvania, New Jersey, and New York, the five states that had representatives present; and, "from motives of respect," the convention sent copies of the report to the legislatures of the other eight states and to Congress. After explaining that the delegates felt they could not "proceed upon the business of their Mission" because of the "partial and defective"

[16] Louis G. Otto to Charles Gravier Vergennes, 10 October 1786, George Bancroft, *History of the Formation of the Constitution of the United States of America* (New York, 1882), II, 399–401.

[17] *New-York Morning Post,* 8 November 1787.

[18] Egbert Benson's Minutes of the Annapolis Convention, Emmet Collection, #9398–9399, New York Public Library.

[19] James Madison to Noah Webster, 12 October 1804, Hunt, ed., *Writings of James Madison,* VII, 164, 165. Hamilton was not, however, an official member of the committee that framed the report, and Madison believed that the first formal suggestion for a second convention was made by Abraham Clark of New Jersey.

representation, the report made a passing reference to that "business," the power to regulate trade, observing that any attempt to deal with the subject would probably "require a correspondent adjustment of other Parts of the Foederal System." Then the commissioners expressed "their unanimous conviction" that every state in the Confederation should appoint commissioners to meet in Philadelphia on the second Monday of the following May in order "to take into Consideration the situation of the United States, to devise such further Provisions as shall appear to them necessary to render the Constitution of the Foederal Government adequate to the exigencies of the Union; and to report such an Act for that purpose to the United States in Congress Assembled." They recommended that Congress treat the report of the Philadelphia convention as suggested amendments to the Articles of Confederation, which, when "agreed to by them and afterwards confirmed by the Legislatures of every State," would become part of the constitution.[20]

On 20 September 1786, the Annapolis report was laid before Congress, but it did not become the order of the day until 21 February 1787, almost four months after it was first presented. The delay resulted from a disagreement between those who endorsed the Annapolis report and those who felt that an amending convention originating with any body other than Congress would be unconstitutional. Those who held the second view wished some state to instruct its delegates in Congress to call for a Congressionally sponsored convention in place of that called by the men at Annapolis.[21] In mid-February, the New York Legislature issued such instructions.

On 15 February 1787, the New York Assembly listened to Alexander Hamilton speak in favor of the Congressional impost and then voted against it. But since Schuyler and Hamilton real-

[20] *Documentary History*, I, 1–5.

[21] *Independent Gazetter* (Philadelphia), 16 March 1787, quoted in Warren, *Making of the Constitution*, p. 43n.; Henry Lee to Henry St. George Tucker, 20 October 1786, Edmund C. Burnett, ed., *Letters of Members of the Continental Congress*, (Washington, 1921–1936), VIII, 489.

ized that the vote did not indicate a desire to weaken the Union, they chose the following day to introduce a proposal to instruct the state's delegates in Congress to call for the meeting of a general convention.[22] The same men who had voted against the impost the previous day now voted in favor of the motion designed to strengthen the Confederation, and it passed in the Assembly without difficulty.[23] In the Senate, Abraham Yates raised some objection, but the motion passed by a vote of ten to nine.[24]

When the New York delegates presented their instructions to Congress, seven states had already appointed delegates to the Philadelphia Convention, and Congress was sharply divided over whether or not to endorse the Annapolis resolutions.[25] But when the New Yorkers introduced the proposal for a convention originating with Congress, specifying no particular time or place, Congress voted against considering it. New York State was suspected of hostility toward the central government, and the motives behind her call for a convention were distrusted. "There was reason to believe . . . from the Language of the instruction from N York," wrote James Madison, "that her object was to obtain a new convention, under the sanction of Congs. rather than to accede to the one on foot, or perhaps by dividing the plans of the States in their appointments to frustrate all of them. The latter suspicion is in some degree countenanced by their refusal of the Impost a few days before the instruction passed, and by their other marks of an unfederal disposition." [26] Madison was certainly wrong in his suspicion; the instruction to the New York delegation had been put through the legislature

[22] Philip Schuyler to Henry Van Schaack, 13 March 1787, Henry C. Van Schaack, ed., *Memoirs of Henry Van Schaack, Embracing Sections of his Correspondence* (Chicago, 1892) p. 150.

[23] *Journal of the Assembly*, 17 February 1787.

[24] *Journal of the Senate*, 20 February 1787.

[25] The Congressional committee endorsed the Annapolis recommendation by a majority of a single vote.

[26] Madison's notes, 21 February 1787, Worthington C. Ford and Gaillard Hunt, eds., *Journals of the Continental Congress, 1774–1789* (Washington, 1904–1937), XXXIII, 723.

at the urging of Alexander Hamilton and Philip Schuyler,[27] men whose federalism cannot be questioned. But the suspicion of New York was real.

Fortunately, Massachusetts immediately proposed a compromise resolution, which did not mention the Annapolis proposal at all, but called for a convention summoned by Congress to meet at the same time and place as that specified by the Annapolis Convention. So it was agreed "that in the opinion of Congress it is expedient that on the second Monday in May next a Convention of delegates who shall have been appointed by the several States be held at Philadelphia for the sole and express purpose of revising the Articles of Confederation and reporting to Congress and the several legislatures such alterations and provisions therein as shall when agreed to in Congress and confirmed by the States render the federal Constitution adequate to the exigencies of Government and the preservation of the Union." [28]

Two days after Congress passed the resolution calling on the states to send delegates to Philadelphia, Governor Clinton laid the resolution before the New York Legislature, and within a week the Assembly had passed a resolution approving the appointment of delegates. Some men from other states had doubted whether New York would send a delegation to Philadephia, so strongly was the federalism of the state supected. Madison, while speculating on the probability of New York sending men to Philadelphia, pointed out again that the New York Assembly "has just rejected the impost which has an unpropitious aspect." [29] But Edward Rutledge was puzzled by the rumor that "the Eastern States [30] will not send delegates to the Convention.

[27] Philip Schuyler to Henry Van Schaack, 13 March 1787, Van Schaack, ed., *Memoirs of Henry Van Schaack*, p. 150.

[28] *Journals of the Continental Congress*, XXXII, 73, 74.

[29] James Madison to Thomas Jefferson, 15 February 1787, *Documentary History*, IV, 70.

[30] The states east of the Hudson River, that is, New England and New York.

They of all others," he wrote, "are more immediately interested in vesting powers in the United Council." [31] The fear that New York and the New England States [32] intended to boycott the Philadelphia Convention was based on a mistaken belief that the denunication of the Annapolis call for a general convention on the grounds that it was unconstitutional was a mere pretext while the states that waited for the Congressional call before appointing delegates really opposed the purpose of the proposed convention to strengthen the general government. Actually the stated objection was the real one, and after the Congressional call every state except Rhode Island chose a delegation.[33]

On 26 February 1787, the New York Assembly passed a resolution calling for the selection of five delegates by joint ballot of the Assembly and the Senate.[34] When the resolution was sent to the Senate, Schuyler noted that a vote by joint ballot would result in an opportunity for the Yates faction "to commit the delegation to creatures of their own complexion." He rose and argued against the Assembly resolution, as he said, "on the specious and well founded reason that the senate would be deprived of the proper share of influence in the appointment." Yates and Schuyler, old foes that they were, understood each other well, and Yates immediately saw the factional motive behind Schuyler's objection. But at a time when party and faction were not respectable, Yates "dared not avow" his conviction that Schuyler was acting for party motives, and he could only argue "most strenuously for adopting the resolution as it then stood," [35] so Schuyler won the move. Schuyler then put his own resolution,

[31] Edward Rutledge to Richard Henry Lee, 27 March 1787, quoted in Warren, *Making of the Constitution*, p. 51.

[32] New Hampshire appointed delegates to the Philadelphia Convention on 27 November 1786, before Congress passed its resolution. Massachusetts appointed delegates on 10 March and Connecticut on 12 May.

[33] Warren, *Making of the Constitution*, p. 43.

[34] *Journal of the Assembly*, 26 February 1787.

[35] Philip Schuyler to Henry Van Schaack, 13 March 1787, Van Schaack, ed., *Memoirs of Henry Van Schaack*, p. 151.

calling for the election of the delegates by separate ballot in the two houses. As he later gloatingly reported to a friend, "Abraham attempted to shackle this, but without success." [36] Two points for Schuyler.

Abraham Yates won the next play, carrying a motion put by his friend John Haring that reduced the size of the delegation from five members to three, but he failed to carry the last resolution in the series, which would have limited the powers of the delegates at Philadelphia to recommendations "not repugnant to or inconsistent with the constitution of this State." [37] For some reason Schuyler believed that such limitation of the power of the delegation "would have rendered their mission absolutely useless." [38]

This parliamentary maneuver is of special interest as an illustration of the extraordinarily amorphous nature of the factional division in New York. The choice of the Philadelphia delegation was an issue that the leaders of both factions recognized as a party question, identifying each other as political enemies. Yet the leaders could not command a party vote. Of the four questions put to a ballot—to approve the Assembly resolution as it stood, to elect the delegates by separate ballot, to limit the size of the delegation to three, and to limit the powers of the delegation —the vote on three is recorded. The separate ballots desired by Schuyler was won by a vote of twelve to six. The size of the delegation was reduced, as Yates wished, by a vote of eleven to seven. On the question that seems most significant, the motion to limit the powers of the delegation, the Senate divided evenly, nine to nine. The casting vote of the president of the Senate, Lieutenant-Governor Pierre Van Cortlandt, won that motion for Schuyler,[39] although Van Cortlandt, who served under

[36] *Ibid.* [37] *Journal of the Senate,* 28 February 1787.

[38] Philip Schuyler to Henry Van Schaack, 13 March 1787, Van Schaack, ed., *Memoirs of Henry Van Schaack,* p. 150.

[39] *Journal of the Senate,* 28 February 1787. There are minor factual errors in the discussions of these votes in Thomas Cochran, *New York in the Confederation: An Economic Study* (Philadelphia, 1932), pp. 178,

George Clinton for six terms, has been identified as a member of the anti-Schuyler faction.[40]

As it was finally decided, the Assembly and the Senate were to meet separately on 6 March and draw up a list of delegates. There was no difficulty in the balloting. In the Assembly each member nominated his own slate. Robert Yates appeared on every man's list; Alexander Hamilton had every vote but his own and that of two others, while John Lansing received twenty-six of the fifty-two votes. The Assembly thus agreed in the nomination of these three men. James Duane won twenty-three votes, but no one else was in the running—there was the merest scattering of votes for R. R. Livingston, Melancton Smith, and John Tayler.[41] Meanwhile the Senate, which was meeting at the same time, recorded that "*the Honorable Robert Yates, Esquire, John Lansing, junior, and Alexander Hamilton, Esquires* were openly nominated." [42] Since both houses agreed on the same men, the matter was settled. About a month later, Hamilton and Schuyler attempted to increase the size of the delegation to five, hoping for the appointment of R. R. Livingston, James Duane, Egbert Benson, or John Jay; [43] but while Hamilton persuaded the Assembly to pass what had been its original plan, the Senate insisted on holding the size of the delegation to three.[44]

Historians who have assumed the existence of a fully developed party system in New York have found it necessary to explain why the members of the "Clintonian" legislature put their political enemy, Alexander Hamilton, on the delegation to Philadelphia. They have concluded that there was a political

180; John C. Miller, *Alexander Hamilton: Portrait in Paradox* (New York, 1959), p. 152; E. Wilder Spaulding, *New York in the Critical Period, 1783–1789* (New York, 1932), p. 187.

[40] Spaulding, *New York in the Critical Period*, p. 73.

[41] *Journal of the Assembly*, 6 March 1787.

[42] *Journal of the Senate*, 6 March 1787.

[43] *Daily Advertiser* (New York), 24 April 1787.

[44] *Journal of the Assembly*, 16 April 1787; *Journal of the Senate*, 18 April 1787.

deal which would allow the minority party to place one member on the delegation.[45] Yet even if parties had existed, there could have been no "deal," since the Schulyer faction had nothing to offer the "Clintonians," who are presumed to have held a commanding majority.[46] In all likelihood, Hamilton gained his place in the delegation simply because the legislators thought him an exceptionally able man.

Whether men loved Hamilton or loathed him, none could deny his ability. "Colo. Hamilton is deservedly celebrated for his talents," wrote William Pierce, one of the delegates at Philadelphia. "He is a practitioner of the Law, and reputed to be a finished Scholar. . . . His manners are tinctured with stiffness, and sometimes with a degree of vanity that is highly disagreeable." [47] Pierce had an unusual opportunity to examine the stiffer side of Hamilton's personality, for while the Philadelphia Convention was in session, Hamilton served as second to Pierce's opponent during preliminaries to a duel.[48] This relationship naturally discouraged any inclination Hamilton might have had to show Pierce his charming side—and he had one. An exceptionally handsome man with fair skin, auburn hair, and deep blue eyes, Hamilton also possessed a captivating smile and an animated, merry manner that his friends, especially the ladies, found irresistible, although one gentleman sniffed that it was "boyish" and "giddy." [49] Hamilton was born in the West Indies

[45] Spaulding, *New York in the Critical Period*, pp. 187, 188; Miller, *Alexander Hamilton*, p. 152.

[46] Miller (*Alexander Hamilton*, p. 152) suggests that the Schuyler group conceded election by joint ballot of the two houses in return for Hamilton's election, but that is not possible since the election was by separate ballot.

[47] Max Farrand, ed., *The Records of the Federal Convention of 1787* (New Haven, Conn., 1937), III, 89.

[48] Alexander Hamilton to Nathaniel Mitchell, 20 July 1787, Syrett, ed., *Papers of Alexander Hamilton*, IV, 226, 227; Alexander Hamilton to William Pierce [20–26 July 1787], *ibid.*, 226; Alexander Hamilton to John Auldjo, 26 July 1787, *ibid.*, 233; Statement of Nathaniel Mitchell, 10 September 1787, *ibid.*, 233n.

[49] William Maclay, *Journal*, E. S. Maclay, ed. (New York, 1890), p. 238.

in 1755 and came to New York before the Revolution. He began his studies at King's College, now Columbia, took the part of the patriots during the war, and emerged at the peace a full colonel married to Elizabeth Schuyler, the daughter of one of New York's most powerful manor lords. When Hamilton won a seat in the New York Assembly in 1786, he was immediately recognized as the leader of the faction corresponding to that led by his father-in-law in the Senate.[50]

Hamilton's factional affiliations were well-known, but those of his colleagues, Robert Yates and John Lansing, were uncertain. Robert Yates had not served in a legislative body since he sat on the committee that framed the state constitution in 1777. In that year he was made a justice of the New York Supreme Court, where he earned a reputation for his legal abilities. Hamilton described him as "upright and respectable in his profession,"[51] and the unanimity with which he was selected for a place in the Philadelphia delegation testifies to the high opinion New Yorkers held of him. He was an Albany man and related to Abraham Yates, yet since he had never voted in the legislature, no one could be certain that he identified himself with either faction.[52]

The politics of the third member of the delegation, John Lansing, were likewise uncertain. Only a year older than Hamilton, Lansing was "large and handsome in person with remarkably fine features."[53] At Philadelphia, a colleague described him as "a Man of good sense, plain in his manners, and sincere in his

[50] Statement by Robert Troup, quoted in Nevins, *American States*, p. 284.

[51] Alexander Hamilton to Robert Morris, 13 August 1783, Syrett, ed., *Papers of Alexander Hamilton*, III, 140.

[52] Allen Johnson and Dumas Malone, eds., *Dictionary of American Biography* (New York, 1928–1937), XX, 601. Spaulding's identification of Robert Yates as an undoubted Antifederalist (*New York in the Critical Period*, p. 187, 187n.) is based on his confusion of Robert with Abraham Yates.

[53] [George R.] Howell and [T. J.] Tenney, *History of the County of Albany, New York, 1609–1886* (New York, 1886), p. 132.

friendships," though he noted that the young man had "a hisitation [*sic*] in his speech, that will prevent his being an Orator of any eminence." [54] Lansing had been a member of the Assembly from 1780 to 1784 and speaker of the Assembly in 1786. In addition, he had spent two terms in the federal Congress and was the appointive mayor of Albany.[55] Despite this active political life, Lansing had not identified himself with either faction. Perhaps holding the speakership in 1786 and sitting in Congress the following year had deprived him of the opportunity to make his allegiances known in the legislature. He was friendly with Hamilton and Schuyler. Hamilton thought him "a good young fellow and a good practitioner of the law," although he believed Lansing's "friends mistook his talents when they made him a statesman." [56] During the Revolution, Lansing had been General Schuyler's confidential clerk,[57] and Schuyler retained a fondness for him. As late as February 1787, Schuyler wrote a warm letter to Lansing, urging him to accept election to Congress and then describing the recent vote on the impost in the state Assembly in a tone showing that he expected Lansing to sympathize in Hamilton's defeat. Schuyler signed himself "Affectionately." [58] On the other hand, Lansing was on excellent terms with George Clinton,[59] and his brother, Abraham G. Lansing, was a close friend of Abraham Yates.[60]

When the membership of the delegation appointed by New York became known, the antifederal reputation of the state attached itself to Yates and Lansing. Hamilton's extreme nationalism was too well known for him to be suspected of antifederal-

[54] Farrand, ed., *Records,* III, 90.

[55] *Dictionary of American Biography,* X, 608.

[56] Alexander Hamilton to Robert Morris, 13 August 1783, Syrett, ed., *Papers of Alexander Hamilton,* III, 140.

[57] B. J. Lossing, *Life and Times of Philip Schuyler* (New York, 1873), p. 439.

[58] Philip Schuyler to John Lansing, Jr., 20 February 1787, John Lansing, Jr., Papers, New-York Historical Society.

[59] Spaulding, *New York in the Critical Period,* p. 187.

[60] Abraham Yates, Jr., Papers, New York Public Library, *passim.*

ism, but Madison noted that the other members of the New York delegation "are supposed to lean too much towards State considerations to be good members of an assembly which will only be useful in proportion to its superiority to partial views and interests." [61] Another Philadelphia delegate who attempted to feel out Yates in conversation, however, concluded that although "some of his Enemies say he is an anti-federal Man, . . . I discovered no such disposition in him." [62] Nevertheless, hindsight and the passing years eventually fastened the antifederal label firmly to Hamilton's colleagues from New York. In 1821 Madison wrote, "whatever may have been the personal worth of the 2 delegates . . . it cannot be unknown that they represented the strong prejudices in N Y agst. the object of the Convention, which was; among other things to take from that State the important power over its commerce," [63] and twelve years later he described the two New Yorkers as "the Representitives of the dominant party in N. York, which was opposed to the Convention & the object of it, which was averse to any essential change in the Articles of Confederation." [64]

And so it has passed into history. A recent writer describes Yates and Lansing as "virtual emissaries of Governor Clinton, sent to protect state claims and to concede as little as possible to national demands." [65] This description is typical,[66] and it is a serious exaggeration, which ought to be corrected. If Robert Yates and John Lansing were antifederal at the beginning of 1787, their antifederalism was neither well-known nor deep-

[61] James Madison to Edmund Randolph, 11 March 1787, Henry D. Gilpin, ed., *The Papers of James Madison* (New York, 1841), II, 621.

[62] Farrand, ed., *Records*, III, 90.

[63] James Madison to Joseph Gales, 26 August 1821, Hunt, ed., *Writings of James Madison*, IX, 69.

[64] James Madison to John Tyler [1833], *ibid.*, 510.

[65] Broadus Mitchell, *Alexander Hamilton* (New York, 1957, 1962), I, 380.

[66] I have seen only one reference to the ambiguous political position of Lansing and Yates before the Philadelphia Convention (Clarence E. Miner,

rooted, and they were by no means official representatives of a faction in the New York Legislature.

Judge Yates and Colonel Hamilton arrived in Philadelphia together and attended the convention for the first time on Friday, 25 May, four days after the date set by the Congressional resolution. Whatever his previous political views may have been, the journey to Pennsylvania in Hamilton's company caused Yates to develop "forebodings" concerning the meeting at Philadelphia, and within a week he was writing to Abraham Yates that his premonitions had been "too much realized." [67] On the very first day Edmund Randolph "candidly confessed" a dislike of "foederal Government" and advocated "a strong, *consolidated* Union in which the Idea of States should be nearly annihilated." [68] The following day Yates and Hamilton divided the New York vote for the first time on a resolution calling for the formation of a "national Government."

John Lansing arrived in Philadelphia on 1 June [69] and attended the convention for the first time the following day. Other members came to think of him as subservient to Judge Yates in his voting. George Mason wrote that neither Yates nor Lansing ever voted with Hamilton.[70] A recent writer, who is usually very careful in checking his facts, has written that "after Lansing with Yates made a New York majority against Hamilton, we find no more divisions recorded for the state, but a ballot contrary to Hamilton's view where we know it." [71] Actually, Lansing voted against Yates at least five times.[72] He

---

The Ratification of the Federal Constitution by the State of New York [New York, 1921], p. 54).

[67] Robert Yates to Abraham Yates, 1 June 1787, Abraham Yates, Jr., Papers, New York Public Library.

[68] Farrand, ed., *Records*, I, 24.

[69] Robert Yates to Abraham Yates, 1 June 1787, Abraham Yates, Jr., Papers, New York Public Library.

[70] Farrand, ed., *Records*, III, 367.

[71] Mitchell, *Alexander Hamilton*, I, 390.

[72] Joseph Reese Strayer, ed., *The Delegate from New York, or Proceedings of the Federal Convention of 1787 from the Notes of John*

voted with Hamilton against Yates on 25 June,[73] and on 21 June Lansing voted yes on a question for which Hamilton and Yates voted no.[74] Still, Lansing and Yates shared a fundamental disagreement with Hamilton, which was reflected in their ballots; they believed in a federal form of government, while Hamilton was perhaps the most extreme nationalist at Philadelphia. The division in the New York delegation appeared openly on the floor of the convention in the middle of June.

On 16 June, John Lansing addressed the convention during the debate on the proposals introduced by Edmund Randolph of Virginia and William Paterson of New Jersey and explained his reasons for preferring the latter. The principles of the two plans, he said, were in direct contrast: "that of Mr. Patterson . . . sustains the sovereignty of the respective states, that of Mr. Randolph distroys it: the latter requires a negative on all the laws of the particular States; the former, only certain general powers for the general good." His chief objections to the Virginia plan were the "want of power in the Convention to discuss & propose it" and "the improbability of its being adopted." Lansing believed that "the power of the Convention was restrained to amendments of a federal nature, and having for their basis the Confederacy in being." He was certain that his own state had intended no more than this. "N. York would never have concurred in sending deputies to the convention," said Lansing, "if she had supposed the deliberations were to turn on a consolidation of the States, and a National Government." He was convinced that the states would not "adopt & ratify a scheme, which they had never authorized us to propose." The people were familiar with the Confederation Congress and "an augmentation of the powers of Congress will be readily approved," but they would never agree to so radical a proposal as Randolph's.[75]

Exasperated by the timidity of his colleagues, Hamilton chose the next session of the convention to describe the form of gov-

---

Lansing, Jr. (Princeton, N.J., 1939), p. 11.

[73] *Ibid.*, p. 83. [74] *Ibid.*, p. 77.

[75] *Documentary History*, III, 128–130.

ernment that he favored and to make a few general remarks that thoroughly horrified the gentlemen from Albany. Hamilton explained that he had not spoken before "partly from respect to others whose superior abilities age & experience rendered him unwilling to bring forward ideas dissimilar to theirs, and partly from his delicate situation with respect to his own State, to whose sentiments as expressed by his Colleagues, he could by no means accede." He himself disliked both the Randolph and the Paterson plans, but he especially disliked the latter, since he was convinced "that no amendment of the confederation, leaving the States in possession of their sovereignty could possibly answer the purpose." He would be for extinguishing the states altogether if it were not for the popular attachment to them. Furthermore, Hamilton doubted whether a republican government could be maintained in an area as large as the United States, and remarked that "in his private opinion he had no scruple in declaring . . . that the British Govt. was the best in the world: and that he doubted much whether any thing short of it would do in America." Since, unfortunately, American public opinion would not permit a monarchy to be established, Hamilton believed the convention "ought to go as far in order to attain stability and permanency, as republican principles will admit." He proposed an executive and an upper house holding office for life, "or at least during good-behaviour," chosen by a method of indirect election, and state governors, appointed by the central government, to have an absolute veto on all state legislation. Hamilton was aware that his plan "went beyond the ideas of most members." He admitted that the people would not accept it, but he did not think they would approve Randolph's proposals either. Nevertheless, there were "evils operating in the States which must soon cure the people of their fondness for democracies," and once the people were "unshackled from their prejudices . . . they will not be satisfied at stopping where the plan of Mr. R[andolph] w[oul]d place them, but be ready to go as far at least as he proposes." [76]

[76] *Ibid.*, 138–151.

The Philadelphia Convention was not prepared to go so far. Hamilton did not offer his plan as a formal proposal, but "only to give a more correct view of his ideas," [77] and the plan was never referred to a committee or acted upon in any way. Everyone thought that Hamilton had made an excellent speech, but "though he has been praised by everybody," a fellow delegate remarked, "he has been supported by none." [78]

Having delivered his one important speech of the convention, Hamilton saw no reason to remain at Philadelphia where he was continually outvoted by Yates and Lansing. About a week later, at the end of June, he left Philadelphia for New York City, probably hoping to arrive in time for the Fourth of July meeting of the Society of the Cincinnati,[79] and expecting to return in ten or twelve days "if I have reason to believe that my attendance at Philadelphia will not be mere waste of time." [80] Meanwhile, Yates and Lansing were planning to go home as well. The sessions of the New York Supreme Court were soon to begin. Robert Yates was a judge and Lansing a practicing attorney. It was clear that the supporters of Paterson's plan were in a minority, and the New Yorkers came to the conclusion that they might as well leave Philadelphia and attend to their business at home. On 10 July they, too, left the convention.[81]

It is frequently assumed that Lansing and Yates left the Philadelphia Convention in July with no intention of returning, that they "flung off in a pet" as one historian puts it,[82] and immediately denounced the convention to Governor Clinton, disre-

[77] *Ibid.*, 149.

[78] Farrand, ed., *Records*, I, 282, 283.

[79] Turner to Webb, 30 June 1787, W. C. Ford, ed., *Correspondence and Journals of Samuel Blanchley Webb* (New York, 1893–1894), III, 81; George Dangerfield, *Chancellor Robert R. Livingston of New York, 1746–1813* (New York, 1960), p. 213.

[80] Alexander Hamilton to George Washington, 3 July 1787, Syrett, ed., *Papers of Alexander Hamilton*, IV, 225.

[81] Yates stopped taking notes in the convention on 5 July, but Lansing continued his until 10 July, and the New York vote is recorded for the last time on 10 July.

[82] Mitchell, *Alexander Hamilton*, I, 392.

garding the convention's rule of secrecy.[83] Actually, their withdrawal from Philadelphia was less dramatic. They left quietly, and none of their colleagues believed at the time that their departure implied any censure of the convention. It seemed understandable that a judge and a lawyer would have business calling them home during the court season,[84] and when the convention was ready to take some important votes, the New Yorkers were politely urged to return in a tone that indicates a belief that nothing other than pressing business had caused them to leave their seats.[85] Moreover, the New York press did not mention the absence of the state delegation from the Philadelphia meeting, although some comment would surely have appeared had the two men returned steaming with indignation and disregarding their pledge to secrecy.

Lansing and Yates did not make their decision to leave the convention permanently until the end of August. The Supreme Court of New York was in session until 8 August, and the circuit court scheduled sessions through the end of September.[86] In the middle of the month Hamilton wrote to his colleagues from New York City, "informing them if either of them would come down, I would accompany him to Philadelphia." These letters have never been located, but they were probably far from persuasive messages. Hamilton wrote them only "for the sake of propriety and public opinion," and no doubt made it clear that he was not anxious to have *both* men return with him to the convention where they would be in a position to outvote him whenever they chose.[87]

Meanwhile, the gossip among the friends of Yates and Lansing in Albany County was that "Mr. Paine (common sense) is employed to write in favor of the British form of Government—

[83] Carl Van Doren, *The Great Rehearsal* (New York, 1948), p. 231.

[84] Farrand, ed., *Records*, III, 367.

[85] William Paterson to John Lansing, 27 July 1787, John Lansing, Jr., Papers, New-York Historical Society.

[86] *New-York Journal*, 16 August 1787.

[87] Alexander Hamilton to Rufus King, 20 August 1787, Syrett, ed., *Papers of Alexander Hamilton*, IV, 235.

and that the system which will be recommended to the States will be similar to that Constitution the Kingly part excepted." [88] Abraham Yates, who was in New York City serving on the Congressional delegation and was expected to learn "at Least the outlines" of the Philadelphia proceedings from "his intercourse with the high perogative Gentlemen," [89] passed on to his friends in Albany what he described as "good information to Yates and Lansing," specifically, that the convention "were now so far from agreeing that it would be a doubt whether they would agree in time so as that this Congress can take up the Matter." [90] About the same time John Lansing confessed to his brother that while he and Robert Yates had been "in sentiment with a respectable *Minority*" at Philadelphia, "they had no prospect of succeeding in the measures proposed," and for the first time he declared "that he was at a stand whether it would not be proper for him to Leave them." [91] The desire to attend to their business at the New York courts, the belief that the convention would propose a highly centralized national government, perhaps as extreme as that proposed by Hamilton in his speech of 18 June, and the information from Abraham Yates that the convention would not be likely to conclude its sessions for many months, combined to convince Yates and Lansing that they should not return to Philadelphia.

After 10 July, New York was never again officially represented at the Philadelphia Convention. Alexander Hamilton attended for perhaps half a dozen days during August and September and he spoke occasionally, but he could not vote since at least two of the state's three delegates were required to be

[88] Abraham Lansing to Abraham Yates, 26 August 1787, Abraham Yates, Jr., Papers, New York Public Library.

[89] *Ibid.*

[90] Abraham Yates to Jeremiah Van Rensselaer and Henry Acthandt [*sic*], 29 August 1787, Burnett, ed., *Letters of Members of the Continental Congress*, VIII, 641, 642.

[91] Abraham Lansing to Abraham Yates, 26 August 1787, Abraham Yates, Jr., Papers, New York Public Library.

present in order to cast a ballot. After Hamilton left the convention at the end of June, George Washington wrote to him urging his return,[92] but Hamilton remained in New York City for several weeks.[93] Sometime after 6 August [94] he left New York to return to the convention and spoke there on 13 August. He did not remain long, however; on 20 August he had been back in New York City for several days.[95] Hamilton was a lawyer, and, like his colleagues, he could not afford long absences during the court season. But he was determined to be at Philadelphia when the convention concluded its business,[96] and after the circuit court ended its sessions in Kings County,[97] he left New York City and returned to Philadelphia.

On 6 September, Hamilton rose in the Philadelphia Convention to say "that he had been restrained from entering into the discussion by his dislike of the Scheme of Govt. in General," but

[92] George Washington to Alexander Hamilton, 10 July 1787, Syrett, ed., *Papers of Alexander Hamilton*, IV, 225.

[93] Manasseh Cutler noted in his journal that Hamilton was in Philadelphia on 13 July. There is, however, no other evidence that he was there. His correspondence shows that he was definitely in New York City on 20 July and gives the impression that he had been engaged in business there for some time (Alexander Hamilton to Nathaniel Mitchell, 20 July 1787, Syrett, ed., *Papers of Alexander Hamilton*, IV, 226). On 3 July, Hamilton told Washington that he would "of necessity" remain in New York City for "ten or twelve days" (*ibid.*, 225), and we know from one of George Washington's letters that Hamilton was not in Philadelphia on 10 July (George Washington to Alexander Hamilton, 10 July 1787, *ibid.*, 225). It is unlikely that Hamilton would make the tedious journey to Philadelphia and back in a period of less than ten days unless he had intended to participate in the convention, and there is no record of his speaking. Cutler was probably mistaken. Broadus Mitchell disagrees (*Alexander Hamilton*, I, 404).

[94] Alexander Hamilton to [?], 6 August 1787, Syrett, ed., *Papers of Alexander Hamilton*, IV, 234.

[95] Alexander Hamilton to Rufus King, 20 August 1787, *ibid.*, 235.

[96] *Ibid.;* Alexander Hamilton to Rufus King, 28 August 1787, *ibid.*, 238.

[97] On 28 August, Hamilton expressed an intention to attend sessions of the circuit court, which was then meeting in Kings County (Alexander Hamilton to Rufus King, 28 August 1787, *ibid.*, 238; New-York Journal, 6 August 1787).

that "he meant to support the plan to be recommended, as better than nothing." [98] On the seventeenth, the final day of the Constitutional Convention, Hamilton urged every man present to sign, remarking that "no man's ideas were more remote from the plan than his own were known to be; but is it possible to deliberate between anarchy and Convulsion on one side, and the chance of good to be expected from the plan on the other." [99] Hamilton was never reconciled to the form of government drawn up in Philadelphia in 1787. Several years later he is reported to have described the Constitution as a "shilly-shally thing of milk and water which could not last and was good only as a step to something better." [100] His own tastes, as he freely admitted in the secrecy of the convention, favored a system of more highly centralized power,[101] but he supported the plan proposed by the convention with all his energy. Much as he disliked it, it was preferable to the weak, decentralized Confederation, and once the plan was adopted it might well be possible to improve it by judicious interpretation.

When the final draft of the Philadelphia plan was laid on the table for the delegates' signatures, Hamilton was the first to pick up a quill. He wrote the names of twelve states on the parchment.[102] The official representatives of eleven states signed, and Alexander Hamilton, in the absence of Yates and Lansing representing no one but himself, signed in the space left for New York State. In this condition the engrossed Constitution was sent to Congress, duly approved by the delegates of eleven states and by "Mr. Hamilton from New York." [103]

[98] *Documentary History*, III, 688.

[99] *Ibid.*, 766.

[100] Paul Leicester Ford, ed., *The Writings of Thomas Jefferson* (New York, 1892), I, 165.

[101] Syrett, ed., *Papers of Alexander Hamilton*, IV, 178–211, 253–274.

[102] Bancroft, *History of the Formation of the Constitution*, II, 367; Syrett, ed., *Papers of Alexander Hamilton*, IV, 274.

[103] Farrand, ed., *Records*, II, 664, 665.

PART II

The New Constitution

IV

First Hostilities

THE newspapers published in New York State while the Constitutional Convention was in session reflect a public sentiment unanimously sympathetic to the Philadelphia meeting. Everyone agreed it was time to reform the federal government. As early as December 1786, a writer in a New York City paper wrote that "the American language has been worn thread bear [*sic*] upon this subject, the most nervous and emphatical expressions that its genius will afford, having been repeatedly culled by writers from one extremity of the United States to the other, to demonstrate the absolute necessity of FOEDERAL POWER." [1] But the torrent of writing was still ahead. Throughout the following spring and on through the summer, the New York newspapers printed articles remarking on the need to give further power to Congress,[2] while no articles at all appeared on the other side.[3]

[1] *New-York Journal*, 14 December 1786.

[2] For instance, *New-York Journal*, 15 March 1787, 29 March 1787, 27 July 1787; *Daily Advertiser* (New York), 3 July 1787, 4 July 1787, 11 July 1787.

[3] Clarence E. Miner (*The Ratification of the Federal Constitution by the State of New York* [New York, 1921], p. 57) states that Antifederalist articles appeared during the spring and summer of 1787, but I have not been able to find any. Charles Warren (*The Making of the Constitution*

One writer expressed his surprise that Abraham Yates and other anti-impost men did not take the opportunity to attack the proposals to increase the power of the federal government. "It is remarkable," he wrote, "that those very men who have not only ransacked their brain for arguments, but every political publication for authorities, to support their favorite measure of withholding the necessary powers from the Union should all at once be fairly silenced. We see or read no more of their elaborate pieces, with long and uninteresting quotations from musty authors. Are they conscious of their errors? Or does the wisdom and dignity of that respectable group of characters now sitting in Convention at Philadelphia for the express purpose of strengthening the Confederacy strike them with awe, or make them apprehensive that their sinister policy will be crushed." [4]

The meeting of the Constitutional Convention set dozens of citizens to writing political essays. The very proposal of the meeting gave an impetus to political speculation. In New York City a gentleman wrote to a friend in Baltimore, "The nature and excellency of the different kinds of governments that have ever existed or have ever been treated upon is here every day discussed, explained, demonstrated, dissected, reviewed and placed in every possible light, by everybody on every occasion; and we have as many predictions of the fate of America as if the prophetic spirit of the ancient Jews had remained among us." [5] The convention itself became a popular subject for "remarks" in the newspapers, which were the eighteenth-century equivalent of letters to the editor. "Whatever measures may be recommended by the Foederal Convention," a citizen wrote in June, "whether an addition to the old constitution, or the adop-

---

[Boston, 1928], p. 341) quotes from an allegedly Antifederalist article that he says originally appeared in New York City on 6 July. I have examined all the papers published on that date but have not seen that article.

[4] *Daily Advertiser*, 18 June 1787.

[5] Quoted in Warren, *Making of the Constitution*, p. 93.

tion of a new one, it will, in effect, be a revolution in government, accomplished by reasoning and deliberation; an event that has never occurred since the formation of society, and which will be strongly characteristic of the philosophic and tolerant spirit of the age." [6] Another writer observed that "the eyes of friends and enemies—of all Europe—nay more—of the whole world are upon the United States." [7]

The convention's secrecy rule prevented commentary on the proceedings at Philadelphia, but the newspaper writers searched for good omens. In July, when the disagreements at Philadelphia were so severe that the meeting nearly broke up altogether, a New York paper printed its latest news from Philadlephia: "So great is the unanimity, we hear that prevails in the Convention, upon all great foederal subjects, that it has been proposed to call the room in which they assemble—*Unanimity Hall*." [8] A month later a writer remarked on the long hours the delegates spent in convention during the heat of the Philadelphia summer: "The punctuality with which the members of the Convention assemble every day at a certain hour, and the long time they spend in the deliberations of each day (sometimes seven hours) are proofs, among other things, how much they are entitled to the universal confidence of the people of America. Such a body of enlightened and honest men perhaps never before met for political purposes, in any country upon the face of the earth." [9]

Respect for the convention naturally turned to an inclination to accept whatever plan it might lay before the country. As it became known that the convention's report would soon be made public, a writer in a New York paper remarked, "The public curiosity will soon be gratified; and it is hoped, from the universal confidence reported in this delegation, that the minds of the people throughout the United States are prepared to receive

[6] *New-York Journal*, 28 June 1787.
[7] *Independent Journal* (New York), 9 June 1787.
[8] *Independent Journal*, 25 July 1787.
[9] *Ibid.*, 25 August 1787.

with respect, and to try with a fortitude and perseverance, the plan which will be offered to them by men distinguished for their wisdom and patriotism." [10] An essay in the *New-York Morning Post* urged that the organization of government be submitted to the council at Philadelphia "with the most respectful confidence," since "it would be better to embrace almost any expedient rather than to remain as we are." [11]

The first intimation that the proposals of the Philadelphia sages might become a subject of controversy in New York appeared late in July, and it came from the Federalists rather than from those who later opposed the Constitution. On 21 July 1787, Alexander Hamilton, who was absent from his seat in Philadelphia, published an anonymous attack on Governor Clinton in one of the New York City newspapers. "It is currently reported and believed," the article began, "that his Excellency Governor CLINTON has, in public company, without reserve, reprobated the appointment of the Convention, and predicted a mischevious issue of that measure." Clinton was said to have asserted that "the present confederation is, in itself, equal to the purposes of the union . . . that the appointment of a Convention is calculated to impress the people with an idea of evils which do not exist," and "that if either nothing should be proposed by the Convention, or if what they should propose should not be agreed to, the one or the other would tend to beget dispair in the public mind." Hamilton followed this description of what Clinton was supposed to have asserted "in public company" with a sharp personal attack on the governor. That a man "high in office" should make such statements, Hamilton insisted, "argues greater attachment to his *own power* than to the *public good*, and furnishes strong reason to suspect a dangerous predetermination to oppose whatever may tend to diminish the *former*, however it may promote the latter." [12]

[10] *New-York Packet*, 3 August 1787. See also *New-York Journal*, 16 August 1787; *Country Journal* (Poughkeepsie), 5 September 1787.

[11] *New-York Morning Post*, 16 July 1787.

[12] *Daily Advertiser*, 21 July 1787. Hamilton was most likely the source of a similar article first published in the *Pennsylvania Herald* (Philadel-

It is not immediately obvious why Hamilton published this letter. The charge that Clinton made public statements of the sort imputed to him was certainly untrue. Almost three months later Hamilton himself wrote to Washington that "the Governor has not publicly declared himself,"[13] and Monsieur Otto, the French chargé at New York City, a gentleman who kept his ears open, thought that there had not been "the slightest provocation" for Hamilton's attack on the governor.[14] Late in October men were still waiting for a public declaration from the governor,[15] and, curiously enough, the declaration never came.[16] As late as January 1788, Antifederalists from other states were unsure whether or not to count Governor Clinton among their friends.[17]

Despite his reticence, Clinton had an antifederal reputation long before the Philadelphia Convention began its meetings, a reputation that dated from his refusal to call a special session of the New York Legislature to consider the Congressional impost. In February 1787, it was "whispered" that the governor personally opposed the impost,[18] and by September of that year a

phia), 1 August 1787, and reprinted in the *Daily Advertiser*, 4 August 1787.

[13] Alexander Hamilton to George Washington [11–15 October 1787], Harold C. Syrett, ed., and Jacob E. Cooke, assoc. ed., *The Papers of Alexander Hamilton* (New York, 1961–), IV, 281.

[14] Louis G. Otto to Armand Marc Montmorin, 25 July 1787, Max Farrand, ed., *The Records of the Federal Convention of 1787* (New Haven, Conn., 1911), III, 63.

[15] Edward Carrington to Thomas Jefferson, 23 October 1787, United States Bureau of Rolls and Library, *Documentary History of the Constitution of the United States* (Washington, 1894–1903), IV, 345; James Madison to Thomas Jefferson, 24 October 1787, Gaillard Hunt, ed., *Writings of James Madison, Comprising His Public Papers and His Private Correspondence* (New York, 1900–1910), V, 35.

[16] Clinton is generally credited with the authorship of the "Cato" letters, a series of Antifederalist articles published in the fall of 1787. It is, however, very improbable that they were written by the governor (see Appendix A).

[17] Hugh Ledlie to John Lamb, 15 January 1788, John Lamb Papers, New-York Historical Society.

[18] "Leo," *Daily Advertiser*, 27 February 1787.

writer in the *Daily Advertiser* could observe that "his Excellency has long been viewed as *secretly hostile* to such measures as were conceived absolutely necessary to the *support of a substantial Federal Government*." [19]

Hamilton was entirely convinced that Clinton would oppose the plan proposed by the Philadelphia Convention. His political opposition to the governor was bitter and he believed any story that reflected discredit on Clinton.[20] In Hamilton's mind, New York's governor was selfish and narrow-minded, bound to oppose any limitations on his power, and in July 1787, Hamilton still half hoped that the limitations proposed by the convention would amount to complete subservience of the states to Congress. Eventually Hamilton even came to believe a story that he had received "through channels which does not permit a public use to be made of it" to the effect that Clinton had "declared the UNION unnecessary." [21]

Since Hamilton was certain that Clinton would be the most dangerous opponent of any plan proposed by Philadelphia (and, after all, Clinton did become an Antifederalist), Hamilton felt it was imperative to disqualify Clinton as a critic of the convention recommendations as early as possible. That an open attack on the popular governor would certainly alienate his followers and cause the growth of feelings unfriendly to the convention even before it had completed its work did not disturb Hamilton. He was not a man willing to wait on events. He had summarized his fundamental principle of political action many years before: "As a general marches at the head of his troops, so ought wise politicians, if I dare use the expression, to march at the head of affairs; insomuch that they ought not to await *the event*, to know what

[19] "Aristides," *ibid.*, 10 September 1787.

[20] "Letters of H. G.," Syrett, ed., *Papers of Alexander Hamilton*, V, *passim*. It is a misfortune that these letters and other writings produced by Hamilton, all distorted by his intense hatred of George Clinton, have been the basis of most historical accounts of Clinton's Antifederalism.

[21] Alexander Hamilton to Gouverneur Morris, 19 May 1788, *ibid.*, IV, 651; Alexander Hamilton to James Madison, 19 May 1788, *ibid.*, 649.

measures to take; but the measures which they have taken ought to produce *the event.*"[22] Accordingly, Hamilton decided on a type of action popular among politicians of his day and described in verse by a Massachusetts rhymester:

> You should in order to accomplish
> Your schemes, and put your foes to non-plus,
> Have first begun, by attacking those
> Who are most likely to oppose
> And thwart your complicated plan;
> These should be silenced to a man.[23]

The anonymous attack clearly placed Governor Clinton in a dilemma. To answer Hamilton he would be obliged either to deny the charge completely, thus, in effect, becoming a public *supporter* of the Constitution even before he had read the document, or he must confess to having the sentiments imputed to him though denying having expressed them publicly. If he chose the second alternative, he would be forced to abandon his habitual reticence on public issues and would give effect to Hamilton's insinuation that he had prejudged the issue. Clinton decided to hold his peace; he made no reply whatever.

The first result of Hamilton's anonymous letter was a disruption of the atmosphere of unanimous approbation that had marked discussion of the Philadelphia Convention in New York State. Although no hostile articles appeared in the press, fears were now expressed that there would be an opposition to the Philadelphia proposals. A few days after Hamilton's letter appeared, "An Admirer of Anti-Federal Men" wrote, "The conduct of several leading men, among us, has, of late, given the friends of liberty much uneasiness. They tremble under an apprehension of becoming dupes to exalted ambition; and they see,

[22] John C. Hamilton, ed., *Works of Alexander Hamilton* (New York, 1891), I, 6.

[23] *The Norwich Packet*, 25 April 1787, quoted in Edward P. Alexander, *A Revolutionary Conservative: James Duane of New York* (New York, 1938), p. 191.

with deep concern, those men, who profess to be the fathers of their country, endeavouring by mean arts, to detach the affections of the people from every thing which bears the name of federal." [24] A few weeks later another writer condemned certain "timid, or perhaps *interested* politicians" who had "expressed apprehensions, that the foederal government will not be adopted by the states, or the people," [25] while still another confessed he did fear that the Constitution would not be adopted because "some people, for some reason or another, have started objections to giving any power out of their hands, as they term it, lest the liberties of the people be endangered. It hath unhappily been the case, when measures have been proposed, in the assemblies of the States, evidently calculated for the benefit of individual and confederate states, for some to mount the political hobby-horse, and set up the cry of—Liberty!" [26] Shortly after, a Federalist writer, using the pseudonym "Rough Carver" in parody of Abraham Yates's familiar "Rough Hewer," stated bluntly, "We have men among us who are assiduously striving to form a party against Federal attachments." [27] Still, there was no reaction from those who later opposed the Constitution.

The first antagonistic reply to Hamilton's attack on Clinton appeared in the *New-York Journal* on 6 September 1787, more than a month after the publication of the Hamilton letter.[28] The man who broke the silence wrote under the name "Republican" and began his piece by observing that "it would be highly

[24] *Daily Advertiser*, 26 July 1787.

[25] *Country Journal*, 15 August 1787.

[26] *New-York Packet*, 14 August 1787.

[27] *Daily Advertiser*, 4 September 1787.

[28] Forrest McDonald writes (*We the People: The Economic Origins of the Constitution* [Chicago, 1958], p. 284): "In September there began . . . a series of attacks on some of the [Philadelphia] delgates, and repeated newspaper articles gratuitously defending Clinton's right to oppose the Convention. . . ." Alexander Hamilton was the only delegate attacked, and he was attacked solely for his abuse of the governor. The articles were not "gratuitous" but were avowedly directed against the anonymous letter that Hamilton had published in the *Daily Advertiser* on 21 July.

improper, in the first magistrate of a respectable state, to enter the lists in a newspaper with an anonymous scribbler; and it cannot but afford pleasure to find, that it has accordingly been treated by him with silent and merited contempt." [29] "Republican" then made the observation "that it is very extraordinary, that expressions, said to be used in a public company, *and currently reported and believed*, should never (as far as I have been able to learn) have reached the ear of a single citizen, before they appeared in the *Daily Advertiser*." "Republican" concluded with an indirect revelation of the authorship of the anonymous attack on the governor, leaving "the application to the reader:"

> Smit with the love of honor, or the pence
> O'er-run with wit and destitute of sense,
> Legions of factious authors throng at once;
> Fool beckons fool, and dunce awakens dunce.
> To Hamilton's the ready lies repair;
> Ne'er was lie made that was not welcome there.
> Thence, on maturer judgment's anvil wrought,
> The polish'd falsehoods into public brought;
> Quick circulating slanders mirth afford,
> And reputation bleeds in every word.[30]

Hamilton was in Philadelphia when the article by "Republican" appeared, but as quickly as he could receive the newspaper and forward a reply, he openly confessed his authorship of the anonymous article, observing that he had left his name with the printers when it first appeared but that no one had approached him to deny the charge.[31] Once it was known that Hamilton was the author of the attack on Clinton, an onslaught against

[29] The New York Senate had resolved some years earlier (*Journal of the Senate*, 27 June 1781) that "it is inconsistent with the Dignity of the Legislature, to take Notice of anonymous Publications which only concern the Character and Conduct of Individuals." The governor's silence was doubtless motivated, at least in part, by a parallel sentiment.

[30] *New-York Journal*, 6 September 1787.

[31] *Daily Advertiser*, 15 September 1787.

him began. His most vitriolic assailant wrote under the title "Inspector," and avoided the crudity of referring to public figures by name by speaking of Governor Clinton as "George Steward," of Philip Schuyler as the "Immaculate Daddy," and of his target, Alexander Hamilton, as "Tom S**t." [32] "Inspector," like "Republican," remarked the general ignorance of what was alledged to have been a public statement by the governor. With heavy sarcasm, "Inspector" praised Hamilton for "discovering that horrid plot of George Steward, which but for Tom S**t would have remained a profound secret to this day; nay, perhaps it would never have been found out at all." [33] It may be noted, incidentally, that "Inspector" may have been a Federalist since he praises the Constitution proposed by the convention at Philadelphia as a defeat for Hamilton, which, in a strict sense, it was.[34]

Other writers shunned the *ad hominem* approach and attacked Hamilton's criticism of the governor's right to speak what he believed. This rebuke had aroused the suspicion of those who believed in a right to free speech even for governors, and the suspicion spread to cover the Constitution, which Hamilton had written his article to aid. "I cannot but express my indignation at the many illiberal publications, which constantly crowd our newspapers, on the subject of politics," wrote "Rusticus" during the final week of the Philadelphia Convention. It seems, by these publications, to be highly criminal, expecially at this particular period, for any man to differ in opinion from a certain Aristocratic junto, who appear determined, by their writings, to silence, and traduce every person who will not subscribe to every part of their political creed." And then appeared the first

[32] *New-York Journal*, 20 September 1787, 4 October 1787, 18 October 1787.

[33] *Ibid.*, 18 October 1787.

[34] *Ibid.*, 4 October 1787. Although the secrecy rule presumably prevented public knowledge of Hamilton's convention speech of 18 June, "Inspector" knew that Hamilton wished an executive appointed for life.

questioning of the Philadelphia Convention to appear in the New York press: "The greatest part of the publications alluded to," "Rusticus" continued, "are artfully calculated to prepare the minds of the people, implicitly to receive *any form* of government that may be offered them. If this is not the design, why anticipate?" [35] Other writers followed the same line of reasoning. Before the Constitution had been published, "Anti-Defamationis," too, insisted that "the free citizens of this continent will never consent to have a constitution crammed down their throats. They have an undoubted right to examine before they accede, and to deny if they do not approve." [36] Gone was the submissive atmosphere of the spring and summer; Hamilton's letter had shattered it.

Hamilton seems not to have anticipated the violent response to his attack on the governor. The first two "Inspector" articles [37] caused Hamilton to write to Washington for help.[38] Washington supplied the appropriate assurances, but took the opportunity to express his "unfeigned concern . . . that a political dispute has arisen between Governor Clinton and yourself." General Washington declared that he had "the highest esteem and regard" for both Clinton and Hamilton and observed that "when the situation of this country calls loudly for unanimity & vigor, it is to be lamented that Gentlemen of talents and character should disagree in their sentiments for promoting the public weal." [39]

The dispute between Clinton and Hamilton was particularly unfortunate for the Federalists. To break into the sympathetic quiet in regard to the Philadelphia Convention and so to arouse

[35] *New-York Journal,* 13 September 1787.

[36] *Ibid.,* 20 September 1787.

[37] *New-York Journal,* 20 September 1787, 4 October 1787.

[38] Alexander Hamilton to George Washington [11–15 October 1787], Syrett, ed., *Papers of Alexander Hamilton,* IV, 280.

[39] George Washington to Alexander Hamilton, 18 October 1787, *ibid.,* 284.

the dormant suspicions of future Antifederalists was hardly wise. Nothing could have assured the opposition of men like Clinton and Abraham Yates more certainly than a statement from a political enemy anticipating their opposition. An opposition that could have been softened, perhaps avoided entirely, was assured in advance by Hamilton's attack. There is, however, no indication that Hamilton regretted having begun the controversy. His sole aim had been to disqualify Clinton as a critic of the Constitution, and when he felt he had succeeded here, he did not concern himself unduly with the violent emotions unfavorable to his cause that had been stirred up.[40]

Hamilton blundered because he misjudged his adversaries. He was a man with great capacity for hatred, which hampered his ability to discern the character of his political enemies.[41] John Adams, Aaron Burr, and Thomas Jefferson appear as almost unrecognizable caricatures of evil when viewed from Hamilton's hate-filled perspective, and Hamilton hated George Clinton as he later hated those men. To Hamilton it was inconceivable that Clinton should voluntarily take the right side of any question or that he could be persuaded to come to the right side by reason and tact. Hamilton believed that the governor's faction would oppose the Constitution and that nothing he might do could conceivably strengthen that opposition. Given this assumption, a frontal attack on the governor was a prudent measure.

Thanks to Alexander Hamilton, George Clinton may almost be said to have passed into history as "Mr. Antifederalist." Clinton's only biographer[42] entitled his volume *His Excellency George Clinton: Critic of the Connstitution*, implying that the governor's Antifederalism in the years 1787 and 1788 was the most significant feature of his long career. Another historian has bluntly stated that "Clinton was the most bitter hater of the

[40] Alexander Hamilton to George Washington [11–15 October 1787], *ibid.*, 280.

[41] Cf. Bower Aly, *The Rhetoric of Alexander Hamilton* (New York, 1941), p. 41.

[42] E. Wilder Spaulding.

Constitution to be found anywhere in the thirteen states."[43] Nevertheless, most of Clinton's unflattering reputation has no better basis than the polemic writings of his bitterest political adversary.[44] While there can be no doubt that George Clinton was an Antifederalist,[45] he was not active in the ratification campaign. Although the Federalists considered the governor the leader of the Antifederalist party,[46] Clinton was not a member of any Antifederalist committee, and he does not appear to have done any personal campaigning. He never made any public declaration in support of the Antifederalists, and when elected a delegate to the Poughkeepsie Convention, he sat quietly in his place most of the time. George Clinton set an example of moderation for his party,[47] and seems to have made a sincere effort to keep an open mind. At the Poughkeepsie Convention he did not attempt to rally the Antifederalists by taking a firm stand himself. On the contrary, he told the Federalists, "I am open to conviction."[48]

Clinton's restraint during the ratification campaign was probably due less to lack of firmness in his views than to his conception of the nature of a governor's office. His private letters, pre-

[43] Edward P. Smith, "The Movement for a Second Convention in 1788," J. Franklin Jameson, ed., *Essays in the Constitutional History of the United States in the Formative Period, 1775—1789* (Boston, 1889), p. 68.

[44] E. Wilder Spaulding, *New York in the Critical Period, 1783–1789* (New York, 1932), p. 184n.

[45] He was regarded as a friend by the recognized leaders of the anti-Schuyler faction of the legislature, and his private letters and remarks in the Poughkeepsie Convention show that he wholly shared their view that the Constitution required amendment.

[46] S. B. Webb to Joseph Barrell, 11 May 1788, W. C. Ford, ed., *Correspondence and Journals of Samuel Blanchley Webb* (New York, 1893–1894), III, 102; Alexander Hamilton to James Madison, 19 May 1788, Syrett, ed., *Papers of Alexander Hamilton,* IV, 649.

[47] James Madison to Thomas Jefferson, 24 October 1787, Gaillard Hunt, ed., *Writings of James Madison, Comprising His Public Papers and His Private Correspondence* (New York, 1900–1910), V, 35.

[48] Jonathan Elliot, ed., *The Debates in the Several State Conventions on the Adoption of the Federal Constitution* (Philadelphia, 1876), II, 252.

served in the Abraham Yates, Jr., Papers and the John Lamb Papers, indicate that Clinton was thoroughly convinced that amendments to the proposed Constitution were imperative, and references by Antifederalist leaders show that they considered the governor a loyal supporter of their views despite his inactivity. In the eighteenth century, when party and faction were not respectable, the governor of a state could not admit to being a party leader. The executive was expected to stand above faction. Clinton's scruples were so great that he conceived his obligation was to avoid all overt political activity. In contrast to the governors of Massachusetts and Virginia, Clinton even shrank from expressing controversial opinions at the state ratifying convention. On one occasion he refused to make any remarks on a disputed question because the delegates might "connect his character as Govr. & representative." [49]

In one of his attacks on Governor Clinton during the gubernatorial campaign of 1789, Hamilton wrote, "Many of our most considerate citizens have long been of opinion that the Governor has possessed an undue and dangerous influence." [50] Since the spoils system had not yet been instituted in New York's politics, Hamilton believed an insinuation that Clinton appointed political supporters to state offices would reflect discredit on the governor. Yet, as might be expected, Clinton was as scrupulous about his appointive powers as he was about all of the gubernatorial prerogatives, and when it came to citing cases, the Federalists, in 1795, could find only two incidents that might conceivably be considered abuses of the appointive power during the seventeen years that George Clinton had served as governor.[51]

There is no evidence that Clinton made any use of the patron-

[49] Gilbert Livingston Reports of the Poughkeepsie Convention, 23 July 1788, New York Public Library.

[50] "To the Electors of the State of New York," 7 April 1789, Syrett, ed., *Papers of Alexander Hamilton*, V, 322.

[51] Hugh M. Flick, "The Council of Appointment in New York State, the First Attempt to Regulate Political Patronage: 1777–1822," *New York History*, XV (1934), 265.

age power to strengthen the Antifederalists during the ratification contest.[52] It was observed at the Poughkeepsie Convention that "the officers of government . . . are perhaps more divided in sentiment than any other class of men," on the question of ratification,[53] and such prominent holders of appointive offices as Egbert Benson, James Duane, Richard Morris, and R. R. Livingston were Federalists. Even after the Constitution had been ratified, and the formidable Federalist machine was set to defeat Clinton, the governor does not appear to have considered politics when making appointments. Aaron Burr, an active Federalist in 1789, was soon after appointed attorney-general of the state. Robert Yates, who deserted Clinton to run on the Federalist ticket for governor in 1789, became chief justice of the Supreme Court of New York the following year. And in 1791, when the formation of several new counties gave Clinton the opportunity to nominate entire lists of county officials, his selections show that he paid little attention to the politics of the appointees.[54]

Governor Clinton's importance in the ratification campaign did not rest on his patronage power, his personal persuasiveness, or even on his political skill. He did not manage a party machine or make public pronouncements and campaign trips, and he did not even direct the parliamentary maneuvers at the Poughkeepsie Convention.[55] Nevertheless, the name of George Clinton was an asset to the Antifederalists and a liability to their opponents.[56] Despite his habitual silence, the frank, conscientious governor was a respected leader in New York, and by attacking him Hamilton guaranteed that a powerful opposition to the Constitution would develop in that state.

[52] *Ibid.*, p. 262; Howard Lee McBain, *De Witt Clinton and the Origin of the Spoils System in New York* (New York, 1907), p. 31.

[53] Elliot, ed., *Debates*, II, 321.

[54] Flick, "The Council of Appointment," p. 262.

[55] Robert Yates was the official chairman of the Antifederalist organization at Poughkeepsie.

[56] S. B. Webb to Joseph Barrell, 13 January 1788, Ford, ed., *Correspondence of S. B. Webb*, III, 90.

V

Official Action

FIVE states—Delaware, Pennsylvania, New Jersey, Georgia, and Connecticut—had called conventions and ratified the Constitution before the New York Legislature met to consider the Philadelphia resolutions in the second week in January. That same week George Washington, speculating on the fate of the Constitution, wrote that "the determinations of new York of all others seem most problematical." [1] Within New York itself there was uncertainty. "The Legislature is now sitting at Poughkeepsie—80 miles up the river," Samuel Blanchley Webb, a City man, wrote to a friend in Boston. "What they will do we are at a loss to determine. That they will appoint a Convention we haven't a doubt, but suppose the antifederalists will be for delaying its meeting to as distant a period as possible." [2]

Nor was it only the Federalists who watched the legislature. Melancton Smith expressed the concern of the Antifederalists in New York City in a letter to Abraham Yates, who was in his

[1] George Washington to Henry Knox, 10 January 1788, United States Bureau of Rolls and Library, *Documentary History of the Constitution of the United States* (Washington, 1894–1903), IV, 437.

[2] S. B. Webb to Joseph Barrell, 13 January 1788, W. C. Ford, ed., *Correspondence and Journals of Samuel Blanchley Webb* (New York, 1893–1894), III, 90.

customary place in the Senate. "You seem to be of the opinion that there is a majority in both houses of the Legislature against the new Constitution," wrote Smith. "We have great doubts here, whether this is the case in the assembly." As one of its first acts, the Assembly chose a new state delegation to the Continental Congress, and although Abraham Yates was elected to a seat, the other four members were Ezra L'Hommedieu, Egbert Benson, Leonard Gansevoort, and Alexander Hamilton—all Federalists. The choice of these men by a supposedly Antifederalist legislature worried the Antifederalists in the City. "You may say they out general you," Smith told Yates, "but it amounts to the same thing, whether you are defeated by the superior skill of your enemy, or by their superior strength, it is a defeat still." Men like Hamilton and Schuyler, as every Anti knew, must be watched carefully. "The *better sort*, have means of *convincing* those who differ from them with which I am unacquainted," Smith reminded his friend. "And how prevalent these kind of means may be, I cannot pretend to say. I confess I fear their power." [3]

The regular annual meeting of the New York Legislature began on 11 January 1788.[4] Governor Clinton opened the proceedings with the customary address, pointing to the need to appoint a new delegation to the Continental Congress and noting that the federal requisition required attention. "I have full confidence that the same spirit which has invariably influenced the legislature of this state will induce you to a cheerful and effectual compliance with every measure founded on the national compact, and necessary to the honor and prosperity of the

[3] Melancton Smith to Abraham Yates, 28 January 1788, Abraham Yates, Jr., Papers, New York Public Library.

[4] Clarence E. Miner (*The Ratification of the Federal Constitution by the State of New York* [New York, 1921], p. 71) says that Clinton deliberately delayed the meeting of the legislature for political reasons. That is incorrect. By law, the second Tuesday in January was set as the time for the legislature's annual meeting. In 1788 the second Tuesday fell on 9 January, and a quorum assembled on the following Thursday.

union," he said. Then the governor passed on to the legislature "the several official communications which have been made to me in the recess." These included "the proceedings of the general convention lately held in the city of Philadelphia, and an act of the United States in Congress for their transmission to the legislatures of the different states," and also a letter from two of New York's delegates to that convention, Robert Yates and John Lansing.[5] Clinton submitted the papers without comment. "From the nature of my office," he explained, "you will easily perceive it would be improper for me to have any other agency in this business than that of laying the papers respecting it before you for your information."[6]

After reading the proposed Constitution, Yates and Lansing were convinced of the wisdom of their decision not to return to the Philadelphia Convention. Their fears that the convention would propose a consolidated government had, they felt, been fully realized and consequently justified their withdrawal. Accordingly, just before the legislature was due to meet, the two men composed a formal letter to Governor Clinton setting out their position on the proposed Constitution.[7] "We do ourselves

[5] *New-York Journal,* 14 January 1788.

[6] New York State, *Messages from the Governors,* Charles Z. Lincoln, ed. (Albany, 1909), II, 281, 282.

[7] The erroneous belief that Yates and Lansing left Philadelphia in an aura of bad feelings, violated the secrecy rule, and immediately began to denounce the convention, is due to improper interpretation of this letter to Governor Clinton. The most convenient sources for the letter print it without a date (Max Farrand, ed., *The Records of the Federal Convention of 1787* [New Haven, 1911], III, 244–247; Robert Yates, *Secret Proceedings and Debates* [n.pub., 1821], 280–283, Jonathan Elliot, ed., *The Debates in the Several State Conventions on the Adoption of the Federal Constitution* [Philadelphia, 1876], I, 480–482), leading historians to assume that it was written in July 1787, immediately after the men left Philadelphia. The true date of the letter is 21 December 1787, and it is included in the newspaper printings: *New-York Journal,* 14 January 1788, 17 January 1788; *New-York Packet,* 15 January 1788; *Independent Journal* (New York), 16 January 1788; *Country Journal* (Poughkeepsie), supp., 22 January 1788.

the honor to advise your excellency that, in pursuance to concurrent resolutions of the honorable Senate and Assembly, we have, together with Mr. Hamilton, attended the Convention appointed for revising the Articles of Confederation, and reporting amendments to the same," they began. Unfortunately, the letter continued, in the prosecution of their mission they found themselves faced with the alternative of exceeding their powers by agreeing to measures "destructive of the political happiness of the citizens of the United States," or standing in opposition to the majority "of a body of those respectable men, to whom those citizens had given the most unequivocal proofs of confidence." They had felt their duty was plain, and while they remained in the convention they gave the consolidationist principles that later received the sanction of the majority "decided and unreserved dissent." After they had left Philadelphia "a persuasion, that our further attendance would be fruitless and unavailing, rendered us less solicitous to return." The letter to Clinton concluded with a request that it "be submitted to the consideration of the honorable legislature." [8]

Consideration of the Philadelphia resolutions began in the New York Assembly on 31 January 1788. Egbert Benson submitted the motion that became the basis of the legislature's action. He proposed that delegates to a ratifying convention be chosen in the same number as Assemblymen by "all free male citizens of the age of twenty-one years, and upwards," and that the meeting be held in the Poughkeepsie court house on the third Thursday in June.[9] There was considerable debate in both houses and many divided votes, but Benson's resolution was finally accepted without change. In fact, Benson's motion itself was barely discussed, since no one objected to calling a convention. Debate centered on the Antifederalists' desire to attach

[8] Robert Yates and John Lansing to George Clinton, 21 December 1787, *New-York Journal*, 14 January 1788.

[9] *Journal of the Assembly of the State of New York* (New York, 1788), 31 January 1788. The one remarkable feature of this resolution, the liberal suffrage requirement, is discussed below, Chap. IX.

some statement of their disapproval of the proposed Constitution to the resolution providing for the election of a ratifying convention.

As soon as Benson was seated after introducing his motion, Cornelius Schoonmaker rose to propose a long amendment to the resolution pointing out at length that the Philadelphia Convention had exceeded its instructions.[10] The Federalists objected that the Constitution should go to the people without commendation or condemnation by the legislature and that Schoonmaker's amendment was not designed to acquaint the people with any necessary information but simply to prejudice their minds.[11] Schoonmaker's amendment was defeated by two votes, twenty-seven to twenty-five.[12] Then Samuel Jones introduced an amendment designed to assure the Poughkeepsie Convention a right to propose amendments to the Philadelphia plan, but his motion lost by five votes.[13] Failing to amend Benson's resolution, the Antifederalists contented themselves with his noncommittal motion, and the Assembly passed it without a recorded division of votes.[14]

The following day, the Assembly resolution was sent to the Senate for its concurrence. Here Abraham Yates led the Antifederalists in an attempt to attach a preface condemning the Philadelphia Convention for exceeding its powers. As soon as James Duane, speaking for the Federalists, had moved that the Senate concur with the Assembly resolution, Yates moved to commit the matter to a committee of the whole. Nathaniel Lawrence objected. He saw no reason for delay: "No one was opposed to calling a convention and the legislature should send this business to the people uninfluenced." Yates admitted that "he had no objections to letting it go to the people,"

[10] *Daily Advertiser* (New York), 12 February 1788; *Country Journal, 26* February 1788.

[11] *Ibid.*

[12] *Journal of the Assembly*, 31 January 1788.

[13] *Ibid.*

[14] *Ibid.*

but he thought it should "go to them properly." The people ought to know that "the delegates went beyond their powers." Yates spoke for some time and indulged in a few eloquent flourishes: "Sir, there is not a step towards this business that I ever agreed to; nor is there a sentence in it that I ever will agree to. Sir, said he, I would be for rejecting it altogether; and I would consider it as a piece of blank paper, only that the other states have let it go to the people." He continued to orate on the usurpation of powers by the Philadelphia Convention, finally remarking that "he had a book at home," meaning the *Journal of the Senate*, "which contained some resolutions," and he promised to "fetch it with him the next time he came to the senate." [15]

When Yates was quite finished, General Schuyler rose and dryly remarked that "the gentleman's observations contained no information; everyone knew the resolutions on which the convention had been called. They had been published in all the papers on the continent." [16] The vote was taken, and Yates was defeated twelve to seven. Yates tried again with a motion to postpone the question; he narrowed the margin, but lost anyway, ten to nine. Finally, the vote was taken on the question of concurring with the Assembly resolution. In the lower house, the Antifederalists yielded when they failed to obtain the amendments they desired, but in the Senate, Abraham Yates and seven others had their votes counted against the resolution. The motion to concur passed by a majority of four.[17]

The New York Legislature determined to hold the election for delegates to the Poughkeepsie Convention at the end of April. Both parties could see some benefit in setting a distant date both for the election and for the meeting of the ratifying convention.[18] The Federalist position would obviously become

[15] *New-York Journal*, 12 February 1788. [16] *Ibid.*

[17] *Journal of the Senate of the State of New York* (New York, 1788), 1 February 1788.

[18] Samuel Blanchley Webb believed that the *Antifederalists* would insist on a distant date for the convention (S. B. Webb to Joseph Barrell, 13

stronger with every state that ratified the Constitution. As Washington put it, "I can hardly entertain an idea that she [New York] would wish to stand alone or with one or two others if the States on her flanks are confederated." [19] On the other hand, the Antifederalists believed that they needed time for campaigning in order to offset the favorable first impression made by the Constitution.[20] With the election set for the end of April, the parties had a full seven months between the publication of the Constitution and the election, and they had been campaigning for four months already when the legislature passed its resolution.

January 1788, Ford, ed., *Correspondence of S. B. Webb*, III, 90). But the fact that the date was originally proposed by Egbert Benson, a Federalist, and that there was no debate on the subject, makes it unlikely that it was a party move.

[19] George Washington to Henry Knox, 10 January 1788, *Documentary History*, IV, 437.

[20] In the Philadelphia Convention both Federalists and Antifederalists remarked that the immediate reaction to the Constitution would probably be favorable but that public feeling would later turn against it (*Documentary History*, III, 658, 659).

VI

Printers and Scribblers

THE Constitution was reported to the United States in Congress assembled on 20 September 1787, and it went straight from the Congress chamber to the print shop. Francis Childs, the owner of the *Daily Advertiser*, was the first to set it in type, and the citizens of New York read the new Constitution for the first time in his newspaper on 21 September. John and Archibald McLean of the *Independent Journal* had it next and printed it as a special supplement to their paper on the following day. In addition they ran off a number of copies as broadsides.[1]

Messengers carried the Constitution north, and on 26 September Nicholas Powers printed it for the men of Dutchess County in his *Country Journal*. By 4 October the Albany printers had it; Charles R. Webster ran it in the *Albany Gazette*, and both he and John Babcock of the *Federal Herald* later printed the Constitution in broadside in a Dutch translation for the benefit of those who could not read it in English.[2]

[1] The New-York Historical Society owns an original of this broadside, and the New York Public Library has a photostatic copy.

[2] Paul Leicester Ford, *Bibliography and Reference List of the History and Literature Relating to the Adoption of the Constitution of the United States, 1787–1788* (Brooklyn, 1888), p. 7; Gedruct voor de Foederale Com-

In the upstate counties, friendliness to the Philadelphia Convention still persisted, and the publication of the Constitution was followed by expressions of the same warm praise that had been lavished on the sages of Philadelphia during the summer. To examine the new Constitution, a subscriber to the *Country Journal* wrote, "is only to feel the instantaneous impressions of ardent gratitude and solid conviction." So far as he could see there was no opposition, but "warmth and congratulation . . . now attend the new system in its progress to every quarter." [3] It was a different matter in the City, where publication of the Constitution and serious debate on it began while the exchange of personal attacks and insults initiated by Hamilton's anonymous letter to the *Daily Advertiser* was still in progress. Discussion of the Constitution merged into the controversy that was already raging, and the Philadelphia plan had no lack of opponents. Indeed, at the end of October, James Madison wrote that to judge from the newspapers "one would suppose that the adversaries were the most numerous and the most earnest." [4]

For seven months the newspapers of New York State published essays that their authors hoped would influence the electorate when it was time to choose delegates to a ratifying convention. It cannot be precisely determined how significant such essays were in the campaign for the Constitution, but it is certain that whatever political significance they had was concentrated in New York City. Of the eleven newspapers published in the state during the ratification campaign, five had their presses in the City. Albany had three newspapers, and Lansingburgh, across the Hudson from Albany, had one. Hudson and Poughkeepsie each had one newspaper.

Not only did the City have the highest concentration of newspapers, but also the papers were of better quality than those

---

mittie by Johannis Babcock, Albany [1788], Broadside Collection, New York Public Library.

[3] *Country Journal* (Poughkeepsie), 3 October 1787.

[4] James Madison to Edmund Randolph, 21 October 1787, Gaillard Hunt, ed., *Writings of James Madison, Comprising His Public Papers and His Private Correspondence* (New York, 1900–1910), V, 16.

published upstate. Two of them—the *Daily Advertiser* and the *New-York Journal*—were dailies, while no paper outside the City published more than one issue a week.[5] Furthermore, since New York City was the state's commercial center and the home of the Continental Congress, the population was practiced in the art of essay writing, and the pieces they produced were usually superior to the contributions sent to the country papers. Indeed, editors of upstate papers were frequently satisfied to fill their pages with clippings from the City press or from Boston, New Haven, or Philadelphia papers. An overwhelming proportion of the essays printed in New York State during the ratification campaign made their first appearance in the City papers. The *Albany Gazette*, for example, printed about twenty-five articles, which had previously appeared in no other New York newspaper,[6] while the *New-York Journal* published at least one hundred fifty such articles besides running a large number of items clipped from other New York papers.

Possibly as a result of having a large number of good newspapers, the City men were more likely to be newspaper readers than their fellow citizens in the country. While it was not usually possible to buy a newspaper by the single issue,[7] a man who was too poor to pay for a year's subscription, could always take his choice of reading matter at a coffee house. If he could not read, there would certainly be someone in the room who could. Moreover, a good many men in the City could easily afford the subscription rates [8] and took subscriptions to two,

[5] Clarence S. Brigham, *History and Bibliography of American Newspapers, 1690–1820* (Worcester, Mass., 1947), II.

[6] All quantitative statements for which no specific source is cited are based on an examination of the surviving files of the newspapers listed in the bibliography. Since the files are not absolutely complete and since it is frequently difficult to distinguish between a news item and a political essay, the figures given are only approximate.

[7] Some people, however, managed to come by a few dishonest pennies by stealing papers from the doorsteps of subscribers and hawking them on the street (*Daily Advertiser* [New York], 7 December 1787).

[8] *The New-York Journal* cost $2.00 a year as a weekly and $6.00 as a daily (*New-York Journal*, 15 November 1787); the *Daily Advertiser* cost

three, or even four of the City papers.[9] In the country the situation was very different. Here, as a Washington County delegate pointed out in the state Senate, many people were "too poor to take the news-papers, and too remote from the common opportunities of information." [10]

Certainly, men who lived any great distance from one of the five towns where newspapers were published cannot have read any great proportion of the political essays which were published on the Constitution. And many voters in the remote parts of the state could not read at all. Alexander Hamilton estimated that between a third and a half of the voters were illiterate in some parts of the state.[11] Nor had the country people developed the custom of reading newspapers, which was already well established in the City. The first country newspaper in New York was established in Poughkeepsie in 1785,[12] and the habit of taking a newspaper developed very slowly. As late as 1802, when there were two newspapers publishing in Poughkeepsie, an editor complained that two-third of the families living along the post-roads, where delivery was prompt and easy, did not subscribe to either Poughkeepsie paper. He observed that "it is a melancholy trait in the history of our country, that there are yet many families of property who do not receive, or read any periodical paper," and he admonished his readers, who, presumably, did not require the rebuke, "No family in the United States ought to be destitute of a Bible and a newspaper." [13]

The circulation of newspapers outside the towns was unpre-

£1/4/0 for six months (Receipt from Francis Childs, 15 October 1787, James Duane Papers, New-York Historical Society).

[9] "A Citizen," *Daily Advertiser*, 27 June 1786; "Twenty-seven Subscribers," *New-York Journal*, 1 January 1788.

[10] *Country Journal*, 19 February 1788.

[11] Harold C. Syrett, ed., and Jacob E. Cooke, assoc. ed., *The Papers of Alexander Hamilton* (New York, 1961–), IV, 31.

[12] Milton W. Hamilton, *The Country Printer, New York State, 1785–1830* (New York, 1936), p. vii.

[13] *Political Barometer* (Poughkeepsie), 8 June 1802, quoted in Hamilton, *Country Printer*, p. 211.

dictable, depending chiefly on individuals who carried papers into the country. Broadsides were a more convenient and effective means of circulating political essays in the country. It was impractical for a man living at any considerable distance from the main post road to subscribe to a newspaper even if he did not object to having it delivered from a week to a month late. The mails were even less efficient than usual during 1788, and the distribution of newspapers was disrupted throughout the Confederation. In February 1788, the *New-York Journal* printed a clipping from a Boston paper headed "Facts!!":

> The several printers on the continent are requested to notice in their papers, that since the commencement of the present year, the printers in the northern states have received scarce a single paper, printed beyond the Hudson. Notwithstanding the public are exceedingly anxious, at the present all-important period, to be acquainted with the progress of political affairs, the printers in Boston, have not received any papers from New-York, for several weeks, tho' before January they were regularly received.[14]

Two weeks later Thomas Greenleaf, the editor of the *New-York Journal*, informed his readers that since the Boston notice appeared he had received nine letters from printers in other states complaining that they had not been receiving his paper, "and requesting that the Editor would, in future, find some other mode than the *post-office*, for conveyance, expressing a desire, that the other Printers might also alter their channel of conveyance if possible." [15]

The difficulty was not limited to interstate movement of newspapers. New Yorkers living to the north of Albany found their subscriptions to the *Albany Journal* failed to arrive. In all of April, "Observer" complained, nothing but the issue of 3 April had reached them. "To whatever cause it may be owing," he warned the printers, "it is proper that the public should be

[14] *New-York Journal*, 25 February 1788.
[15] *Ibid.*, 10 March 1788.

informed of this extraordinary circumstance—whether it is to be attributed to the spirited exertions of some of the Foederalists to prevent their fellow citizens from being informed, that the opposition to the adoption of the New-Constitution without previous amendments is still persevered in: whether they like not the complexion of some late publications contained in those papers, or whether you intend the subscriptions for your papers should cease."[16]

For the Antifederalists, it was an easy assumption that the interruption of communications was politically motivated. Believing, as they did, that it was necessary to destroy the original favorable impression made by the Philadelphia report, the Antifederalists saw any hindrance of free discussion as in the Federalist interest.[17] Federalists seem never to have blamed the Antis for the interruption of mail service, although the New York papers carried far more Federalist than Antifederalist material. But while the assumption that Ebenezer Hazard, the postmaster general, had political reasons for preventing the free circulation of newspapers was widely made by Antifederalists, Hazard's ill-timed attempt to reform the postal service by substituting post riders for stagecoaches, which resulted in serious interruptions of communication at this politically important period, seems to have had no political motivation.[18]

Despite the disruption of mail service, printers in New York City seem to have had no difficulty obtaining copies of publications from other states. Even if papers did not come in by post, they were brought by the many visotors from out of state who constantly arrived in New York City. Out of a total of approximately 350 political essays dealing with the Constitution that

[16] "From the ALBANY JOURNAL," *New-York Journal*, 13 May 1788.

[17] "Centinel," IX, *New-York Journal*, 14 January 1788; "Notes from a Correspondent," *ibid.*, 25 January 1788; "Centinel," XIV, *ibid.*, 15 February 1788; "A True Federalist," *ibid.*, 25 March 1788.

[18] Oliver W. Holmes, "Shall Stagecoaches Carry the Mail?—A Debate of the Confederation Period," *William and Mary Quarterly*, third series, XX (1963), 555–573.

appeared in one or more of the state's papers between September 1787 and the election of April 1788, more than 125 had their first publication outside New York State. The proportion of clippings in these papers was doubtless even higher than these figures indicate since the printers were not scrupulous about acknowledging the source of the essays they published, and it is not always possible to identify an item if the printer does not label its source. The greatest number of clippings were taken from the Philadelphia papers: thirty Federalist essays and fifty-five Antifederalist essays. Most of the remaining pieces came from New England papers with a scattering from Maryland, Viriginia, and South Carolina, which may have been taken secondhand from the Philadelphia publications.

Throughout the period between the first publication of the Constitution and the election for members of the ratifying convention, and even beyond, the new Constitution was the chief topic of discussion in the pages of the New York newspapers. The papers of 1787–1788 were single folio sheets, and of the four pages, one, two, or even three, were devoted to advertisements. That left at the most three pages for which the printer would set type for political essays and news. Most of this space was devoted to discussion of the Constitution during the ratification campaign—but not all of it.

Some papers, like the *Independent Journal* and the *New-York Morning Post*, felt obliged to continue their reports of European news. Other editors were pressed by their readers to devote an occasional inch or two to other subjects. Thomas Greenleaf was persuaded to relax his "stern *constitutional* politics" in order to print an article on the safety of the frontier.[19] One Pat O'Balaghan wrote to Nicholas Powers in Poughkeepsie to "beg a nook in your paper for the insertion of a piece which I think contains many beauties." He enclosed his translation of some Irish verse, observing that "little effusions of this kind, may tend to smooth the public brow, perhaps too much contracted from

[19] *New-York Journal*, 5 December 1787.

the austerities of politics."[20] At the end of April, barely a week before the election, the *New-York Journal* devoted the whole space available for political essays in four issues to an extract from a pamphlet published in 1769 dealing with the union of England and Scotland.[21]

In addition, New Yorkers found other subjects to disagree on during the ratification period that drew their attention from politics. In New York City, the newspapers served as a battlefield for "Philalethes" and "Filetus" who held conflicting opinions on the value of studying classical Greek,[22] and for "Humanio" and "Student"who differed on the propriety of grave robbing,[23] while in Poughkeepsie, Nicholas Powers set his type for "Sidney" and "Aristides" who respectively attacked and defended a justice of the peace who had fined a hairdresser for prosecuting his trade openly on Sundays.[24]

The Constitutional essays appeared in the New York newspapers accompanied by such ephemeral material. Most of them had as little permanent value as Pat O'Balaghan's verses, and even their immediate political effect may not have been very great. Perhaps, as Henry Knox suggested, they represented just so much spoiled paper and wasted ink and were "never read on either side."[25] Yet since enterprising penmen continued to forward a great number of pieces to the printers' offices, the production of these political essays must be considered a significant part of the ratification campaign in the urban areas of New York.

By the end of April 1788, about 180 Federalist essays and 160

[20] *Country Journal*, 19 December 1787.

[21] "Caledonia," *New-York Journal*, 22–25 April 1788.

[22] *Daily Advertiser*, April 1788, *passim*.

[23] *Ibid.*, February 1788, *passim*.

[24] *Country Journal*, 19 September 1787, 10 October 1787, 12 October 1787.

[25] Quoted in Broadus Mitchell, *Alexander Hamilton* (New York, 1957, 1962), I, 417.

Antifederalist essays had appeared in one or more New York newspapers. Some of them were very long and filled several issues. But fewer than half the essays printed were serious discussions of the Constitution of the sort found in *The Federalist* by "Publius" or the *Letters from a Federal Farmer.* Satire, sarcasm, and verse were the contributions of many writers. A favorite technique was to parody the serious arguments of one's opponents, as in this rousing Rabelaisian appeal, clipped from a Philadelphia paper by the *Daily Advertiser:*

Rouse then, my friends, my countrymen, my fellow-citizens!—Rouse, ye Shayites, Dayites, and Shattuckites!—Ye Insurgents, Rioters, and Deserters!—Ye Tories, Refugees, and Antifederalists! . . . Do not you see the Aristocrats, Monocrats, Demagogues, Pedagogues, Gogamagogs, Brobdingnags, Conspirators, and Federal Hobgoblins, are preparing to govern you, to enslave you, enthral you, and bemaul you. . . .[26]

One of these articles, Hugh Henry Brackenridge's "Cursory Remarks," which was reprinted in the *Daily Advertiser,* is worth quoting at some length since it is typical of so much that was written:

The first thing that strikes a diligent observer, is the want of precaution with regard to the *sex* of the president. Is it provided that he shall be of the male gender? The Salii, a tribe of the Burgundians, in the eleventh century, excluded females from the sovereignty. Without a similar exclusion, what shall we think if, in progress of time, we should come to have an *old woman* at the head of our affairs? . . . But what avails it to dwell on these things? The want of a *bill of rights* is the great evil. There was no occasion for a bill of *wrongs;* for there will be wrongs enough. But oh! a *bill of rights!* . . . A bill of rights is wanting, and all those things which are usually secured under it— . . . the *liberty of the press*—that is gone at the first stroke. Not so much as an advertisement for a stray horse or a runaway negro, can be put in any of the gazettes

[26] *Daily Advertiser,* 23 February 1788.

. . . . I would submit it to any candid man, if in this constitution there is the least provision for the privilege of shaving the beard? . . . Whence is it then, that men of learning seem so much to approve, while the ignorant are against it? The cause is perfectly apparent, viz., that reason is an erring guide, while instinct, which is the governing principle of the untaught, is certain. Put a pig in a poke, carry it half a day's journey through woods and by-ways, let it out, and it will run home without deviation. Could Dr. Franklin do this? [27]

The Antifederalists wrote as much of this sort of thing as the Federalists, as in thirteen "Maxims" published in the *New-York Journal,* which listed as number seven, "Trial by jury was *never known in Sweden,* and therefore we ought not to have it in America." [28]

Almost a third of both Federalist and Antifederalist articles were devoted to *ad hominem* attacks, either on prominent members of the opposite party, or on opposing scribblers. The art of personal invective was cultivated with relish, and the desire to practice it was only incidentally political. At times the writers would be so carried away by the simple joy of mudslinging that it is quite impossible to tell the Federalist writer from the Antifederalist.[29] Most of the writers [30] stopped short of obscenity, and limited themselves to such remarks as "A monkey has more unexceptionable claim to reason than the Examiner to elegance or satire," [31] and, as "Examiner" wrote the same day, "As to that sniviling blockhead, Democritus, his drunken performance does not indeed merit a reply, but. . . ." [32] The hottest scorching was likely to go to writers unfortunate enough to have their true identities discovered. Richard Henry Lee, Alexander Hamilton, and most of all, Abraham Yates, were excoriated by the

[27] *Ibid.,* 5 May 1788. [28] *New-York Journal,* 15 January 1788.

[29] L. Elmendorf, *Country Journal,* 29 April 1788; John Addison, *ibid.,* 6 May 1788.

[30] But not all: "Democritus," *New-York Journal,* 21 December 1787.

[31] "A Friend to Common Sense," *ibid.,* 18 December 1787.

[32] "Examiner," III, *ibid.*

scribblers who suspected that they stood behind "Federal Farmer," "Publius," and "Sydney." [33]

About a quarter of the articles published consisted of serious argument clothed in an informal style. Perhaps the most effective of these were the "Countryman" essays written by the governor's nephew, De Witt Clinton, who was then eighteen years old. He had graduated from Columbia at the head of his class two years earlier and in 1787 was reading law under Samuel Jones in New York City,[34] but the young De Witt was clever enough to realize that the Antifederal arguments of a precocious law student from the City would win few votes. He therefore adopted the character of "Countryman," a simple, uneducated soul from Dutchess County, who had a healthy suspicion of lawyers [35] and a common-sense approach to politics.[36] De Witt's brother thought the "Countryman" letters "better adapted to the understanding of the Common People than any piece in the newspapers." [37]

Every essay that appeared in print did not receive the same circulation. A paragraph that appeared once in the Lansingburgh *Northern Centinel*, for example, would have few readers compared to one of the "Publius" letters, which might be reprinted by practically every newspaper in the state. Thus, while the Antifederalists were able to supply almost as large a number of essays to the printers as did the Federalists, relatively few of their essays were reprinted, and, consequently, the prevailing tone of the New York press was overwhelmingly Feder-

[33] For example, "A Landholder," Albany Gazette, 3 January 1788; *New-York Journal*, 4 February 1788; *Federal Herald* (Albany), 18 February 1788.

[34] William W. Campbell, *Life and Writings of De Witt Clinton* (New York, 1844), p. xxvi.

[35] "Countryman," IV, *New-York Journal*, 10 January 1788; "Countryman," VI, *ibid.*, 14 February 1788.

[36] *Ibid.*, 6 December 1787, 13 December 1787, 10 January 1788, 17 January 1788, 14 February 1788.

[37] George Clinton to De Witt Clinton, 22 December 1788, De Witt Clinton Papers, Special Collections, Columbia University.

alist. Of the approximately 160 Antifederalist essays published in New York, more than 130 appeared in a single paper: Thomas Greenleaf's *New-York Journal*. The 180 Federalist articles, on the other hand, made close to fifty appearances in the *Daily Advertiser*, twenty-five appearances in the *New-York Journal*, and twenty in the Poughkeepsie *Country Journal*. All of the other papers also ran large numbers of Federalist essays in fairly equal proportions. The disproportionately large number of Antifederalist articles that was run by the *New-York Journal* was not the result of deliberate partiality in the newspapers. There was no established party press in the 1780's, for in the absence of organized political parties, a party newspaper, as it was known in the later decades, could not exist. Party was an evil, and the appropriate sentiments for a newspaper editor were those expressed in the masthead of the Poughkeepsie *Country Journal:*

> In my Free Page let different Works reside
> Tho' Party's hostile Lines those Works divide.
> Party! whose murdering Spirit I abhor
> More subtly cruel, and less brave than war.[38]

Only one paper in the state carried its support of the Constitution so far as totally to exclude Antifederalist pieces,[39] but when forced to choose between printing a contribution from an Antifederalist reader and reprinting, say, one of the "Publius" essays, all of the printers except Thomas Greenleaf customarily chose

[38] This verse first appeared in the *Country Journal* masthead on 3 October 1787.

[39] The exception is the *Independent Journal* (New York), which was principally concerned with foreign news and, with the notable exception of the *Federalist*, printed almost nothing on the Constitution. Jackson Turner Main (*The Antifederalists, Critics of the Constitution, 1781–1788* [Chapel Hill, N.C., 1961], pp. 250, 251) is mistaken in believing that popular pressure stopped the *New-York Morning Post* from printing Antifederalist articles after 9 January 1788. The *Post* devoted most of its space to foreign news and advertisements. It printed only two original articles on the Constitution after 9 January 1788; both were carried in March, and both were Antifederalist.

the latter. Their sympathies were with the Federalists,[40] as they would sometimes openly admit,[41] although even those who confessed a party preference still affirmed that "to be IMPARTIAL shall be their steady aim." [42]

There was considerable complaint from Antifederalists that printers discriminated against them,[43] but, strangely enough, it is the *New-York Journal* that historians most frequently accuse of partiality.[44] Actually Greenleaf published a great quantity of original Federalist articles and Federalist clippings from the philosophy of "Publius" to the billingsgate of "Examiner," and the printer reported the progress of the Consitution without editorializing.[45] It seems likely that more Antifederalist essays were submitted to Greenleaf than to other editors since he had room for more contributions in his daily paper. Greenleaf, himself, insisted that he was impartial and merely set type for what was put in the boxes at his office door. To those who complained that the newspapers were partial, he observed that printers "doubtless print what is sent them—for a *printer* as a *printer*, has no choice. . . ." He added that if newspapers "should happen to appear *partial*, *pray*, leige, our readers, whoever are so nicely distinguishing, do not stigmatize the printers, but take one paper of each sort." [46]

There is no reason to believe that what was printed in the newspapers had a decisive influence in the ratification campaign, if only because the distribution of the papers was relatively limited. Moreover, most of the essay and verses—the "voluminous

[40] E. Wilder Spaulding, *New York in the Critical Period, 1783–1789* (New York, 1932), p. 39.

[41] The *Independent Journal* sometimes editorialized for the Federalists in news articles, (e.g. 16 February 1788); *Federal Herald*, 31 March 1788.

[42] *Federal Herald*, 31 March 1788.

[43] For instance, John Lansing to Melancton Smith, 1 March 1788, Abraham Yates, Jr., Papers, New York Public Library.

[44] William F. Swindler, "The Letters of Publius," *American Heritage*, XII (1961), 4–7, 92–97.

[45] *New-York Journal*, 17 January 1788.

[46] *New-York Journal*, 27 December 1787.

conscribulations"[47] of a "Montezuma"[48] or an "Alexander the Great"[49]—were hardly worth a single reading,[50] and it is quite possible that no one but the authors gave them any more than that. When writing of the Constitution, Vernon L. Parrington noted with surprise "how little abstract political speculation accompanied its making and adoption."[51] A contemporary rhymester gaily made the same observation in his "Newsmongers' Song: For the winter of 1788:"

> Good news brother dealers in metre and prose!
> The world has turn'd *buffer* & coming to blows;
> Write *good-sense* or *non-sense*, my boys, it's all one,
> All persons may fire when the battle's begun.
> *Down, down, down derry down.*
> Our tutors and sages would oftentimes say,
> "Sit omnibus hora," each dog has his day:
> Queen Anne's was the aera of genius 'tis known,
> *Arguendo* this day is for scribblers alone
> *Down, down, &c.*
>
> . . . . .
>
> Old Time, with his brass-eating teeth shall consume,
> The works of a *Homer*, a *Newton*, a *Hume;*
> And who, when all things are consum'd by Old Time
> Can tell but we scribblers were writers sublime?
> *Down, down, down derry down*[52]

There was, however, one series of articles produced in the "age of scribblers" that became an enduring classic of political literature: *The Federalist Papers* of Hamilton, Madison, and Jay.

[47] "A Lunarian," *Daily Advertiser*, 20 December 1787.

[48] *New-York Morning Post*, 24 October 1787.

[49] *Country Journal*, 22 April 1788.

[50] The best pieces to appear, besides the *Federalist*, were in opposition to the Constitution: "Cato," "Sidney" (and "Sydney"), "Brutus," "Countryman," "Centinel," and the "Federal Farmer." These were reprinted all over the state and the last two circulated as pamphlets as well.

[51] *Main Currents in American Thought* (New York, 1927), I, 283.

[52] *Daily Advertiser*, 23 November 1787.

These essays, seventy-six of which were published before the New York election, stood out in the newspapers of the time the way "The Waste Land" would stand out in a high school literary magazine. They differed in kind and in merit from the other essays printed that year, and the facts of their production and their possible influence in the ratification campaign are the subject of the following chapter.

VII

Publius

THE first of the *Federalist* essays was published late in October 1787, a month after the appearance of the first Antifederalist "Cato" letter, and several weeks after the publication of the first "Federal Farmer" letter. The decision to write the "Publius" [1] series must have been made by Hamilton and Jay early in October, for Hamilton's widow recalled many years later that Hamilton wrote the first number of the series on board one of the North River sloops during a week-long journey to attend the fall session of the Supreme Court in Albany,[2] and John Jay was ready with the second number of the series four days after the first number appeared.

Originally, the two New Yorkers probably intended to write

[1] The pseudonym was adopted from the prenomen of Publius Valerius, who, Plutarch records, established a just and stable republican government in Rome after the overthrow of Tarquin, the last Roman king (Madison to Pauling, 24 July 1818, quoted in W. C. Rives, *History of the Life and Times of James Madison* [Boston, 1866], p. 484n.).

[2] Interview with Mrs. Hamilton, August 1851, Joel Munsell, ed., *The Annals of Albany* (Albany, 1850–1859), VIII, 227). The story, as it usually appears, is that the piece was written while Hamilton was *returning* to New York. It appeared in this form in John C. Hamilton, *History of the Republic of the United States as Traced in the Writings of Alexander Hamilton and his Contempories* (Philadelphia, 1864), p. 369, and in the

the entire series themselves. John Jay wrote rapidly and contributed three more essays in less than two weeks. Then, early in November, Jay suffered a severe attack of what was diagnosed first as tuberculosis and then as rheumatism,[3] which lasted throughout the winter. He was still tortured by pain in February [4] and was unable to attend to any business, even the most pressing, until near the middle of that month.[5] Not until March 1788 was Jay well enough to do another piece for "Publius," [6] and then, scarcely more than a month later, the unfortunate man was struck with a brick during the Doctors' Riot [7] and attempted no more essays for the series.

Alexander Hamilton was thus deprived of his collaborator less than a month after beginning the "Publius" series, and since he was unable to write all of the projected essays himself, he approached James Madison in the middle of November [8] and requested his aid. Hamilton would have preferred to have another New Yorker assist him in composing the series, which was directed to "the People of the State of New York," but Gouverneur Morris declined an invitation to take part,[9] and William Duer, although he did his best, was unable to produce long

same author's edition of *The Federalist* (Philadelphia, 1864), pp. lxxxv, lxxxvi. The earlier version of Elizabeth Hamilton is probably more trustworthy, although neither the memory of a ninety-four-year-old woman nor the family tradition repeated by the son can be regarded as absolutely reliable.

[3] Frank Monaghan, *John Jay* (New York, 1935), p. 290.

[4] John Jay to George Washington, 3 February 1788, H. P. Johnston, ed., *Correspondence and Public Papers of John Jay* (New York, 1891), III, 323.

[5] [John Jay] to Aides of General Greene, 12 February 1788, John Jay Manuscripts, Catalogued Collection, Columbia University.

[6] Number LXIV. [7] See below, pp. 149–151.

[8] James Madison to Edmund Randolph, 18 November 1787, Gaillard Hunt, ed., *Writings of James Madison, Comprising His Public Papers and His Private Correspondence* (New York, 1900–1910), V, 56. Madison had been contemplating a trip to Virginia—an impossibility once he had begun to write as "Publius."

[9] Jared Sparks, ed., *The Life of Gouverneur Morris* (Boston, 1832), III, 339.

essays, and his two or three paragraph pieces were finally published separately over the signature "Philo-Publius." [10]

Madison contributed his first paper to the series, the classic *Federalist* X, on 24 November 1787. He and Hamilton worked together until the beginning of the new year when Hamilton took time off to attend the winter term of the New York Supreme Court and Madison wrote twenty-one successive essays. After Hamilton's return, pieces by both men appeared in late February and early March, with a single contribution from Jay appearing on 5 March.[11] Three days after the publication of Madison's final number, he left for Virginia, arriving the day before Virginians were to elect members to their ratifying convention,[12] and Hamilton was left to complete the remaining essays. But the New Yorker could not carry the burden alone, and when the Court of Chancery and the Circuit Court began their sessions, Hamilton had to give up his literary enterprise and devote his full time to business.[13] Consequently, after 2 April, during the final weeks of the campaign, "Publius" sent nothing to the newspapers. Hamilton wrote eight more essays, bringing the

[10] Duer wrote three essays over this signature during October and November 1787. They are published in Hamilton, ed., *The Federalist*, pp. 655–659; James Madison to George Washington, 18 November 1787, United States Bureau of Rolls and Library, *Documentary History of the Constitution of the United States* (Washington, 1894–1903), IV, 381.

[11] The authorship of certain numbers of the *Federalist* has been disputed with much heat and at great length for more than 150 years (Jacob E. Cooke, ed., *The Federalist* [Cleveland, 1961], pp. xx to xxx; Harold C. Syrett, ed., and Jacob E. Cooke, assoc. ed., *The Papers of Alexander Hamilton* [New York, 1961–], IV, 292–301). The most recent contribution to the controversy is Frederick Mosteller and David L. Wallace, *Inference and Disputed Authorship: The Federalist* (Reading, Mass., 1964), a computer analysis of the papers. The evidence heavily favors Madison as the author of all the disputed essays.

[12] By remaining so long in New York, Madison imperiled his chance of election (Douglass Adair, "The Authorship of the Disputed Federalist Papers," *William and Mary Quarterly*, third series, I [1944], 252, 253).

[13] Hamilton to Madison, 3 April 1788, Syrett, ed., *Papers of Alexander Hamilton*, IV, 644. He was even too "engaged in private business" to

total number of papers to eighty-five, but these appeared for the first time in the bound second volume of the *Federalist*, published on 28 May 1788,[14] a month after the New York election.

In view of the differences in the political philosophies of Madison and Hamilton, it is remarkable that symptoms of haste and schizophrenia are so little apparent in the *Federalist*. The two men had no opportunity to consult on every essay. Frequently one half of "Publius" would not know what the other half had said until he read the article in the newspaper. "Though carried on in concert," Madison wrote to Jefferson, "the writers are not mutually answerable for all the ideas of each other, there seldom being time for even a perusal of the pieces by any but the writer before they were wanted at the press, and sometimes hardly by the writer himself." [15] Even for two men, "Publius" turned out essays at a furious rate. At first the articles appeared at the rate of two a week, one in each issue of the *Independent Journal*, which published on Wednesdays and Saturdays. Then, on Saturday, 17 November, less than a month after the series began, "Publius" announced: "In order that the whole subject of these Papers may be as soon as possible laid before the Public, it is proposed to publish them four times a week, on Tuesday in the *New-York Packet* and on Thursday in the *Daily Advertiser*." [16] For five months "Publius" kept to his demanding schedule and missed the printer's deadline only once.[17]

The *Federalist* essays were reprinted by the New York papers more frequently than any other piece on the Constitution. In

---

attend Congress (Samuel Alleyne Otis to George Thatcher, 13 April 1788, Edmund C. Burnett, ed., *Letters of Members of the Continental Congress* [Washington, 1921–1936], VIII, 711).

[14] *Independent Journal* (New York) 28 May 1788.

[15] James Madison to Thomas Jefferson, 10 August 1788, Hunt, ed., *Writings of James Madison*, V, 246.

[16] The *Independent Journal* was the only newspaper to publish or reprint the entire series.

[17] *Independent Journal*, 29 December 1787.

New York City, they were given saturation distribution. Some of the essays were reprinted by four of the five City papers.[18] Thomas Greenleaf began to print "Publius" in mid-December. He published the *Federalist XXIII* on 18 December, informing his readers that it had been sent to him in manuscript the previous day "with an assurance, that his press should be preferred, in future, for the first ushering into public view, the succeeding numbers."[19] No doubt he was annoyed to find the piece printed in the *New-York Packet* on the same day, but he continued to print "Publius" essays despite the fact that he was given the first publication of no other number.

Some of Greenleaf's patrons protested. "Twenty-seven Subscribers"[20] rebuked him for printing essays they had already read elsewhere. They subscribed to the *New-York Journal*, they said, "merely for variety and to have an opportunity of seeing the arguments as fully as possible on both sides." Now they were disgusted with Greenleaf "for cramming us with the voluminous PUBLIUS." They subscribed to the *Independent Journal*, the *Daily Advertiser*, and the *New-York Packet* as well as to Greenleaf's paper. "We take M'Lean," they explained, "to read Publius in the best edition, and he gives us two at a time; and Childs for the daily news and advertisements, but they are curtailed, and we are disappointed for the purpose of serving up the same Publius at our expense; Loudon we take for his morality and evangelic sentiments; but here again we are imposed upon, by being made to pay for the very same Publius, who has become nauseous, by having been served up to us no less than in two other papers on the same day." And now Greenleaf was giving them "Publius" "a fourth time before breakfast and no less

[18] The *New-York Morning Post* devoted little space to the Constitution.

[19] *New-York Journal*, 18 December 1787.

[20] Jacob E. Cooke incorrectly cites this letter as "45 Subscribers" (*The Federalist*, p. 600n.; and Syrett, ed., *Papers of Alexander Hamilton*, IV, 289n.). William F. Swindler ("The Letters of Publius," *American Heritage*, XII [1961], 93) improperly identifies it as a "signed petition of thirty subscribers."

than two at a time." If Greenleaf was not going to give them variety, he ought to return the money they had paid for subscriptions.[21] Greenleaf printed "Publius" for another month and then stopped. He had long before declared to his readers that he would prefer almost any stigma "to that of a slavish copiest." [22]

Outside of New York City, the *Federalist* was reprinted much less frequently, although the republication it received was still impressive compared to that granted to most of the City essays. In Albany, twelve numbers appeared in the *Albany Gazette* between mid-November and March, while number *LXIX* was inserted by special request in the *Federal Herald*.[23] Across the river, the *Northern Centinel* carried the first ten essays. Farther south, James Kent, then a young Poughkeepsie lawyer, sent copies of the "Publius" essays to Nicholas Powers but was informed that the pieces were too long to print regularly in the weekly paper.[24] Nevertheless, Powers obliged by printing some special supplements to the *Country Journal*, and seven of the *Federalist* essays ran in January and February. It was not very much, but it was wider distribution than most newspaper essays received.[25]

Circulation of the "Publius" essays did not depend entirely on the distribution of newspapers. Hamilton contracted with the publishers of the *Independent Journal*, which first published the essays, to publish five hundred copies of the *Federalist* as a book.

[21] *New-York Journal*, 1 January 1788.

[22] *Ibid.*, 18 December 1787.

[23] Numbered in that newspaper as *LXVIII*, 31 March 1788.

[24] "A Country Federalist," *Country Journal* (Poughkeepsie), supp., 19 December 1787.

[25] The republication of "Publius" outside New York State is equally unimpressive. Mr. Leonard Rapport of the National Archives informs me that a search of all extant newspapers for this period reveals no surviving record of the publication of the essays in Connecticut, New Jersey, Delaware, Maryland, North Carolina, South Carolina, or Georgia—a majority of the states—or in the territories of Maine, Vermont, or Kentucky. In fact, outside the large cities of Boston and Philadelphia, no more than twelve "Publius" essays appeared, and these few were concentrated in seven newspapers published in six towns.

It was expected that the series would run to twenty or, at most, to twenty-five numbers.[26] McLean began to solicit subscriptions for the book in January,[27] but it was April before it came from the press. Then it contained thirty-six essays, and a second volume was in progress.

The Federalists began to distribute the volumes of "Publius" during the last three weeks of the ratification campaign. We know the fate of something over one hundred of the five hundred copies printed. Fifty-two copies were sent to Virginia addressed to the care of Governor Randolph.[28] This batch probably included the copy for George Washington.[29] At least one member of Congress sent a copy of the *Federalist* to a friend in his home state,[30] and there were doubtless others who did the same. Sixty copies were sent to Albany in care of Stephen Van Rensselaer—forty for Albany subscribers and twenty for subscribers in Montgomery County.[31] Finally, James Kent reported that "a large number" of the volumes were sent to him and Egbert Benson in Poughkeepsie "for gratuitous distribution." [32] Most of the remaining volumes were probably sold in New York City where they were advertised by the printers.

The effect of these bound volumes of the *Federalist* on the Poughkeepsie election, if any, was minuscule, since it is doubtful whether copies so much as reached subscribers in remote parts

[26] Archibald McLean to Robert Troup, quoted in Hamilton, ed., *The Federalist*, p. lxxxvix n.

[27] *Independent Journal*, 1 January 1788.

[28] Alexander Hamilton to James Madison, 19 May 1788, Syrett, ed., *Papers of Alexander Hamilton*, IV, 650.

[29] George Washington to Alexander Hamilton, 28 August 1788, *ibid.*, V, 207.

[30] Charles Thomson to James McHenry, 19 April 1788, Burnett, ed., *Letters of Members of the Continental Congress*, VIII, 722.

[31] Archibald McLean to Stephen Van Renselaer [*sic*], 10 April 1788, The Henry E. Huntington Library and Art Gallery.

[32] James Kent to Elizabeth Hamilton, 10 December 1832, William Kent, ed., *Memoirs and Letters of James Kent, Late Chancellor of the State of New York* (Boston, 1898), p. 302.

of the state before the election days.[33] Furthermore, it may be assumed that most of the men who ordered copies (and we know of only sixty subscribers outside New York City) [34] had read at least a few of the essays previously and agreed with the sentiments expressed in them. The volumes sent to Poughkeepsie for "gratuitous distribution" were taken to the nominating meeting of the Dutchess County Federalists, and, Kent reports, "the volumes were there circulated to the best of our judgements." [35] Certainly none would fall into the hands of an Antifederalist in that company.

It is tempting to exaggerate the importance of the *Federalist* in the ratification campaign. It is common to read that the "Publius" essays were "extensively circulated and generally read," [36] and John Fiske believed that the essays "probably accomplished more toward insuring the adoption of the Constitution than anything else that was said or done in that eventful year." [37] Actually, the circulation of the "Publius" essays was relatively small. Despite extensive reprinting in the New York City newspapers, the total circulation of the essays was much smaller than that of the Antifederalist "Federal Farmer" or "Columbian Patriot." [38]

[33] The copies for Montgomery County were forwarded from New York City via Albany on 10 April (Archibald McLean to Stephen Van Renselaer [*sic*], 10 April 1788, The Henry E. Huntington Library).

[34] *Ibid.*

[35] James Kent to Elizabeth Hamilton, 10 December 1832, Kent, ed., *Memoirs and Letters of James Kent,* p. 302.

[36] Jabez Delano Hammond, *History of Political Parties in the State of New York* (Cooperstown, N.Y., 1846), I, 20; Monaghan, *John Jay,* p. 291.

[37] John Fiske, *The Critical Period of American History* (Boston, 1888), p. 342.

[38] In addition to considerable republication in the newspapers, the sales of the "Federal Farmer" pamphlet were counted in the thousands (Forrest McDonald, ed., *Empire and Nation* [Englewood Cliffs, N.J., 1962], p. xv; Charles Warren, *The Making of the Constitution* [Boston, 1928], p. 767). More than 1600 copies of the "Columbian Patriot" pamphlet were distributed by the New York City Federal Republican Committee alone (Paul Leicester Ford, *Bibliography and Reference List of the History and Literature Relating to the Adoption of the Constitution of the United States, 1787–1788* [Brooklyn, 1888], p. 27).

There is no evidence that Publius converted a single Antifederalist, but he may well have made additional enemies for the Constitution. Today the best known number of the *Federalist* is number ten, but in 1787 number nine attracted more attention from Antifederalists. Both essays deal with the same topic; John Quincy Adams described them as "rival dissertations upon Faction and its remedy." [39] In number ten, Madison argued that the new Constitution would prevent the formation of dangerous factions and guarantee that no further outbreaks similar to Shays's Rebellion would occur. Hamilton, on the other hand, wrote the ninth essay to show how the new Constitution would allow the government forcibly to suppress such outbreaks. The Hamilton argument aroused those Antifederalists who feared a standing army. A gentleman who arrived in Philadelphia at the beginning of 1788 reported that there was not "the smallest probability" of New York adopting the Constitution, and he believed the "Publius" essays had done most to assure that result: "The common talk is, *Well what do you think of being surrounded with a standing army?*" [40]

The *Federalist* actually had little value as propaganda. The pieces were long and learned, and there were far too many of them. The *Federalist* is certainly the longest piece to come out of the campaign. It finally ran to two good sized volumes, eighty-five numbers, while "Centinel" wrote fewer than twenty pieces, and the "Federal Farmer" essays made only a slim pamphlet. The scribblers began to sneer at "the dry trash of Publius in 150 numbers" [41] and to poke fun at the author's erudition:

A correspondent, having observed the attempt of the present *voluminous* writer upon the new constitution, to explain the meaning of its several abstruse parts . . . begs leave to propose . . . that he next have recourse to CONIC SECTIONS, by which he will be

[39] Quoted in Alpheus T. Mason, "The Federalist—A Split Personality," *American Historical Review*, LVII (1952), 636.

[40] *New-York Morning Post*, 4 January 1788.

[41] *New-York Journal*, 16 May 1788.

enabled, with greater facility, to discover the *mazy windings* of his favorite system.[42]

De Witt Clinton, who was quick to take advantage of the opening, wrote in "Countryman," "As to Mr. Publius, I have read a great many of his papers, and I really cannot find out what he would be at; he seems to me as if he was going to write a history, so I have concluded to wait and buy one his books, when they come out." [43] Monsieur Otto reported that the essays were "of no value whatever to well-informed people, and . . . too learned and too long for the ignorant." [44] Or, as a North Carolina Federalist more charitably expressed it, "He is certainly a judicious writer, though not well calculated for the common people." [45]

More serious than its elevated tone was the irrelevance of the "Publius" essays to the questions that were actually at issue between Federalists and Antifederalists. The irrelevance of the essays was complained of constantly. De Witt Clinton, as "Countryman," wrote:

The only thing I can understand from him, as far as I have read, is that it is better to be united than divided—that a great many people are stronger than a few—and that Scotland is better off since the union with England than before; and I think, he proves too, very clearly, that the fewer nations there are in the world, the fewer disputes will be about the law of nations . . . but I do not learn that anybody denies these matters, or that they have anything to do with the new constitution. Indeed I am at a loss to know, whether Mr. Publius means to persuade us to return back to the old government, and make ourselves as happy as Scotland has by its union, or to accept of the new constitution, and get all the world to join with us, so as to make one large government.[46]

[42] *Ibid.*, 7 January 1788. [43] *Ibid.*, 10 January 1788.

[44] Louis G. Otto, "Liste des Membres et Officiers du Congrès," Max Farrand, ed., *The Records of the Federal Convention of 1787* (New Haven, 1911), III, 234.

[45] Ford, *Bibliography*, p. 11.

[46] *New-York Journal*, 10 January 1788.

A month later he wrote in the same vein, "The Foederalist, as he terms himself, or Publius, puts me in mind of some of the gentlemen of the long robe, when hard pushed, in a bad cause, with a rich client. They frequently say a good deal, which does not apply; but yet if it will not convince the judge nor jury, may, perhaps, help to make them forget some part of the evidence—embarrass their opponent, and make the audience stare, besides encreasing the practice." [47] The fiery "Centinel" from Philadelphia poured out his scorn for "Publius," calling him "a New York writer, who, mistaking sound for argument, has with Herculean labour accumulated myriads of unmeaning sentences . . . he might have spared his readers the fatigue of wading through his long winded disquisitions . . . as totally inapplicable to the subject he was *professedly* treating; this writer has devoted much time, and wasted more paper in combating chimeras of his own creation." [48]

"Publius" was devoted to confounding the Antifederalist position as he misunderstood it. He mistakenly assumed that it was necessary to convince the Antifederalists of the need for a stronger federal union, when what was needed was to convince them that the stronger union proposed by the Philadelphia Convention would not endanger personal liberty.[49] "Publius" does not so much as touch on the chief Antifederal objection to the Constitution, the absence of a bill of rights, until the eighty-third and eighty-fourth numbers, which were not published until late May 1788, and here he but repeats the unsatisfying argument first advanced by James Wilson that a bill is unnecessary since guarantees of personal liberty are implicit in the Constitution.

Although it was poorly calculated as propaganda, the *Federalist* was widely recognized at the time as a work of genius.

[47] *Ibid.*, 14 February 1788.

[48] *Ibid.*, 21 January 1788. See also, "An Observer," *ibid.*, 19 November 1787.

[49] Cf. below, Chap. XII.

Thomas Jefferson wrote to Madison from Paris that he thought it "the best commentary on the principles of government which was ever written," [50] and young James Kent, who not only read the essays but committed whole passages to memory,[51] could not think of "any work on the principles of free government that is to be compared, in instruction, and intrinsic value, to . . . *The Federalist*, not even if we resort to Aristotle, Cicero, Machiavel, Montesquieu, Milton, Locke, or Burke." [52] Still, it should never be supposed that the brilliance of these essays in any way discouraged the Antifederalists. Shortly after the second volume of the *Federalist* came from McLean's press, New Yorkers were enjoying a new political song, and there was an unanswerable reply to the learned lucubrations of "Publius" in its boistrous chorus:

> Federal, falderal, federalist,
> Your thumb to your mouth, and your nose to your fist.[53]

[50] Thomas Jefferson to James Madison, 18 November 1788, *Documentary History*, V, 120.

[51] John Theodore Horton, *James Kent: A Study in Conservatism, 1763–1847* (New York, 1939), p. 55.

[52] Quoted in Swindler, "The Letters of Publius," p. 93.

[53] *New-York Journal*, 28 June 1788.

PART III

Federalists and Antifederalists

VIII

The Campaign

PREDICTING the results of an election is an uncertain business, and it was an even less trustworthy practice in the eighteenth century than it is today. Yet predicting election results was as necessary to politicians then as it is now, and the attempt was made. John Jay wrote to Thomas Jefferson after the Constitution had circulated for about a month that "the Majority seem to be in favor of it, but there will probably be a strong opposition in some of the States, particularly in this. . . ." [1] Alexander Hamilton noted in a private memorandum at the end of September 1787 that "it will be Eight or Nine months before any certain judgement can be formed respecting the adoption of the Plan," [2] and a month later he told Washington, "The event cannot yet be foreseen." For what it was worth he added, "The constitution proposed has in this state warm friends and warm enemies," but he thought the first impressions were generally favorable.[3] James Madison wrote from New York City early in

[1] John Jay to Thomas Jefferson, 24 October 1787, John Jay Papers, Catalogued Collection, Columbia University.

[2] Harold C. Syrett, ed., and Jacob E. Cooke, assoc. ed., *The Papers of Alexander Hamilton* (New York, 1961–), IV, 277.

[3] Alexander Hamilton to George Washington, 30 October 1787, *ibid.*, 306.

October that he had heard "nothing decisive as yet concerning the general reception given to the acts of the Convention," but he was sceptical of what Hamilton had interpreted as the favorable first impression made by the Constitution. "The advocates for it come forward more readily than the adversaries," wrote Madison.[4] He admitted that "the general voice of this City seems to espouse the new Constitution," but pointed out that "the country must finally decide, the sense of which is as yet wholly unknown." [5]

Reliable intelligence from the country was difficult to come by. The population was not concentrated as it was in New York City, and a resident could do little more than speak for himself and his near neighbors and speculate about the sentiments in more remote areas. Peter Tappen wrote to Governor Clinton from Dutchess County at the end of September, "I find the New Constitution Sirculating here. It has but few warm friends here . . . I make no doubt but the common people here will generally oppose it. I should think that the Northern part of the County will be for adopting it. I judge from the leading men." [6] Throughout the campaign such speculation continued. A writer in the *New-York Journal* purported to know the sentiments of every voter in one of the Ulster County towns:

> There are but three federalists (as they are called) in the town of Goshen. . . . The first . . . was a Lieutenant in the Continental Army, and lately a tavern-keeper in the town—The second is a School-master lately imported from Scotland—and the third a young man, whom I am informed was lately elected a constable for the precinct of Goshen.[7]

[4] James Madison to Edmund Randolph, 7 October 1787, Henry D. Gilpin, ed., *The Papers of James Madison* (New York, 1841), II, 647.

[5] James Madison to George Washington, 30 September 1787, *ibid.*, 646.

[6] Peter Tappen to George Clinton, 29 September 1787, George Clinton Papers, New York Public Library.

[7] "A Citizen," *New-York Journal*, 12 April 1788.

Ultimately, the view of public sentiment that emerged was that expressed in a letter from a New York City Federalist: "This City is true—but the Country wants mending." The politicians directed their activities on that assumption. "We are busy," the letter continued; "so are the Anti's." [8]

Although there was heated controversy in the newspapers from September on, there was no organized campaign activity until February 1788, after the New York Legislature had called for the election of delegates to a ratifying convention. The first formal campaign organization was founded in the city of Albany. The gentlemen of that district had a club, established for "hearing news, smoaking tobacco & drinking grogg." There a party of Antifederalists met on the evening of 13 February 1788 and "appointed a Committee to manage the election for Convention." [9] The Committee had about thirty members, including Abraham Yates; Jeremiah Van Rensselaer was the chairman.[10]

The first official action of the "Anti-Federal Committee" was to attempt to set up an "impartial paper" in Albany. Charles Webster, who published the *Albany Gazette,* was a confessed Federalist, and the Antis distrusted him. Even before the formation of the Anti-Federal Committee, the Albany Antifederalists had written to friends in New York City asking that Thomas Greenleaf be requested "to send one of his Journeymen to set up a printing office here." [11] On 1 March 1788, seven members of the Albany Anti-Federal Committee formally requested Melancton Smith in New York City "to procure a printer and to send

[8] S. B. Webb to Joseph Barrell, 9 March 1788, W. C. Ford, ed., *Correspondence and Journals of Samuel Blanchley Webb* (New York, 1893–1894), III, 97.

[9] Major North to Henry Knox, 13 February 1788, Knox Papers, XXI, 143, Massachusetts Historical Society.

[10] See the signatures on the Anti-Federal Committee's "Objections to the Adoption of the Constitution," 10 April 1788, Joel Munsell, ed., *The Annals of Albany* (Albany, 1850–1859), IV, 342, 343.

[11] Abraham Lansing to Abraham Yates, 31 January 1788, Abraham Yates, Jr., Papers, New York Public Library.

him up without Delay with his press." They proposed to call the new newspaper the *Albany Register* and were willing to guarantee the new printer two hundred subscriptions as well as to advance him "a sum of Money on Account, immediately on his arrival." The "impartial printer" was expected to print Antifederalist essays willingly and without having them "accompanied with others to counteract their Effects." Webster's *Albany Journal*, they complained, printed their pieces rarely and always "with Reluctance," [12] and the Anti-Federal Committee feared that Webster "will deceive us when his services should be most wanted." [13]

The Anti-Federal Committee busily solicited subscriptions for its new paper—Robert Yates took six copies [14]—but for some reason it was impossible to induce a printer to come to Albany. Finally, near the end of March, the Albany Antifederalists wrote, "Despairing of receiving any aid from New York we have made explicit Arrangements here which we have every Reason to suppose will answer our purpose. We therefore wish you not to persist in engaging the printer." [15] The "Arrangements" were doubtless with Webster himself, for a number of the Committee's broadsides printed in March and April bear his name.[16]

The Federalists were impressed by the industry of their opponents. "They use every art, & strain every nerve to gain their points," an Albany Federalist wrote the day following the organization of the Anti-Federal Committee, "& if the Federalists

[12] John Lansing, Jeremiah Van Rensselaer, Peter W. Yates, Henry Oothoudt, Richard Luch, Matthew Vesscher, and Abraham G. Lansing to Melancton Smith, 1 March 1788, Abraham Yates, Jr., Papers, New York Public Library.

[13] Abraham G. Lansing and Henry Oothoudt to [Abraham Yates], 2 March 1788, *ibid.*

[14] *Ibid.*

[15] John Lansing and Abraham G. Lansing to [?], 23 March 1788, John Lamb Papers, New-York Historical Society.

[16] Broadside Collection, SY-1788-14, SY-1788-24, New-York Historical Society.

do not exert themselves (which they never have done, nor ever will do sufficiently) they will be beaten."[17] The Federalists never did establish an organization comparable to that established by the Antis at Albany. There were Federal Committees in New York and Albany, the first headed by Thomas Randal[18] and the second by Robert McClallen,[19] but these did little more than circulate the local election list and a few broadsides. The leaders of the Federalist party acted independently of them. For instance, when Peter Van Schaack, a member of a leading Columbia family and a Federalist candidate for the Poughkeepsie Convention, believed that an alliance with the Albany County Federalists might be useful, he did not write to Robert McClallen's Federal Committee but to Philip Schuyler.[20] The Federal Committees were purely local and did not maintain the state-wide connections that marked the Albany Anti-Federal Committee.

The smaller communities in the different counties also appointed political committees, but very little is known of their activities. A number of the freeholders of the town of Kingston "met on 14 February 1788 and appointed three men to meet in a general county committee of the different towns and precincts of Ulster County to deliberate on the Constitution and propose a list of delegates for the Poughkeepsie Convention."[21] In mid-March "the inhabitants of the respectable district of Scatakoke" in Albany County held a general meeting on the Constitution and polled the sentiments of those present: "there appeared a

[17] Major North to Henry Knox, 13 February 1788, Knox Papers, XXI, 143, Massachusetts Historical Society.

[18] The Randal Committee proposed the slate of candidates most frequently reprinted in the New York City newspapers.

[19] McClallen's Committee nominated a slate of candidates on 14 March 1788 (Broadside Collection, SY–1788–13, New-York Historical Society). Like Randal's list in New York City, the McClallen list was frequently reprinted in the local newspapers.

[20] Peter Van Schaack to Philip Schuyler, 3 April 1788, Philip John Schuyler Papers, Vol. XXXVI, New York Public Library.

[21] *New-York Journal*, 29 February 1788.

majority of 27 in favor of its adoption, and but 5 against it."[22] These meetings, and other similar, seem to have had no purpose but to express the approbation or displeasure of the attending electors and in some cases to nominate a slate of candidates. They were not proselytizing campaign organizations.

There is an amusing description of the proceedings of one rural political meeting which may well have been typical. On 7 February 1788, a group of Antifederalists numbering between 100 and 600 met at Montgomery.[23] One report insists that no general notice of the meeting was given in advance,[24] but it seems unlikely that so large a group would have assembled spontaneously. The Federalist description of the affair insists that prior notice was given:

> About eight or ten days previous to this great meeting, it was noised about in the two counties [Ulster and Orange], that effigies of three gentlemen of respectable characters in the city of New-York were to be burnt at Ward's bridge . . . in the county of Ulster, for having heretically asserted that they were for the adoption of the proposed Constitution; in consequence of which a number of people, who usually frequent such scenes, from the county of Ulster attended, and some few from Orange County.[25]

The Antifederalists, of course, insisted that the participants were "respectable inhabitants,"[26] and that they assembled merely "in order to ascertain the general sentiment respecting the proposed constitution."[27] What transpired at the meeting was described by "A Friend to Truth" thus:

> After passing the grog freely, it was determined to appoint a Committee. . . . [W]hile the other persons present were intent on

[22] *Federal Herald* (Albany), 17 March 1788.

[23] "A Friend to Truth," *Daily Advertiser* (New York), 4 March 1788; "Letterbox," *New-York Journal*, 23 February 1788.

[24] *New-York Journal*, 28 February 1788.

[25] "A Friend to Truth," *Daily Advertiser*, 4 March 1788.

[26] *New-York Journal*, 28 February 1788.

[27] "Letterbox," *New-York Journal*, 23 February 1788.

the real (getting grog) business of their meeting . . . they in grand procession marched to ward's bridge, about two hundred yards . . . with the Constitution on a long pole . . . followed in procession by fifteen men, out of the number of perhaps one hundred present (who probably would have followed had they been able to do so) . . . and the copy they had jointly purchased of the Constitution . . . was burned.[28]

Such activity may have been neither intellectual nor edifying, but it was the stuff political campaigns were made of.

Abraham Yates was pleased with the political situation in New York at the end of February, noting that "Antifederal Business is carried on in [Dutchess] County and so they tell me in Ulster Orange and Weschester [*sic*] with Spirit. . . . And by the reports we have lately had federalist are in greater Doubt about their success in the County of Albany." The only difficulty was in Suffolk, Richmond, Kings, and New York counties, where Yates feared the Federalists would be entirely successful.[29] In New York City, the Antifederalists were few and sensitive of their weakness,[30] and they did not establish a campaign organization of any sort until the beginning of April, less than a month before the election.

The first evidence of the existence of a formal Antifederalist organization in New York City is a draft letter in the hand of Melancton Smith dated 6 April 1788. The name "Federal Republican Society," which was later used by the New York City organization, had not yet been adopted, and the letter is directed from the "Committee of N. York." Copies were sent to Antifederalist campaign leaders in other counties. The purpose of the communication was to transmit copies of a pamphlet entitled "Observations on the New Constitution" by the "Columbian Patriot," which the New Yorkers wished to have distributed—although not at their expense. "The cost of Printing,"

[28] "A Friend to Truth," *Daily Advertiser*, 4 March 1788.

[29] Abraham Yates to [Abraham G. Lansing], 28 February 1788, Abraham Yates, Jr., Papers, New York Public Library.

[30] *Ibid.;* Melancton Smith to Abraham Yates, 23 January 1788, *ibid.*

Smith wrote, "you will find in the Packages."[31] Thomas Greenleaf printed 1630 copies of the pamphlet,[32] more than three hundred copies of which were sent to Dutchess County in care of four different Antifederalists.[33] Most of the remainder probably went to the Albany Anti-Federal Committee.

At the beginning of April, the Albany Anti-Federal Committee was directing the campaign activity in the three largest counties of the state: Washington (and Clinton), Montgomery, and Albany.[34] They were exceedingly industrious; the chairman, Jeremiah Van Rensselaer, reported on 3 April that "we are in close action from morning to night so that little time is spent with me on any other subject."[35] On 12 April, the Albany Committee acknowledge the receipt of letters from the Antifederalist group in the City and thanked them for the package of "Columbian Patriot" pamphlets. That work, by the Massachusetts bluestocking Mercy Warren, the Albany Committee considered "a well composed piece but in a stile too sublime & florid for the common people in this Part of the Country." They planned to distribute the pamphlets, they said, "but do not expect to pay for them." The membership of the Anti-Federal Committee was small, and they had "already incurred a considerable expence inclusive of throwing away the Money for Greenleafs Pamphlets."[36]

The last remark probably referred to a collection of Antifederal material including the "Reason of Dissent of the Minority

[31] Committee of N. York to [?], 6 April 1788, John Lamb Papers, New-York Historical Society.

[32] Paul Leicester Ford, *Bibliography and Reference List of the History and Literature Relative to the Adoption of the Constitution of the United States, 1787–1788* (Brooklyn, 1888), p. 27.

[33] Staughton Lynd, *Anti-Federalism in Dutchess County, New York* (Chicago, 1962), p. 13.

[34] The Committee of Albany to the Committee of New York, 12 April 1788, John Lamb Papers, New-York Historical Society.

[35] "J——V——R——," *Daily Advertiser,* 10 April 1788.

[36] The Committee of Albany to the Committee of New York, 12 April 1788, John Lamb Papers, New-York Historical Society.

of Pennsylvania," the "Letter of Edmund Randolph," the "Letters of Centinel," and the Constitution itself, 225 copies of which had been bound together in a pamphlet by Thomas Greenleaf.[37] The Antifederalists in the City were expected to supervise the delivery of the material to Albany, but by mid-April it had not arrived. With some annoyance the Anti-Federal Committee wrote that they were sending "a special Messenger to find out what is become of them and if found to bring them up," but ruefully added "they will at any rate arrive too late to be of any service." [38]

"Too late"—and far too little. That describes the acitivity of the Antifederalist organization in New York City. It is ironically characteristic of the City Antifederalists that the ten members of the Federal Republican Society did not organize formally until 30 October 1788,[39] several months after New York had ratified the Constitution. There is no evidence of any participation in the state campaign by the group except for their encouragement of the circulation of the "Columbian Patriot" in April, and the only other activity of the City organization was a tardy and ineffective correspondence with out-of-state Antifederalists beginning in May.[40] The group was so dispirited that it did not even nominate a list of candidates to oppose the official Federalist slate in New York City.[41]

For some reason, probably because a large quantity of the Federal Republican Society correspondence has survived, historians have depicted that small and incompetent group as a

[37] Ford, *Bibliography*, p. 38.

[38] The Committee of Albany to the Committee of New York, 12 April 1788, John Lamb Papers, New-York Historical Society.

[39] "Proceedings," 30 October 1788, John Lamb Papers, New-York Historical Society. Marinus Willet was chairman and Charles Tillinghast secretary. John Lamb conducted the correspondence with out-of-state Antifederalists. Other members included two delegates to the Poughkeepsie Convention: Melancton Smith and Samuel Jones.

[40] John Lamb Papers, box 5, New-York Historical Society.

[41] No official Antifederalist list appeared in any New York City newspaper.

powerful, efficient machine, directing not only the New York State campaign, but serving as "the national center on anti-Federalist organization."[42] Forrest McDonald declares that the New York committee was "a clearinghouse for the writing of anti-ratificationist propaganda and for the selection and distribution of the best of it throughout the United States." He claims to have traced the "influence of propaganda emanating from this center . . . in newspapers in every state," and declares that the "machinery in New York was the national center of anti-Federalist organization, as the Robert Morris headquarters in Philadelphia was the center for Federalist activities."[43] McDonald's comparison with a Federal headquarters directed by Robert Morris is itself puzzling, for the New York State Federalists had no contact with such an organization. Hamilton's correspondence does not so much as mention Morris at any time during the year the Constitution was under consideration. Moreover, McDonald does not explain how he identified the Federal Republican Committee as the source of the newspaper essays traced through the newspapers of other states. Certainly the better essays from New York—"Cato," "Brutus," "Sydney"—were clipped and published all over the country. There is no need to inject a hypothetical "clearinghouse" for which there appears to be no evidence in order to explain the phenomenon. It was commonplace for publishers to clip from one another.

The flow of propaganda to the New York City newspapers was obviously not regulated in any way. Those who felt capable of writing political essays wrote them and sent them to the printer with no attempt to time them for maximum political im-

[42] Forrest McDonald, *We the People: The Economic Origins of the Constitution* (Chicago, 1958), p. 285. Also, E. Wilder Spaulding, *New York in the Critical Period, 1783–1789* (New York, 1932), p. 221; Clarence E. Miner, *The Ratification of the Federal Constitution by the State of New York* (New York, 1921), p. 122; Jackson Turner Main, *The Antifederalists, Critics of the Constitution, 1781–1788* (Chapel Hill, N.C., 1961), pp. 233, 234.

[43] *We the People*, pp. 285, 285n.

pact. The greatest quantity of material was produced in November, December, and January, while in April, the month of the election, the quantity of political matter published fell off sharply.[44] Toward the end of January, Melancton Smith wrote to Abraham Yates begging him to "employ all your leisure in thinking and making remarks" and promising to arrange for publication in the City, but Yates sent all of his pieces to Albany and wrote nothing for the New York papers until June.[45]

At any rate, it would hardly have been worth the trouble for New York's politicians to attempt to manipulate their staunchly "impartial" printers. Newspapers were relatively scarce and costly, particularly outside New York City. The broadside, not the newspaper, was the most significant instrument of written propaganda. Pamphlets could be carried into the country and sold, and less expensive handbills could be left for distribution at a country store or carried to a crossroads and nailed to a tree or fencepost where they would deliver the political message to an audience that did not subscribe to the newspapers.[46]

Even before the organization of the Anti-Federal Committee in Albany, the Antifederalists in that part of the state were distributing broadsides. A Federalist, piqued at the inactivity of his own party complained, "The Centinel, the farmers letters [*Letters of a Federal Farmer*], & every other publication against the Constitution are scattered all over the County, while the federal-

[44] On 18 October, 27 December, and 7 January, the *New-York Journal* commented on the great number of essays it was receiving. In April, comparatively little was published in that paper, and the quantity of material published in the other New York papers reflected the break in production of *Federalist* essays during the month of April.

[45] "Sidney" published in the *Albany Gazette* in February and March; the "Sydney" series began in the *New-York Journal* on 13 June 1788. Although the "Sydney" essays are usually attributed to Robert Yates, it is fairly clear that Abraham Yates was the author (Abraham Yates to Abraham G. Lansing, 28 May 1788, 15 June 1788; Abraham G. Lansing to Abraham Yates, 22 June 1788, Abraham Yates, Jr., Papers, New York Public Library).

[46] Dixon Ryan Fox, *The Decline of Aristocracy in the Politics of New York* (New York, 1919), p. 64.

ist [the "Publius" essays] remains at New York, & not a single piece (of which there are many more intelligible to the common people) is sent abroad." [47] Not until April did the *Federalist* circulate outside the City and a "more intelligible" pamphlet, the *Address to the People of the State of New York* by John Jay, find readers in Dutchess County.[48] And only in April did the Antifederalists in Albany discover any Federalist broadsides competing with their own. In that month New York Federalists directed the preparation of addresses by the members of the German Society and the Scotsmen of the St. Andrews Society in New York City and sent them to Albany.[49] They also had Thomas Lloyd's debates of the Pennsylvania ratifying convention, which recorded no Antifederalist argument, printed and sent to Albany County.[50] In addition, the Albany Federal Committee prepared some broadsides of its own and circulated them in the countryside.[51] An interesting feature of this broadside battle was the care taken to prevent any of the sheets from falling into the hands of confirmed opponents. The chance of converting a member of the opposition was not considered great enough to justify the loss of an expensive bit of printed material, particularly since it would most likely be used by the recipient to compose a rebuttal.[52]

When broadsides were too expensive, the parties circulated

[47] Major North to Henry Knox, 13 February 1788, Knox Papers, XXI, 143, Massachusetts Historical Society.

[48] *Country Journal* (Poughkeepsie), 3 June 1788.

[49] Leonard Gansevoort to Stephen Van Rensselaer, 6 April 1788, #4069, New York State Library; Broadside Collection, SY–1788–25, New-York Historical Society. Syrett (*Papers of Alexander Hamilton,* IV, 646n.) incorrectly identifies this piece as an appeal to New York City Scotsmen.

[50] Leonard Gansevoort to Stephen Van Rensselaer, 6 April 1788, #4069, New York State Library.

[51] Broadside Collection, SY–1788–23, SY–1788–24, New-York Historical Society. These are Antifederalist broadsides, which make reference to Federalist pieces that have not survived.

[52] *Ibid.*, SY–1788–24.

rumours, sometimes helped on by the newspapers. In November, Philadelphia Antifederalists started the story that John Jay, "a gentleman of first-rate abilities, joined to a good heart," had become an Antifederalist and denounced the Constitution as "as deep and wicked a conspiracy as has ever been invented in the darkest ages against the liberties of a free people." [53] Needless to say, the story was false.[54] "Tricks of this sort," Madison observed, "are not uncommon with the enemies of the new Constitution." [55] In December, a Poughkeepsie Federalist declared that the tales spread by the Antifederalists of plots against the liberties of the people "can find no parallel but in the records of ancient supersitition, of witchcraft, hobgoblins and fairies." He described some of them in detail: "In one county we are told that General Washington is to be appointed King: in another, that the inhabitants of the east end of Long-Island are to be called to the German Flatts to give their votes; in a third, that Prince William Henry is expected from Canada to assume regal government in the name of his father; in a fourth that the militia is to be embodied, and sent to France to pay off the congressional debt." [56] The Federalists had a few stories of their own, the most popular being that George Washington had solemnly declared that civil war would result if the Constitution was not ratified.[57]

The most useful campaign weapon of the Federalists was the "influence" of prominent men. The use that was made of Washington's name to win support for the Constitution is one indication of the extent to which the average man was expected to decide his vote according to what important people thought about the issue. "It is the duty of every man . . . to think for him-

[53] *Daily Advertiser*, 29 November 1787.

[54] *Independent Journal* (New York), 15 December 1787.

[55] James Madison to George Washington, 20 December 1787, Gilpin, ed., *Papers of James Madison*, II, 659.

[56] "Cato," II, *Country Journal*, 19 December 1787, supp.

[57] *Daily Advertiser*, 3 November 1787, supp.

self," the newspapers were fond of repeating, but added that it was the duty "especially of every man of influence." [58] Most of the influential men in New York, "the balance of abilities and property," [59] as John Jay expressed it, supported adoption of the Constitution. And as the democratic ideology of a later day did not inhibit them, they were not backward in exerting their influence over the poor, uneducated men of the community. In 1792, the tenants of Judge William Cooper described how he sought to win their votes in an election. His method was simple; he went "round to the people and told them that they owed him, and that unless they voted for Mr. Jay, he would ruin them." [60] When one tenant protested, Judge Cooper replied in surprise, "What, then, young man, you will not vote as I would have you—you are a fool, young man, for you cannot know how to vote as well as I can direct you, for I am in public office." [61]

Patronage was another valuable political tool for men of influence in eighteenth-century New York. In addition to militia commissions and the big offices of sheriff, coroner, and justices of the peace, other prizes were such posts as "cullers of staves and headings," "packers of beef," "inspectors of pearlash and potash," and "inspectors of flour." Minor customs offices were also desirable: "port, land and tide waiters," "gaugers" and "recoverers of goods from wrecks." The state constitution left appointments to the Council of Appointment, of which the governor was chairman, but, as in England, the leading families were thought to have the right to recommend the men who should fill offices in their localities. Almost all the leading families in New York supported the Constitution, and although Governor Clinton apparently made no use of his opportunities, there was con-

[58] *New-York Morning Post*, 6 October 1787.

[59] John Jay to George Washington, 3 February 1787, H. P. Johnston ed., *The Correspondence and Public Papers of John Jay* (New York, 1891), III, 322.

[60] Fox, *Decline of Aristocracy*, p. 140.

[61] *Ibid.*, pp. 140, 141.

siderable use of patronage in the ratification campaign by the Federalists.

In March 1788 James Fairlie of Albany proposed a candidate for the office of sheriff in Montgomery County, observing that he "is an Excellent Federalist" and "might do some good to our Cause." [62] Early in April, Leonard Gansevoort forwarded a number of commissions to Stephen Van Rensselaer for appointments in Albany County. There were several military commissions, three appointments of "Cullers of Staves," one for "Measurer of Boards, Timber &c.," and one for "repacker of Beef & Pork." Gansevoort advised Van Rensselaer that "Good Use may be made of them as they were severally appointed by our Recommendations." Van Rensselaer was told to inform one Maris R. Van Vranker that he had been appointed Justice of the Peace by Gansevoort's recommendation, and Gansevoort added that he had obtained the appointment of one Jonathan Hilton although he knew nothing of his politics, since he considered Hilton "a friend to your Family." Gansevoort reminded Van Rensselaer that the four men recently appointed coroners should be advised that Gansevoort's intervention had given them their jobs: "It may give a Spur to Action," he remarked. Gansevoort also thought "it would be well to suggest to Genl. Schuyler the propriety of writing official Letters to the newly appointed Justices." [63]

In order to exploit their prestige to the best advantage, the Federalists in the northern part of the state began a chain correspondence by which prominent men were persuaded to use their influence in the local community and to induce other men of high standing with whom they had connections to do the same. The Federalists in Albany took as many pains to insure the delivery of such letters as their opponents did to insure the deliv-

[62] James Fairlie to Philip Schuyler, 9 March 1788, Philip John Schuyler Papers, Vol. XXXVI, New York Public Library.

[63] Leonard Gansevoort to Stephen Van Rensselaer, 6 April 1788, #4069, New York State Library.

ery of a package of broadsides. For instance, the chairman of the Albany Federal Committee, Robert McClallen, who was a mere merchant without influence, enlisted the support of James Duane: "Knowing your sincere attachment to the federal side of the question in the present political controversy, we take the freedom to request your influence, among the Inhabitants of Duanesburgh in favor of the Gentlemen named . . . for members to Convention. . . . We would at the same time consider you as rendering an essential service to the *Federal Cause* by requesting Mr. Watts, Mr. Dirck Lefferts, Mr. Augustus Van Cortlandt, Mr. Augustus Van Horn, Mr. Peter Kissam, the Proprietors of Kayaderosiras, and any other Gentlemen in this County, to use their influence also, by letters or otherwise." McClallen promised to receive any letters that were written and to "take the most speedy measures for having them forwarded." [64]

Duane's attempts to exert his influence in Schenectady and Duanesburgh were frustrated by "the unexpected Exertions there was made in this place in opposition to the Adoption of the Constitution," as Duane's overseer at Schenectady wrote. Those who tried to persuade the tenants to vote Federalist, he said, "were looked upon as belonging to the tyrannical party." [65] The overseer at Duanesburgh wrote to his employer, "I hope you will Lett me know a Lettel how our present Plan the New Constitution Comes on as I am Sure that I have had a good Dele of trubel . . . in be halfe of the Same Not to my profit." [66]

The Federalist campaign ran into difficulty in Columbia, the other important manor county, as well, although there was no organization comparable to the Albany Anti-Federal Committee to combat. The Federalists were industrious enough; there was

[64] Robert McClallen to James Duane, 12 March 1788, James Duane Papers, New-York Historical Society; Leonard Gansevoort to Stephen Van Rensselaer, 6 April 1788, #4069, New York State Library.

[65] Abraham Oothoudt to James Duane, 19 May 1788, James Duane Papers, New-York Historical Society.

[66] John Myers to James Duane, 23 June 1788, James Duane Papers, New-York Historical Society.

so much oratory that a candidate told a friend that "were you here you would be reminded of the days of ancient Greece and Rome." Nor was it a mere "war of tongues, but a few bloody noses have been the consequence." [67] The root of the Federalists' trouble was a schism in the Livingston family. The manor and Clermont branches were at odds, and effective cooperation between men of influence in the county was consequently almost impossible. In a political climate where personality rather than principle dominated, confusion was inevitable:

Thus Mr. Jacob Goes, though still calling himself a "foederalist," was offended with the Van Rensselaers for not inviting him to an interesting March meeting at Claverack; the citizens of little Hudson, while friendly to the Chancellor [R. R. Livingston], could not abide the manor Livingstons; John Livingston, who had been placed on the Assembly list along with Thomas Jenkins, of Hudson, and William H. Ludlow, said that he would oppose the election of Mr. Jenkins and of every person unfriendly to his (the manor) family; while Henry Livingston, in spite of the most tactful hints by Philip Schuyler, would not yield his place on the convention list to the more popular Edward Livingston, the Chancellor's youngest brother.[68]

And to make matters worse, the tenants in the eastern part of Columbia County were engaged in "Controversies about their Lands," and they were "wonderfully poison'd against all the manor lords." [69]

In April, the New York delegates in Congress, who were all men of influence, grew anxious to return home and campaign. Stephen Van Rensselaer believed it was "indespensably necessary" for him to return to Albany County, and Ezra L' Hommedieu "was very apprehensive of the Issue of the Election in

[67] Peter Van Schaack to Henry Walton, 3 June 1788, Henry C. Van Schaack, *The Life of Peter Van Schaack* (New York, 1842), p. 426.

[68] George Dangerfield, *Chancellor Robert R. Livingston of New York, 1746–1813* (New York, 1960), pp. 218, 219.

[69] Peter Van Schaack to Philip Schuyler, 3 April 1788, Philip John Schuyler Papers, Vol. XXXVI, New York Public Library.

Suffolk unless he could be at Home to concert Measures to procure a federal representation from thence to the Convention." Consequently, Leonard Gansevoort wrote to Albany that he felt obliged to remain in Congress since he could "be better spared than . . . the others" except, of course, for the Antifederalist Abraham Yates, "who is not wanted here at all." [70]

The Antifederalists had some small influence on their side, and they used it as best they could.[71] Abraham Yates himself was requested to come to Albany County and "take a Ride to Montgomery and Schoharrie." [72] He finally went up, together with Judge Robert Yates,[73] although he was not at all sure that it was wise to do so. "I am determined to do what is Desired from me let it be to what part of the Country it May," he wrote. "But I wish that it may be Considered that last fall it was the Business of the federalist to hold out in Idea that the opposition was a meer party affair, that otherwise the Constitution was a good one—and that a party (and sometimes they Honour me with being at the head of that party . . .) opposed the Constitution was for fear of getting out of office." Yates believed that that line of argument had not been used recently, but he feared that it might be revived if he began "going round." He suggested that it might be wiser for him to confine his activity to political correspondence, although he confessed to having a much smaller group of influential acquaintances than he had had twenty or thirty years earlier. "Those that I know are Chiefly Dead," he said, "and others on the Stage that I do not know." [74]

The Federalist men of influence rode through the country

[70] Leonard Gansevoort to Stephen Van Rensselaer, 6 April 1788, #4069, New York State Library.

[71] *Daily Advertiser*, 2 June 1788; Peter Tappen to George Clinton, 29 September 1787, George Clinton Papers, New York Public Library.

[72] Abraham G. Lansing to Abraham Yates, 12 March 1788, Abraham Yates, Jr., Papers, New York Public Library.

[73] Abraham Yates to [Abraham G. Lansing], 18 March 1788, Abraham Yates, Jr., Papers, New York Public Library.

[74] Abraham Yates to Abraham G. Lansing, 14 March 1788, Abraham Yates, Jr., Papers, New York Public Library.

trying to gather a group of voters whom they might address and to whom they could distribute their broadsides and election lists. Town meetings were ready-made for their purposes, and when these meetings were held in Albany County at the beginning of April, the city of Albany "was almost Destitute of the Better Kind of People" who had gone to "Several Polls in the Country Dispersing their General Letter Hand Bills Lists of Delegates and Assemblymen." [75] If there was no meeting in a district, men of influence had other means of collecting a crowd. Militia officers could call a meeting of two or three companies, and so have an opportunity to address the men.[76] Or they might formally summon a meeting for political discussion. An Antifederalist gleefully described the failure of one such meeting:

> A few days since, three of the *well-born* of the city of Albany made an excursion to Nestegeuna, where they employed *nine* persons (whom they paid well for their services) to ride through the country and endeavour to collect the freeholders and freemen of that quarter to meet them at a certain place to *confer on the proposed new constitution.* When the day appointed came, their influence extended so far as to collect *seven* freeholders who were all good whigs (or in other words those distinguished by the appelation of Antes) who assured the three *rich* and *well-born* gentlemen they had but one observation to make which was the following, "*We think you are come out on a very foolish errand.*" [77]

The Antifederalists were in the habit of following the Federalist parties, and addressing the crowd after they had left. Then the Antis would "Deel in plain Simple Truth." [78] No doubt they found it advantageous to have the last word with the voters.

[75] Henry Oothoudt to John McKesson, 3 April 1788, John McKesson Papers, New-York Historical Society.

[76] *Ibid.*

[77] "Fidelia," *New-York Journal,* 10 April 1788.

[78] Henry Oothoudt to John McKesson, 3 April 1788, John McKesson Papers, New-York Historical Society; Abraham Yates to Abraham G. Lansing, 14 March 1788, Abraham Yates, Jr., Papers, New York Public Library.

The campaign was fought strenuously on both sides, particularly in Albany and Columbia Counties, reaching its height in March and April. "I do believe Since the Settlement of America Such Exertions have not been Made upon a Question of any Kind as the present upon the New Constitution," [79] wrote an Albany Antifederalist. A week before the election John Jay told George Washington, "The Constitution still continues to cause great Party Zeal and Ferment among us; and the opposition is yet so formidable that the Issue appears problematical." [80] There would be no certainty until the votes were counted.

[79] Henry Oothoudt to John McKesson, 3 April 1788, John McKesson Papers, New-York Historical Society.

[80] [John Jay] to George Washington, 20 April 1788, John Jay Papers, Monaghan Collection, Columbia University.

IX

The Electorate

THE New York Legislature's resolution calling for the election of a ratifying convention provided that "all free male citizens of the age of twenty-one years, and upwards, be admitted to vote, and that any person of that description be eligible." [1] Only New York State made so liberal a provision, universal manhood suffrage, for the electors who would decide on the Constitution. The suffrage in most of the other states was specifically restricted to those who were qualified to vote for members of the lower house of the state legislature.[2]

Historians have been astonished by the New York provision and have puzzled over the political motivation of the measure.[3]

[1] *Journal of the Assembly of the State of New York* (New York, 1788), 31 January 1788.

[2] Charles Warren, *The Making of the Constitution* (Boston, 1928), p. 352n.

[3] Orin Grant Libby, *Geographical Distribution of the Vote of the Thirteen States on the Federal Constitution, 1787, 1788* (Madison, Wis., 1897), p. 26, 26n.; Charles A. Beard, *An Economic Interpretation of the Constitution of the United States* (New York, 1913), p. 241; David M. Ellis, *et. al, A Short History of New York State* (Ithaca, N.Y., 1957), p. 125; E. Wilder Spaulding, *New York in the Critical Period, 1783–1789* (New York, 1932), pp. 199, 200; Nathan Schachner, *Alexander Hamilton* (New York, 146), p. 215; Forrest McDonald, *We the People: The Economic*

The mystery is deepened because what appears to be a radical extension of the suffrage was accepted without a division of votes in the legislature and with no significant debate. The Assembly did not debate the provision at all. In the Senate, the only debate arose on the mild objection of John Williams from Washington County. Might not, Williams wondered, "a person of influence on the borders of the State . . . hire 100 men to come into the state to work for him; could they not give him 100 votes?" James Duane pointed out that any prospective voter would have to give the voting inspectors evidence of citizenship, and Mr. Williams acknowledged himself satisfied, observing that "there would be no danger of a thing of this kind in that part of the country he came from." [4] And nothing more was said on the subject.

The debate in both houses showed general agreement that the proposed Constitution, as fundamental law, ought to be ratified by the whole people. True, New York's own Constitution of 1777 had not been submitted to any kind of popular ratification, but many such niceties were sacrificed in wartime, and even in 1777 there had been some demand for a popular vote.[5] Ten years later no one wished to dispute the point. Not only was there no debate in the legislature, but there is no record of any comment on the legislature's action either in newspapers or in private letters. The universal manhood suffrage provision was accepted as a matter of course. The apparent extension of suffrage that has so astounded historians was obviously not a controversial measure.

It is unlikely that any extension of suffrage would have gone unopposed if it had greatly increased the number of citizens who would be permitted to go to the polls. Actually the increase

---

Origins of the Constitution (Chicago, 1958), p. 286n.; George Dangerfield, *Chancellor Robert R. Livingston of New York, 1746–1813* (New York, 1960), p. 219.

[4] *Country Journal* (Poughkeepsie), 12 February 1788, 26 February 1788.

[5] Charles Sumner Lobinger, *The People's Law* (New York, 1909), pp. 157–161.

was very small, since, in effect, New Yorkers enjoyed universal manhood suffrage in every Assembly election. The seventh article of the New York State Constitution of 1777 provided that every adult male who had resided in one of the New York counties for at least six months was qualified to vote for assemblyman, provided that he held a freehold worth at least fifty dollars, or paid taxes to the state and a rent of at least five dollars, or was a freeman of Albany or New York City.[6] The freemen were a small group—in 1790 only 138 men claimed the right to vote because of that status.[7] They were merchants, artisans, and professional men who paid the city corporation for the privilege of engaging in their occupations.[8] Slightly more than 25 per cent of the state electorate claimed the right to vote because they paid taxes and a five-dollar rent. Most men voted in the Assembly elections as freeholders; about a third of all the voters held freeholds worth two hundred and fifty dollars. They were qualified to vote for senators and governor as well as for assemblymen. The rest of the voters, more than half the total, held fifty-dollar freeholds.[9]

A "freehold" was not necessarily an absolute ownership of land. It might be an estate "in fee simple" that granted the occupant possession "forever," but stipulated that rent must be paid. Or it might be an estate "in fee tail," which restricted the right of the occupant to dispose of the property. It might be an estate

[6] The constitution named the sums as £20 and 40 shillings. Dollar equivalents were substituted in 1811 (Franklin Ellis, *History of Columbia County, New York* [Philadelphia, 1878] p. 46). The values had not changed since 1788 (*Letters from the Federal Farmer, VI,* in Forrest McDonald, ed., *Empire and Nation* [Englewood Cliffs, N.J., 1962], p. 141).

[7] "A Census of Electors and Inhabitants of the State of New York," 11 January 1791, Broadside Collection, SY–1791–26, New-York Historical Society.

[8] Carl Lotus Becker, *The History of Political Parties in the Province of New York 1760–1776* (Madison, Wis., 1909), p. 10.

[9] "A Census of Electors," 11 January 1791, Broadside Collection, SY–1791–26, New-York Historical Society.

held only for life, or for an indefinite period such as two or three lives. It might even be a mere leasehold for a long term of years.[10] Most of the lands held by tenants of the manor lords qualified as freeholds, and there were more leaseholds qualifying as freeholds in New York State than anywhere else except perhaps in Virginia.[11] Due to this circumstance, and to the liberal provision that those who paid taxes and a rent of five dollars yearly might vote, there was an unusually large electorate in New York State.

Historians have wondered at the extension of the franchise to include all adult white males in the election of 1788 because they have grossly underestimated the size of the electorate that was regularly entitled to vote for the Assembly. Albert E. McKinley said that only one-ninth to one-fourteenth of the New York City population could vote under the qualifications required by the 1777 constitution.[12] Carl Becker believed that "the proportion of voters for assemblymen to the total population was approximately twelve percent." [13] These figures, however, distort the question, since the important ratio is that of qualified voters to adult white males. Women, children, and slaves were automatically excluded from voting, and not more than 20 per cent of New York's population consisted of white males over twenty-one.[14] Even today the eligible voters in the United States compose no more than 60 per cent of the total population.[15]

Even writers who have dealt with the significant ratio have tended to underestimate the size of the New York electorate. Chilton Williamson cautiously speculates "possibly 65 to 70 per-

[10] Spaulding, *New York in the Critical Period*, pp. 60, 61.

[11] *Ibid.;* Chilton Williamson, *American Suffrage from Property to Democracy* (Princeton, 1960), pp. 27, 28.

[12] *The Suffrage Franchise in the Thirteen English Colonies in America* (Philadelphia, 1905), pp. 218–221.

[13] *Political Parties,* p. 264.

[14] Nicholas Varga, "Election Procedures and Practices in Colonial New York," *New York History*, XLI (1960), 273n.

[15] *Ibid.*, 252.

cent of all adult males could vote about 1790 for assemblymen." [16] The largest estimate is that of Milton M. Klein, who has stated that almost all of the adult white male population in the cities of Albany and New York had the right to vote and that at least 65 per cent of the men in the country had the suffrage, adding that the percentage of country men qualified to vote may possibly have been as large as that in urban areas.[17]

There is sufficient statistical evidence available for fifteen of New York's seventeen counties to permit a reasonably precise estimate of the voting population in 1790. The New York constitution provided for a periodic census of electors to apportion representation in the legislature. Such a census was made in 1790, and reports were submitted by every county except Clinton and Ontario.[18] Since lists of electors must have been kept by voting inspectors, the census is probably fairly accurate. In the same year, the first federal census reported the number of white males over sixteen who lived in New York State. Large families and war meant a young population, and a large proportion of the men over sixteen years were under twenty-one. In 1790 the median age of white males was less than sixteen years.[19] Milton M. Klein, writing of the period before the Revolution, has estimated the proportion of men over sixteen who were under

[16] *American Suffrage*, p. 111.

[17] "Democracy and Politics in Colonial New York," *New York History*, XL (1959), 221–246.

[18] Broadside Collection, SY–1791–26, New-York Historical Society. The census of Assembly electors printed in the *New-York Journal*, 27 January 1791, improperly calculated the electorate by adding £20 freeholders and 40 shilling tenants without including £100 freeholders. The two listings of freeholders in the state census are exclusive—in some counties £100 freeholders outnumber the £20 freeholders so that the former cannot have been included in the figure given for the latter—and the wealthier group must be added to the number of Assembly electors given by the *New-York Journal*.

[19] United States Bureau of the Census, *Historical Statistics of the United States: Colonial Times to 1957* (Washington, 1960), p. 11. In 1950 the median was close to thirty years.

twenty-one at 25 per cent.[20] Using that estimate, which is conservative for the post-war period, together with the 1790 federal census returns and the 1790 state census of electors, Table 1 may be constructed.

As that table indicates, in no county in New York State did the ratio of qualified voters to adult white males fall much below 80 per cent, and if it be assumed that the conditions in Clinton and Ontario counties did not differ significantly from those in neighboring areas, it may be said that the ratio for the state as a

Table 1. Percentage of adult white males qualifying as Assembly electors in New York State, 1790

County	Voters qualified in Assembly elections	White males over 16	White males over 21	% of electors
Albany	13,064	18,549	13,912	94
Columbia	5,568	6,573	[5,568]	100
Dutchess	6,308	10,968	8,227	78
Kings	881	903	[881]	100
Montgomery	5,153	7,837	5,818	88
New York	5,184	8,500	6,375	82
Orange	2,674	4,600	3,450	78
Queens	3,109	3,554	[3,109]	100
Richmond	741	749	[741]	100
Suffolk	3,580	3,756	[3,580]	100
Ulster	4,591	7,058	5,293	87
Washington	2,372	3,606	2,704	88
Westchester	4,303	5,877	4,408	97
Total	57,528	82,500	61,875	92

whole was 92 per cent. The statistical evidence supports Alexander C. Flick's generalization that "only paupers and lodgers or sons living with their parents" could not vote in Assembly elections.[21] In practice, men were rarely turned away from the polls even if they did not qualify under the suffrage law. Any man interested enough to attend the election was usually permitted to

[20] "Democracy and Politics," pp. 245, 246.

[21] Alexander C. Flick, *Loyalism in New York during the American Revolution* (New York, 1901), p. 91.

vote without too much searching of his qualifications.[22] When, in 1786, the right of some of James Duane's tenants to cast votes for senators and governor was challenged, one of the men remarked, "Had we bin all of one mind thair would have bin no objactions to our vote." [23]

Thus, the New York Legislature's provision that all adult white males would be permitted to vote for the state ratifying convention was not a radical measure and actually differed little from the provision of other states that all voters qualified as electors in Assembly elections might vote for convention delegates.

Some of the most aristocratic gentlemen in New York State remarked during the ratification campaign on the intelligence of the electorate and on the degree to which they had informed themselves on the Constitution. John Jay wrote to Thomas Jefferson that there was "a Degree of Intelligence and Information in the Mass of our People, which affords much Room for Hope that by Degrees our Affairs will assume a more consistent and pleasing Aspect." [24] Peter Van Schaack observed that "we have . . . a wonderful degree of information among the common people." [25] Nevertheless, it is important not to overestimate the electorate of 1788. There is a temptation to make plaster images of the entire Revolutionary generation and to assume that the men who cast their votes for the Constitution were superhumanly intelligent, well-informed, and rational.

While it is clear that the Constitution was more widely and more thoroughly discussed than any other political topic since the Revolution, not everyone believed that wide discussion was beneficial. One man who had observed some artisans discussing politics in a New York City coffee house wrote to the *New-York Journal* to express his indignation. "It must be considered,"

[22] Williamson, *American Suffrage*, p. 50. [23] *Ibid.*, p. 16.

[24] John Jay to Thomas Jefferson, 8 September 1787, United States Bureau of Rolls and Library, *Documentary History of the Constitution of the United States* (Washington, 1894–1903), IV, 276.

[25] Peter Van Schaack to Henry Walton, 3 June 1788, Henry C. Van Schaack, *The Life of Peter Van Schaack* (New York, 1842), p. 426.

he wrote, "that government is a very abstruse science, and political disquisition is very arduous talk, far beyond the reach of common capacities."[26] His remarks found some sympathetic readers, for two days later his piece was reprinted "by particular desire."[27] Moreover, while the public was well-informed in the cities, it was far less so in the country districts despite the efforts of the parties in distributing broadsides and orating before public meetings. Illiteracy was a formidable obstacle. In some places illiteracy may have run as high as 50 per cent of the adult male population.[28] Staughton Lynd speculates that in Dutchess County, "the number of men who read the proposed Constitution before voting for or against it may have been quite small."[29]

It is also important not to overestimate the interest New Yorkers took in the ratification campaign. It is true that in the seven months the Constitution was debated in the state, more interest was aroused in the election for ratifying convention delegates than in the usually uncontested Assembly elections. Madison reported in February that the men in New York City were "much agitated by the proposed foederal Constitution and . . . attentive to little else."[30] Those who were naturally interested in politics found unusual excitement in a campaign that involved the adoption of a new fundamental law for the continent. Even the ladies filled their letters to female friends with political remarks, so that one Boston girl complained to her correspondent in New York City, "Patience, patience!—the dogs take the new

[26] "Honestus," *New-York Journal*, 26 April 1788.

[27] *Ibid.*, 28 April 1788.

[28] Alfred Fabian Young, "The Democratic-Republican Movement in New York State, 1788–1797" (unpublished Ph.D. dissertation, Northwestern University, 1958), p. 24; Harold C. Syrett, ed., and Jacob E. Cooke, assoc. ed., *The Papers of Alexander Hamilton* (New York, 1961–), IV, 31.

[29] *Anti-Federalism in Dutchess County, New York* (Chicago, 1962), p. 13.

[30] James Madison to Thomas Jefferson, 19 February 1788, *Documentary History*, IV, 510.

constitution—it robs us of all those endearing sentences of chit-chat, &c. with which your letters used to be replete, and which we always classed among our choicest treasures." [31] But interest in the Constitution, while intense where it existed, was not widespread. As a newspaper essayist pointed out, "at this crisis, when the minds of men are *on one side violently agitated and active;* on the other, and the greater part, *a sleepy indolence and inattention seems to prevail.*" [32]

During the seven months of campaigning, New Yorkers found many personal and public matters competing with the Constitution for their attention. It is not possible to judge what topics were most before the public by an examination of newspapers, since at a time when cities were small, men did not wish to pay to read what they already knew by gossiping with their neighbors.[33] In New York City, where the Constitution was more widely discussed than anywhere else in the state, a completely unrelated event occurred in April, a scant two weeks before the election, which halted all political thought and activity for many days.

On Sunday, 13 April 1788, a group of young boys were playing behind the hospital in New York City. The building had been used as a British barracks during the war and had been badly damaged. In 1788 only a few doctors used it, for lectures and for dissecting,[34] while it was undergoing repairs. A ladder was leaning against the building and one of the youngsters climbed up and peeped into a window. There he saw a medical student engaged in dissecting a cadaver, and when the operator noticed the boy, he cheerfully waved one of the severed arms, telling the boy it belonged to his mother. The remark was ill-

[31] *New-York Journal,* 25 June 1788.

[32] "Timolean," *New-York Journal,* supp., 1 November 1787.

[33] For instance only one New York City newspaper carried an article on the Doctors' Riot (*New-York Packet,* 25 April 1788).

[34] I. N. Phelps Stokes, *The Iconography of Manhattan Island, 1492–1909* (New York, 1915–1928), I, 374; *New-York Morning Post,* 6 October 1787.

timed, for the boy's mother had recently died.[35] The child ran in horror to tell his father what he had seen, and the father marched straight to the hospital, collecting a crowd of sympathetic citizens on the way.

For several months reports of grave-robbing had circulated in the City, and the populace had been inflamed by the stories.[36] When the crowd reached the hospital, the men were ready for violence. They broke in, destroyed some of the apparatus, and carried off what cadavers they could find and buried them. The student doctors were threatened, but thanks to the personal intervention of Mayor James Duane at a crucial moment, the doctors were rescued and placed in jail for their protection.

When night came, most of the crowd dispersed, but small groups continued to move through the streets, and on Monday morning the size of the mob was even greater than it had been before, numbering about two thousand[37]—almost as many men as cast ballots in the election two weeks later. In the morning they roamed through the City, breaking into the homes of doctors suspected of engaging in the dissection of corpses. At one point they approached the home of Sir John Temple, British consul-general, and as the word passed through the crowd that they were coming to Sir John Temple's house, the syllables slurred and a party launched a vigorous attack on what they supposed was the home of a Surgeon Temple.[38]

In the absence of a municipal police force, the only alternative to calling out the militia against the populace was for the authorities to move among the people personally in an attempt to persuade them to return to their homes. Governor Clinton,

[35] John C. Hamilton describes this event as "the indecent exposure of bodies, recently disinterred for anatomical purposes" (*History of the Republic of the United States as Traced in the Writings of Alexander Hamilton and His Contemporaries* (Philadelphia, 1864), p. 454.

[36] *New-York Packet*, 25 April 1788.

[37] Frank Monaghan, *John Jay* (New York, 1935), p. 290.

[38] Martha J. Lamb and Mrs. Burton Harrison, *History of the City of New York*, (New York, 1877), p. 307.

Mayor Duane, and Chancellor R. R. Livingston all mingled with the crowd but did not succeed in dispersing it. On Monday afternoon the mob moved to the jail, broke down some fences, smashed windows, and threatened to hang the doctors who were within on the public gallows, a gaudy affair of red and yellow shaped like a Chinese pagoda, which stood conveniently close and had facilities to accommodate the gentlemen of science six at a time. Governor Clinton finally called out the militia, although he was reluctant to direct them to fire. At dusk, a party of influential citizens arrived to relieve the guard at the jail, and the mob began to hurl bricks and stones. Several men, including John Jay, were badly injured, and Clinton finally gave the order to fire. Three of the rioters were killed and many others were wounded.[39] The crowd soon dispersed.[40]

When John Jay was carried to his home, his wife was horrified to see the "two large holes in his forehead." [41] For a time it was feared that Jay's brain had been damaged, and there was great relief when, at the end of a week, he was finally out of danger.[42] Jay did not dwell on his experiences in the Doctors' Riot. He immediately turned his mind back to politics and while convalescing published a very able pamphlet entitled *Address to the People of the State of New York,* which was said to have "a most astonishing influence in converting Antifederalists." [43] It is doubtful, however, that many men were able to put the Doctors' Riot out of mind as quickly and completely as did John Jay. As election day approached in the City, the riot surely competed with the Constitution as a topic of common conversation.

[39] *Country Journal,* 22 April 1788.

[40] Where other sources are not cited, this narrative is based on *New-York Packet,* 25 April 1788, and William Alexander Duer, *Reminiscences of an Old New Yorker* (New York, 1867), pp. 33, 34.

[41] Mrs. Jay to her mother, 17 April 1788, quoted in Monaghan, *John Jay,* p. 291.

[42] Monaghan, *John Jay,* p. 291.

[43] S. B. Webb to Joseph Barrell, W. C. Ford, ed., *Correspondence and Journals of Samuel Blanchley Webb* (New York, 1893–1894), III, 99.

X

The Election

IN the period prior to the development of parties, it was customary for any individual or group of citizens that cared to do so to suggest the names of men they thought fit for office. In New York City more than a dozen lists of delegates for the Poughkeepsie Convention were proposed and printed in the City papers. As early as February the lists began to appear over such pseudonymns as "Montgomery," "Minerva," and, most frequently, simply "Citizen." Most of the men nominating delegates concentrated on choosing candidates who agreed with them on the adoption of the Constitution. One of the earliest lists to appear explained that the men named had been selected for their "Federalism and talents, without totally disregarding property." [1] A few days later, a citizen observed as he presented his list, that "as the object of deliberation is definite, and every elector, perhaps, has by this time, made up his mind on the subject, we are rather to nominate those who coincide with us in opinion then to choose on the score of general abilities." [2]

But a great many men disagreed with that view and believed that the opinions of a candidate should not be the prime con-

[1] *Daily Advertiser* (New York), 18 February 1788.

[2] *Independent Journal* (New York), 20 February 1788.

cern. "A Free Man" remarked, as he presented his list, that the opinions of several of the gentlemen he named were wholly unknown. He had selected them for their "general interest, ability, and coolness, if not disinterestedness," as he believed that "great and obvious interest on either side, will excite suspicion and calumny." [3] The lists presented by other men indicate that they, too, selected candidates on the basis of their ability rather than for their opinions—although they did not demand coolness. Numerous lists name prominent Federalists and Antifederalists, side by side. "A Citizen" named R. R. Livingston and Melancton Smith; Alexander Hamilton and Samuel Jones.[4] "A Freeman" suggested Hamilton and Livingston, John Lamb and John Lawrence.[5] Hamilton and Livingston headed the list made up by "Minerva," which closed with John Lamb and Melancton Smith,[6] while "A Citizen," "Marcus," and "A Friend of Good Order" offered lists topped by George Clinton and John Jay.[7]

On 9 April 1788, order was introduced into the confusion of nominating lists by the proposal of an official Federal ticket drawn up by the New York City Federal Committee, of which Thomas Randal was chairman. The list was headed, "In Supporting the present Nomination let ONE AND ALL BE OUR MOTTO." It was reprinted every few days in the *Independent Journal, Daily Advertiser*, and *New-York Journal*. Special meetings of the "Germans, inhabitants of the city of New-York," [8] "The Master Carpenters of the city of New York," [9] and a group of "Mechanics and Tradesmen" [10] formally endorsed the Randal list, and as an aid to memory, a Federalist poet put it into typically bad verse:

> Mr. Jay, Col Hamilton, Harrison [*sic*], Low,
> Are honest, good patriots all of us know;
> Mr. Livingston Rosevelt [*sic*], his Worship the Mayor,

[3] *New-York Journal*, 13 March 1788. [4] *Ibid.*, 17 March 1788.
[5] *Ibid.*, 22 March 1788. [6] *Daily Advertiser*, 22 March 1788.
[7] *New-York Journal*, 5 April, 22 April, 14 April 1788.
[8] *Daily Advertiser*, 28 April 1788.
[9] *Independent Journal*, 26 April 1788. [10] *Ibid.*, 20 April 1788.

Will look to your interests with very great care.
Judge Morris and Hobart are true to the cause,
They'll preserve us from ruin by strength'ning our laws.[11]

The Antifederalists, meanwhile, had already given up the contest in New York City. The only activity that can be traced to them there was the publication of counterfeit "Federal Lists," which listed the official Randal committee candidates, but was headed by George Clinton,[12] and the circulation of a few handbills on the first day of the election.[13] In fact, the Antifederalists openly announced that they would not contest the election in the City.[14]

The Antifederalists made up for their inactivity in New York City by efforts in the rest of the state. Samuel Jones and Melancton Smith, both City men, were put on the official Antifederalist list for Dutchess County,[15] and George Clinton headed the official Antifederalist list in Ulster County. The party leaders had considered placing Clinton on the Albany ticket and the New York City Antifederalists intended to attempt to gain a City seat for him, but they insisted that he be run in Ulster, his native county, as well. "For he had better be chosen in two Places, than not to be elected at all." [16]

Farther north, in Albany County, individuals sent lists of nominations to the newspapers as was done in New York.[17] In

[11] *Daily Advertiser*, 29 April 1788.

[12] Broadside Collection, SY–1788–9, New-York Historical Society; *New-York Journal*, 19 April 1788, 24 April 1788.

[13] S. B. Webb to Joseph Barrell, 11 May 1788, W. C. Ford, ed., *Correspondence and Journals of Samuel Blanchley Webb* (New York, 1893–1894), III, 102.

[14] *Daily Advertiser*, 26 April 1788.

[15] *Country Journal* (Poughkeepsie), 15 April 1788. The nominating meeting had been held at Oswego in February.

[16] Melancton Smith to [?], 6 April 1788, John Lamb Papers, New-York Historical Society.

[17] For example, *Federal Herald* (Albany), 25 February 1788, 3 March 1788.

addition, both Antifederal and Federal committees proposed official lists, which were printed in the newspapers and circulated as broadsides.[18] As the election days approached, special preparations were made. The chairman of the Anti-Federal Committee wrote to local party workers enclosing handbills and giving them last minute instructions. The Antifederalists at Stephen Town were requested "to attend at the Poll constantly until it is closed to see that all Matters are properly conducted." He had been informed, he wrote, that "the Patroons Tenants are to fold up their Ballots in a particular Manner—if they do, you will direct the anti Voters to do the same." [19]

During the election days politicians were busy at the polls in Columbia County also. Robert Livingston wrote to James Duane that three influential Federalists were attending the different voting places. "They had good Success Yesterday at millers, this day they are at Tachkanick & tomorrow at Ancram." Meanwhile, he reported, "there are a number of emissaries daily going about to poison the Tenants." The Antifederalists, apparently, were getting their licks too. Livingston ruefully noted that "they do considerable mischief among the Ignorant." [20]

In New York City the election days were anticipated with special joy by those who enjoyed rioting. A New Yorker wrote to a friend in Boston, "You have no Idea of Electioneering business—with you 'tis all fair & quiet, but with us, 'tis all confusion—for parties for different sides appear publicly—and sometimes blows ensue." [21] To his sweetheart he boasted that during the last election "your Hum. Servt. was so beat and

[18] Broadside Collection, SY–1788–13, SY–1788–14, New-York Historical Society.

[19] Jeremiah Van Rensselaer to Benjamin Egbertsen, Jonathan Niles, and others, 28 April 1788, #2135, New York State Library.

[20] Robert Livingston to James Duane, 30 April 1788, James Duane Papers, New-York Historical Society).

[21] S. B. Webb to Joseph Barrell, 11 May 1788, Ford, ed., *Correspondence of S. B. Webb*, III, 102.

bruised that he was confined to his room for four days." [22] The City election, however, was disappointingly quiet. Perhaps those who usually participated in its wilder aspects were still recovering from the Doctors' Riot. Besides, the Antifederalists were so few, that they did not appear at the polls at all after the first day.[23]

The polls opened on the morning of Tuesday, 29 April, and closed at two o'clock on Friday, 2 May,[24] while for four days all regular business activity was suspended in the city.[25] In March, John Jay had predicted that the election would be "the most contested of any we have had since the Revolution," [26] and the reality exceeded his expectation. On the third day of the election, the *New-York Journal* announced that "a greater number of votes have already been presented at this election, than was ever known, at any one time, to be presented in this city, and the poll not yet closed." [27] Even the great contests between the De Lanceys and the Livingstons prior to the Revolution never called out more than 2,700 voters in New York City, while 2,836 ballots were taken for delegates to the ratifying convention.[28]

But how great was the percentage of qualified electors who participated in the election? The statistical evidence available is summarized in Table 2. The great contested election did not draw more than 45 per cent of the qualified voters to the

[22] S. B. Webb to Catherine Hogeborn, 27 April 1788, Ford, ed., *Correspondence of S. B. Webb*, III, 98.

[23] S. B. Webb to Joseph Barrell, 11 May 1788, *ibid.*, 102; *New-York Journal*, 1 May 1788.

[24] *New-York Journal*, 29 April 1788, 2 May 1788.

[25] *Ibid.*, 1 May 1788; S. B. Webb to Catherine Hogeborn, 4 May 1788, Ford, ed., *Correspondence of S. B. Webb*, III, 100.

[26] John Jay to William Bingham, 24 March 1788, H. P. Johnston, ed., *Correspondence and Public Papers of John Jay* (New York, 1891), III, 325.

[27] *New-York Journal*, 1 May 1788.

[28] S. B. Webb to Joseph Barrell, 11 May 1788, Ford, ed., *Correspondence of S. B. Webb*, III, 103; *Independent Journal*, 31 May 1788.

Table 2. Participation in the election for assemblymen and Poughkeepsie Convention delegates, 1788

County	A. electors	Votes cast for A.	% A.	Adult white males	Votes cast for P.	Votes cast P. – A.	% P.
Albany	13,064	6,710	52	13,912	7,449 *	739	54
Columbia	5,568	2,575	22	5,568	3,361	789	60
Dutchess	6,308			8,227	2,657		30
Kings	881			881			
Montgomery	5,153			5,818	2,020		35
New York	5,184	1,650 *	38	6,375	2,836 *	1,186	45
Orange	2,674	368	14	3,450	340	–28	10
Queens	3,109	729	23	3,109	934	205	33
Richmond	741			741			
Suffolk	3,580			3,580			
Ulster	4,591			5,293	1,440		27
Washington & Clinton	2,731			3,112			
Westchester	4,303			4,408	1,093		25

Sources: Table I, p. 146; *Independent Journal,* 31 May 1788; *Daily Advertiser,* 3, 4, 6, 7, and 14 June 1788; *New-York Journal,* 5 June 1788; and Matthew Vesscher to Abraham Yates, John McKesson, and Melancton Smith, 30 May 1788, Abraham Yates, Jr., Papers, New York Public Library.

* Where the exact total of ballots cast is known, it is given and marked with an asterisk; where it is not available it has been calculated as the sum of the highest Federalist plus the highest Antifederalist vote. The method proved approximately accurate when tested for the counties where complete data is available. It should be remembered that the number of adult white males is an estimated figure.

polls in New York City nor more than 60 per cent anywhere in the state.[29] The percentage that participated in the

[29] If it is permissible to generalize from nine counties, 34 per cent of the adult white males in New York State voted for delegates to the Poughkeepsie Convention. E. Wilder Spaulding (*New York in the Critical Period, 1783–1789* [New York, 1932], p. 91) and Henry Noble MacCracken (*Old Dutchess Forever! The Story of an American County* [New York, 1956], p. 438) give percentages that are far too low, since they have calculated on the basis of *all* males in New York, including children and slaves.

Assembly election, which was held concurrently, was even lower—except in Orange County where the 340 men who went to the polls showed more interest in who was to represent them in the Assembly than they did in the Constitution.

It is not justifiable to assume, as is frequently done,[30] that the smaller number of votes cast for the Assembly represents the number of men normally disqualified by property requirements for voting. There is evidence for fewer than half the counties in New York, and in one of the counties for which evidence is available more men voted for the Assembly than cast ballots for the Constitution. The disparity most likely resulted from a combination of spoiled ballots and apathy. A new election law required that ballots be written, outlawing printed lists.[31] Adjusting to the change certainly resulted in a large number of spoiled ballots, particularly in the less interesting part of the election, and probably exceeded 10 per cent of the ballots cast in some places.[32] And to most men the Assembly election was decidedly less interesting. If a man wished to vote for assemblyman as well as for convention delegates he could not mark both choices on the same ballot, but he must stand in line a second time to qualify for another voting inspector.[33] Doubtless many men did not think it worth the bother, and having saved the United States from despotism, or alternatively from anarchy and confusion, went off to the grog shop without concerning themselves about the local assemblyman.

The generally low level of participation in the election re-

[30] For instance, Spaulding, *New York in the Critical Period*, p. 200; Lee Benson, *Turner and Beard: American Historical Writing Reconsidered* (Glencoe, Ill., 1960), p. 184.

[31] *Journal of the Assembly of the State of New York* (New York, 1788), 13 February 1788; *Daily Advertiser*, 28 April 1788.

[32] V. O. Key, Jr., *Politics, Parties, and Pressure Groups* (4th ed.; New York, 1958), p. 625n.

[33] Senate debate of 1 January 1788, *New-York Journal*, 13 February 1788.

quires no special explanation. Indeed, for an eighteenth-century election it was very well attended. In the absence of an organized party system to stir interest in politics, voting had scant attraction for the average man. Going to the polls at the end of April involved a trip to town along roads blocked by mud and ruts, although, thanks to the new election law,[34] it was no longer necessary to go all the way to the county seat. It is noteworthy that the percentage of participation was highest in Albany, New York, and Columbia Counties, areas where we have evidence of vigorous party activity. Americans have never been noted for a large attendance at elections, and it took many years to form a habit of voting in men who, either because they disliked the inconvenience or because they believed that common people should leave the business of government to their betters, were not accustomed to attending the polls.

[34] *Journal of the Assembly*, 13 February 1788.

XI

The Parties

IN December 1787, when political essays had all but driven news from the columns of the *New-York Journal,* Thomas Greenleaf apologized to those of his patrons who expected "NEWS, as well as POLITICS," by explaining that "the PAROLE of the day is NEW CONSTITUTON, the countersign STATE CONVENTIONS, and the RAGE of the season is, Hallow, damme, Jack, what are you, boy, FEDERAL or ANTI-FEDERAL?" [1] When the votes were cast in April, almost two-thirds of the citizens refused to express a preference for either party. But what of the third that did take an interest in politics? What sort of people were Federalists and Antifederalists, and how did they differ from each other?

It was an early and tenacious belief of the Federalists that the only persons of sound mind who would oppose the Constitution were government officers. While the Philadelphia Convention was still in session and before any sign of opposition had appeared, the following paragraph was clipped from a Philadelphia paper and printed in New York:

This govenment will be opposed *only* by our *Civil officers,* who are afraid of new arrangements taking place which shall jostle them out

[1] *New-York Journal,* 17 December 1787.

of office. . . . [T]he public are desired to beware of all essays and paragraphs that are opposed to a reform of our government, for they all must and will come from *Civil officers,* or persons connected with them.[2]

A similar paragraph actually had its origin in New York:

The principal difficulty in the way of necessary alterations in our Government will arise from the officers of Government. Their interest, it is imagined, will be affected by the alterations. . . . But it is to be hoped the people will neither be influenced by such men nor their connections in the adoption of a Foederal Government.[3]

After the release of the Constitution, Hamilton made a private estimate of the forces he thought would oppose ratification and noted particular danger in "the influence of many *inconsiderable* men in possession of considerable offices under the state governments, who will fear a diminuation of their consequence, power, and emolument, by the establishment of the general government, and who can hope for nothing there—the influence of some *considerable* men in office possessed of talents and popularity who partly from the same motives and partly from a desire of *playing a part* in a convulsion for their own aggrandisement will oppose the quiet adoption of the new government." [4] Hamilton expressed the same opinion in the first number of the *Federalist.*

The basis of all the remarks linking office-holders with opposition to the new Constitution was axiomatic, not empirical. As one writer says, there was a tendency in the eighteenth century to consider "desire for office as a disease which fed upon office-holding." [5] A contemporary essayist justified his generalization about "persons who hold posts of profit and honor," by point-

[2] *Ibid.*, 28 June 1787.

[3] Quoted in Charles Warren, *The Making of the Constitution* (Boston, 1928), p. 340. Cf. *Daily Advertiser* (New York), 24 September 1787.

[4] Harold C. Syrett, ed., and Jacob E. Cooke; assoc. ed., *The Papers of Alexander Hamilton* (New York, 1961–), IV, 275.

[5] Merrill Jensen, *The Articles of Confederation: An Interpretation of the Social-Constitutional History of the American Revolution, 1774–1781* (Madison, Wis., 1940), p. 242.

ing out that "such is the weakness of frail nature, that none of us can act, or even think, with impartial justice, on any subject that interferes with our interest or ambition." [6] Even Antifederalists accepted the truism that men are motivated by their selfish interests—although they, of course, drew the conclusion that Federalists were seeking advancement under the new government. "Publius," it was said, "pants for a fat office." [7]

Mere desire for office was, in fact, more apt to convert men to the support of Federalism than to Antifederalism. In addition to the patronage of prominent Federalists in New York State offices, a new federal government would open many places to reward a loyal Federalist, particularly if the national capital were retained in New York City. One Federalist recorded his satisfaction after the Constitution had been ratified by cheerfully noting, "As the new government of the United States will soon take place, and of course all appointments be made, it behooves us all to look around and try what we can get." [8] Another man may have had similar thoughts when he wrote to his sweetheart in February 1788 that "probably both your and my future happiness is depending upon the issue of this business." [9]

The assumption that the new Constitution would adversely affect any considerable number of established offices was quite groundless. "It is suggested, that state officers, from interested motives will oppose the constitution presented," wrote the "Federal Farmer," "I see no reason for this, their places in general will not be affected, but new openings to offices and places of profit must evidently be made by the adoption of the constitution in the present form." [10] Even William Duer, "Philo-

[6] *Albany Gazette*, 1 November 1787.

[7] *New-York Journal*, 14 January 1788; "Countryman," IV, *ibid.*, 10 January 1788.

[8] James Seagrove to S. B. Webb, 2 January 1789, W. C. Ford, ed., *Correspondence and Journals of Samuel Blanchley Webb* (New York, 1893–1894), III, 121.

[9] S. B. Webb to Catherine Hogeborn, 17 February 1787, *ibid.*, 94.

[10] *Letters from the Federal Farmer, V*, in Forrest McDonald, ed., *Empire and Nation* (Englewood Cliffs, N.J., 1962), p. 132.

Publius," admitted that few offices would be affected by the Constitution. "Most of the departments of the State Governments," he wrote, "will remain, untouched, to flow in their accustomed channels." [11]

New York State officers were far from united in their political sentiments, and those who opposed the Constitution frequently had little to fear personally from the new system. Men like Egbert Benson, James Duane, and R. R. Livingston held important state offices and were Federalists. And those Antifederalists who held state offices, such as George Clinton, John Lamb, and Abraham Yates, not only continued to hold office after ratification but actually aggrandized their positions. There were probably as many state officers favoring ratification as there were opposing it,[12] and on the level of inferior offices, the patronage of influential Federalists may have won over a disproportionately large number. Unfortunately, too little is known of the politics of lesser office holders to be certain.

Members of both parties gladly offered abundant explanation of what divided Federalists from Antifederalists. The Antis thought of themselves as common people, "the democracy," [13] opposing Federalist aristocrats. They were "poor poltroons," [14] "the Yeomanry," [15] and they loved to take such pen names as "One of Yourselves," [16] and "One of the Common People." [17]

The Federalists believed Antis were either knaves or fools. An Antifederalist sarcastically observed that the final article of the "Political Creed of every Federalist" was, "I believe that every

[11] *Daily Advertiser*, 30 October 1787.

[12] E. Wilder Spaulding, *New York in the Critical Period, 1783–1789* (New York, 1932), pp. 105, 106; Jonathan Elliot, ed., *The Debates in the Several State Conventions on the Adoption of the Federal Constitution* (Philadelphia, 1876), II, 220, 221.

[13] "Cincinnatus," IV, *New-York Journal*, 6 December 1787.

[14] "Philadelphiensis," *ibid.*, 1 January 1788.

[15] Robert Yates to George Mason, 25 June 1788, Emmet Collection, #9528, New York Public Library.

[16] *New-York Morning Post*, 17 October 1787.

[17] *New-York Journal*, 12 December 1787.

person, who differs from me in belief is an infernal villain,"[18] while another remarked when forwarding his list of nominations to the newspaper, "It may be said, that I am antifederal, and of course a *knave*, a *fool*, and an *interested man*."[19] Federalist writers describe the opposition to the Constitution as supporters of "Shayism,"[20] as "the *weak*, the suspicious, and the *interested*,"[21] as "the less knowing part of the country,"[22] and as "men much in debt."[23] Parodying Federalist essays, Antifederalist scribblers described themselves as "rabble."[24] One Antifederalist put a choice bit of zoologic imagery into a Federalist's mouth: "The great mass of the people are . . . mere *orang outangs*—blockheads, numskulls, asses, monkeys, sheep, owls, and lobsters."[25]

When Federalists described the men who supported ratification, they said they were persons of "abilities and property,"[26] "the commercial interest," and "the public creditors,"[27] while Antifederalists called them the "wealthy and ambitious,"[28] "the lazy and great,"[29] the sort of man who "powders his hair and wears silk stockings,"[30] and, most popular epithet, the Federalists were the "well-born."

[18] "One of the Nobility," *ibid.*

[19] *New-York Journal*, 14 April 1788

[20] "Caesar," II, *Daily Advertiser*, 11 October 1787.

[21] "Caesar," I, *ibid.*, 1 October 1787.

[22] Paine Wingate to Timothy Pickering, 29 March 1788, Edmund C. Burnett, ed., *Letters of Members of the Continental Congress* (Washington, 1921–1936), VIII, 711.

[23] Syrett, ed., *Papers of Alexander Hamilton*, IV, 275.

[24] "Montezuma," *New-York Morning Post*, 24 October 1787.

[25] "One of the Nobility," *New-York Journal*, 12 December 1787.

[26] John Jay to George Washington, 3 February 1788, H. P. Johnston, ed., *The Correspondence and Public Papers of John Jay* (New York, 1891), III, 322.

[27] Syrett, ed., *Papers of Alexander Hamilton*, IV, 275.

[28] "To the Freemen of Pennsylvania," *New-York Morning Post*, 17 October 1787.

[29] "Address to the Minority of the State Convention of Pennsylvania," *New-York Journal*, 15 January 1788.

[30] "Nancy Feather," *New-York Packet*, 9 November 1787.

The danger of accepting these contemporary descriptions uncritically should be obvious. The prejudices of both friends and enemies result in defective vision, and hate is at least as blind as love. During the nineteenth century, historians usually followed the Federalist party line, describing Antifederalists as demagogues and debtors, while writers influenced by Charles Beard have followed the Antifederalist line by condemning the Federalists as self-seeking enemies of the common people. Recently Forrest McDonald has openly adopted the old Federalist "knaves and fools" interpretation of Antifederalism, arguing that "as a general rule the verdict of history has been the view held by the winner." [31] If so, it is a dangerous rule. Overstatement is characteristic of political rhetoric, and it is rare indeed that a man or a cause is so evil that its opponents have no need to exaggerate its faults in order to justify their own hatred or to stir uncommitted men. As Louis Hartz very sensibly points out, "In politics men who make speeches [or write essays] do not go out of their way to explain how differently they would speak if the enemies they had were larger in size or different in character. On the contrary whatever enemies they fight they paint in satanic terms." [32] That is why Federalist propaganda "is filled with 'levellers' even worse than Babeuf, just as the anti-Federalist world is filled with 'aristocrats' even worse than the Guises," [33] and it is also the source of the many demagogues, despots, and disunionists in the propaganda of the ratification campaign.

There is, however, some support for the most important line of party division described by contemporaries, what might be called the socio-economic division. Both parties agree in assigning the balance of property and ability to the Federalists, despite their vigorous disagreement on where the balance of patriotism lay. Naturally, it cannot have been a fact that all New York

[31] Forrest McDonald, "The Anti-Federalists, 1781–1890," *Wisconsin Magazine of History*, XLVI (1963), 214.

[32] Louis Hartz, *The Liberal Tradition in America* (New York, 1955), p. 6.

[33] *Ibid.*, p. 70.

Federalists were rich and well-born—there were far too many of them—but it was true that most of the rich and well-born in the state were Federalists. The great manor lords of New York State favored ratification with very few exceptions. Only three Antifederalists had land holdings large enough to rank them among the manor lords, and one of these, John Williams, held land in the wilderness of Washington County and his estate was sparsely settled.[34] Only Pierre Van Cortlandt held an estate that compared with those of such Federalists as Stephen Van Rensselaer, Philip Schuyler, R. R. Livingston, Philip Van Cortlandt, William Cooper, and James Duane, and there is reason to doubt that Pierre Van Cortlandt was an Antifederalist in 1788.[35] As a rule, the Antifederalist landowners had relatively small holdings, and, as one writer puts it, they were not "to the manor born."[36]

That the Federalist party was supported by the propertied men of New York State is easily established, but that is all that can be said in support of the socio-economic interpretation. It is not even possible to say that, as most wealthy men were Federalists, most debtors were Antifederalists, for on the two occasions when debtors recorded their sentiments on the Constitution, they toasted its success.[37] Furthermore, neither debtors nor aristocrats were sufficiently numerous in New York State to have held the balance in either party. Wealth and breeding, or the lack of it, cannot have been the quality that distinguished Federalists from Antifederalists. Both parties drew the bulk of their supporters from the large middle group.

[34] Spaulding, *New York in the Critical Period*, p. 74n.

[35] Spaulding (*ibid.*, p. 74) identifies Pierre Van Cortlandt as an Antifederalist, but I have been unable to find any record of his political activity in 1788. His son, Philip, voted as a Federalist in the Poughkeepsie Convention (*ibid.*, p. 246).

[36] Alfred Fabian Young, "The Democratic-Republican Movement in New York State, 1788–1797" (unpublished Ph.D. dissertation, Northwestern University, 1958), p. 51.

[37] *Country Journal* (Poughkeepsie) 24 October 1787; *Daily Advertiser*, 25 July 1788.

Another hypothesis is that Federalists and Antifederalists were distinguished by some sectionally-related characteristic. Table 3 illustrates the sectional features of the vote for the Poughkeepsie Convention. Sectional features are not sufficiently prominent to explain the nature of the party division in New York. Libby's belief that New York "presents the problem in its simplest form," [38] resulted from his practice of ignoring the minority when mapping the distribution of votes. True, the counties that

Table 3. Sectionalism in the vote on the Constitution in New York State *

County	Ballots cast	% participation	Highest Fed vote	Highest Anti vote	% cast for victor
Albany	7,449	54	2,627	4,681	63
Columbia	3,361	60	1,498	1,863	56
Dutchess	2,657	30	892	1,765	66
Montgomery	2,020	35	811	1,209	60
New York	2,836	45	2,735	134	95
Orange	340	10		340	100
Queens	934	33	416	518	55
Ulster	1,440	27	68	1,372	95
Westchester	1,093	25	694	399	64

* Figures are not available for Kings, Richmond, Suffolk, and Washington counties. The first two elected Federalists and the second two elected Antifederalists (*Independent Journal* (New York), 31 May 1788; *Daily Advertiser* (New York), 3, 4, 6, 7, 14 June 1788; *New-York Journal*, 5 June 1788; see above, p. 157.

had Federalist majorities are all clustered around New York City, but in almost every other county there were substantial Federalist minorities, and there were sizable Antifederalist minorities in every Federalist county except New York.

Lee Benson's sectional interpretation of the vote on the Con-

[38] Orin Grant Libby, *Geographical Distribution of the Vote of the Thirteen States on the Federal Constitution, 1787–1788* (Madison, Wis., 1897), p. 18.

stitution in New York State is also stronger than the evidence will support. Benson writes:

> Since Ulster was agrarian and New York was urban, their diametrically opposed patterns—95.2 per cent Antifederalist, 95.3 per cent Federalist, suggests a sharp political cleavage between agrarians and non-agrarians. More precisely, it suggests that, as far as we have tested the relationship, a sharp political cleavage existed between men who lived in urban and agrarian communities. Our inference about the strong relationships between agrarianism and Antifederalism and urbanism and Federalism is supported by the available voting statistics; they indicate that the more remote from New York City, the more strongly agrarian communities supported the Antifederalists.[39]

Actually, the Ulster and New York patterns cannot be considered "diametrically opposed," since in the first county only 27 per cent of the eligible voters cast ballots, while the percentage in New York City was 45 per cent. In other words, only 25.7 per cent of the adult white males in Ulster were Antifederalists while 42.7 per cent of New York's citizens were Federalist. Moreover, Benson is mistaken in believing that support for Antifederalism increased proportionally with the distance from New York City. The statistics show that Orange County, just across the river from the City, was unanimous in its support of Antifederalism, and Ulster County, one more step up the Hudson, was almost as strongly agreed. But in Montgomery County, the most remote from New York City, 40 per cent of the voters were Federalists.

There is, however, some evidence connecting urban environment and a propensity to vote Federalist. New York City was the only county to combine a high level of voter participation with a landslide victory for one party, and other urban areas, even though located in Antifederal counties, reported Federal

[39] *Turner and Beard: American Historical Writing Reconsidered* (Glencoe, Ill., 1960), p. 196.

majorities. Lansingburgh was said to be four-fifths Federalist,[40] Hudson was reported to be as unanimous as New York City,[41] and Albany had "a respectable majority" for the Federalists.[42] Nevertheless, most of those who voted for Federalists in the New York election did not live in a city. An adequate explanation of New York Federalism will have have to explain its apparent connection with an urban environment, but it cannot be based on that factor.

There is insufficient evidence to differentiate the individuals who voted Federalist and Antifederalist in the election for the delegates to the Poughkeepsie Convention with any degree of precision. Generalizations based on wealth, social standing, or sectionalism fail for lack of data or because there are too many known exceptions. Fortunately, it is not necessary to relate Federalism and Antifederalism to other factors in order to point out a significant distinction between the parties. One need not know the social status or psychological characteristics of Baptists and Episcopalians in order to describe their theological differences. In fact, an excessive preoccupation with determining what sort of men tended to vote Federalist or Antifederalist tends to distract attention from what the two parties wanted. How did Federalists and Antifederalists differ in the programs they advocated? That, it would seem, is the crucial question.

[40] *Hudson Weekly Gazette*, 24 June 1788.
[41] *New-York Packet*, 13 June 1788. [42] *Ibid.*

XII

The Issue

THE terms "federal" and "antifederal" predated the campaign for the Constitution by at least two years.[1] The first was a term of praise used to describe patriots—those who supported the Confederation. The second was a term of opprobrium used to describe those who were enemies of the central government; it was most frequently used by nationalists to describe men who did not wish to grant Congress the impost on the terms demanded. When the Constitution came before the country, the supporters of the plan promptly appropriated the name Federalist and dubbed the opposition Antifederalist. The term was an insult to the Antis. The Constitution's supporters might as well have called themselves Patriots and the opposition Traitors. The assumption of the name Federalist by the supporters of the Philadelphia proposals was misleading as well, since it was the Federalists who wished to abandon the Confederation. Naturally, the men who believed that the Constitution required amendment resented being attacked under the title Antifederal-

[1] James Madison to James Monroe, 7 August 1785, Gaillard Hunt, ed., *Writings of James Madison Comprising His Public Papers and His Private Correspondence* (New York, 1900–1910), II, 158; Jackson Turner Main, *The Antifederalists, Critics of the Constitution, 1781–1788* (Chapel Hill, N.C., 1961), pp. i, ii.

ist, and they were never entirely reconciled to the name. As late as February 1789, Joshua Atherton apologized for using "so improper a Term" when he referred to the friends of the Constitution as Federalists.[2]

A few of the opponents of the Constitution stubbornly clung to the term Federalist,[3] but there was obvious inconvenience in conducting a political campaign in which both parties operated under the same name. Elbridge Gerry analysed the situation after the Constitution had been ratified and attempted to set the record straight:

> Those who were called Anti-Federalists at that time complained that they had injustice done them by the title, because they were in favor of a federal government, and the others were in favor of a national one; the Federalists were for ratifying the Constitution as it stood, and the others, not until amendments were made. Their names ought not to have been Federalists and Anti-Federalists, but Rats and Anti-Rats.[4]

Gerry's analysis was entirely just, and no doubt the Antis would have been well pleased had they been permitted to address their opponents as the Rats, but at the time they did not think of it. Abraham Yates believed the parties might be called Federal and Extra Federal,[5] which would have been inoffensive enough, but the preferred terms were Republicans and Anti-Republicans.[6] The New York Federal Republican Committee gave the Antifederalists a particularly respectable title. It was, of course, unfair to call the Federalists anti-republican, for most Federalists

[2] Joshua Atherton to John Lamb, 23 February 1789, John Lamb Papers, New-York Historical Society.

[3] For instance, " A Real Federalist," *Country Journal* (Poughkeepsie), 11 March 1788.

[4] Quoted in Francis N. Thorpe, *Constitutional History of the United States* (Chicago, 1901), II, 238.

[5] Abraham Yates to Abraham G. Lansing, 28 May 1788, Abraham Yates, Jr., Papers, New York Public Library.

[6] "Rusticus," *New-York Journal*, 23 May 1788; *ibid.*, 26 May 1788; *ibid.*, 20 June 1788.

were as determined in their opposition to monarchy as any Anti.

At any rate, the Antifederalists were not able to drop the label that had been pinned on them by their opponents, and so, like many groups from the Quakers to the muckrakers, they made the best of the situation. Official Antifederalist committees formed under the name,[7] and in newspapers and private letters most Antifederalists spoke of "Feds" and "Antis" as freely as the men of the other party did.[8] Forrest McDonald is in error when he writes, "Anti-Federalists did not use the term to designate themselves;" [9] all but the pedants of the party promptly adopted the name.

But while they accepted the name, the Antifederalists continued to insist that their disposition was truly federal. They valued federal government, but they sincerely feared national government. The consolidation of the thirteen states into a single monolithic unit, they believed, was certain disaster for liberty and republicanism. All Antifederalists would have agreed with this statement by Thomas B. Wait:

> I consider the several States to stand in a similar relation to the Nation, and its Constitution—as do individuals to a State and its Constitution—the former have certain rights, as well as the latter that ought to be secured to them—otherwise . . . the whole will be "*melted down*" into one nation; and then, God have mercy on us—our liberties are lost—The vast Continent of America cannot be long subjected to a Democracy, if consolidated into one Government—you might as well attempt to rule Hell by Prayer.[10]

[7] Broadside Collection, SY–1788–14, New-York Historical Society; "A Dutchess County Antifederalist," *Country Journal*, 8 April 1788.

[8] For example, "A New Federal Song," *New-York Journal*, 2 May 1788.

[9] "The Anti-Federalists, 1781–1789," *Wisconsin Magazine of History*, XLVI (1963), 206.

[10] Quoted in Samuel Bannister Harding, *The Contest over Ratification of the Federal Constitution in the State of Massachusetts* (New York, 1896), p. 38; "On the New-Constitution," *New-York Journal*, 14 February 1788.

The Federalists admitted that the Constitution proposed a government somewhat less federal than the Confederation, but they insisted that it safeguarded individual liberty. Nevertheless, it took some boldness for Federalists to believe that a republic the size of the United States could endure. All accepted political theory and the unanimous testimony of history was against them. There had never been a large republic that did not fall to tyrants, and in 1788 the United States was far larger in terms of time than it is now. The distance from one end of the country to the other is now measured in hours, then in weeks. One does not have to believe in states' rights for the twentieth century in order to sympathize with the Antifederalists' concern in 1788.

Before discussing what the Antifederalists wanted, it is well to be clear that they were not in favor of everything that Federalists and historians have believed. First, they did not favor the dissolution of the Union. Hamilton honestly believed that the Antifederalists were hostile to the Union,[11] and some historians have expressed a like opinion.[12] There is not a jot of evidence to support the belief. Nor is there evidence to support the charge that Antifederalists endorsed the plan to divide the Union into three smaller confederacies.[13] On the contrary, what support the plan had came from Federalists.[14]

It has also been charged that the New York Antifederalists were primarily opposed to the federal impost rather than to the Constitution. The New York opposition to ratification, wrote "A Landholder," "is confined wholly to salary men and their

[11] Alexander Hamilton to James Madison, 8 June 1788, Harold C. Syrett, ed., and Jacob E. Cooke, assoc. ed., *The Papers of Alexander Hamilton* (New York, 1961–), IV, 3.

[12] Irving Brant, *James Madison: Father of the Constitution, 1787–1800* (Indianapolis, 1950), pp. 196, 229.

[13] I have found only one contemporary making this charge (*Daily Advertiser* [New York], 8 September 1787). Francis N. Thorpe (*Constitutional History of the United States* [Chicago, 1901], II, 137) implies that Melancton Smith and Richard Henry Lee favored separate confederacies. Neither man did so.

[14] Main, *Antifederalists,* pp. 283, 284.

connections, men whose salary is paid by the State Impost." [15] Stated in this form, the accusation is obviously untrue; there were too many Antifederalists in New York for all of them to have been on the state payroll. Thomas C. Cochran describes a more subtle connection between the impost and opposition to the Constitution. He believes that New Yorkers opposed the Constitution because they feared that the federal government would deprive them of the income from the state impost and so force them to lay heavy land taxes.[16] There is some support for Cochran's analysis. John Williams wrote to his friends in Washington County in January 1788:

> What hath kept the taxes so low in this state—the reason is obvious, impost duties. . . . Let our imposts and advantages be taken from us, shall we not be obliged to lay as heavy taxes as Connecticut, Boston, &c. What hath kept us from those burthens but the privileges, which we must lose if the present proposed constitution is adopted.[17]

Unfortunately, Williams seems to have been the only Antifederalist to use this line of argument, and even he grounded his objections chiefly on the great powers of the President and the right of Congress to determine the place of elections.[18] While Cochran's conclusion may apply to some few New Yorkers, it was not the foundation of Antifederalism in the state.[19]

[15] *Daily Advertiser*, 1 January 1788.

[16] *New York in the Confederation: An Economic Study* (Philadelphia, 1932), pp. 133, 134.

[17] *Country Journal*, 4 March 1788; *New-York Journal*, 29 February 1788.

[18] *Ibid.*

[19] I agree with Forrest McDonald in minimizing the significance of the Cochran thesis, but I do not agree that the thesis "would seem to wither" on the evidence McDonald presents. McDonald (*We the People: The Economic Origins of the Constitution* [Chicago, 1958], p. 296n.) cites an article by Philip Schuyler which "attempted to win support for ratification by pointing out to the voters that the state would profit handsomely from the funding and assumption of the debts by the United States," and also "similar articles" in the *Daily Advertiser* for 2 February 1788 and

The Antifederalists feared the national power of the new government and the absence of a bill of rights, but they recognized the need to alter the Confederation in order to increase the power of the federal government. The most popular Antifederalist pamphlet asserted that the Constitution proposed by the Philadelphia Convention was "a better basis to build upon than the confederation." [20] Although in the heat of debate, Antifederalist writers condemned the Constitution in the strongest terms, there is no evidence that any New York Antifederalist urged an outright rejection of the Philadelphia proposal.[21] On the other hand, the Federalists did not oppose amending the Constitution on principle, although the pressure of campaigning induced them to demand immediate ratification of the Philadelphia proposals without changes. In doing so, the Federalists were not motivated by a conviction that the Philadelphia plan was the best of all possible Constitutions, but by a belief that the situation of the nation was too critical to allow of the delay and possible convulsion that would result if every state convention proposed amendments.[22] The Antifederalists were sceptical of the

5 February 1788. The Schulyer article was published almost a full year after ratification (*Country Journal*, 10 March 1789) and was in no sense an argument for ratification. The other "articles" are a single piece by "A Citizen of the State of New York" published in two parts in successive issues of the *Daily Advertiser*. The article makes no mention of federal assumption, federal funding, or of the proposed Constitution. The only piece dealing with the Constitution in the issues of the *Daily Advertiser* cited by McDonald is number forty-six of the *Federalist*.

[20] *Letters from the Federal Farmer, VI*, in Forrest McDonald, ed., *Empire and Nation* (Englewood Cliffs, N.J., 1962), p. 134.

[21] It is difficult to believe that New York contained a more outspoken Antifederalist than Abraham Yates, but even he wanted the state to ratify —after previous amendments had been obtained (Abraham Yates to Abraham G. Lansing, 25 June 1788, Abraham Yates, Jr., Papers, New York Public Library).

[22] The Philadelphia fathers were the first to regret that the Constitution was imperfect and to wish that improvements could be made (Homer C. Hockett, *Constitutional History of the United States* [New York, 1939], p. 222; Charles Warren, *The Making of the Constitution* [Boston, 1928], pp. 733–742).

Federalists' concern, which does occasionally seem excessive, and they suspected that the warnings of confusion if amendments were insisted upon was a cover for a more sinister desire to force the acceptance of a potentially despotic government. Attempting to be reasonable, an Antifederalist penman wrote, "The truth is, that we cannot exist without a general government, and that great thanks are due to the convention for the plan they offer, but should the body of the people, or even a majority of the states, wish for alterations, before they ratify the work, surely they may be obtained without bloodshed, without the ULTIMA RATIO. And the minority with usual American candour, will yield to their brethren." [23]

When the exaggerations of campaign propaganda are torn away, the essential practical difference between the Federalists and the Antifederalists was when and how to amend the Constitution.[24] Ignoring mythical antirepublicans and disunionists, it is clear that both parties favored increasing the power of the central government and doing so on the basis of the Philadelphia Constitution. Both parties, however, recognized imperfections in the plan, and their differences, although clouded with emotion during the campaign, can be reduced to disagreement over whether the imperfections were so critical as to require immediate correction or whether it would be more dangerous to attempt amendment before the plan was ratified. The narrowness of the division between the parties frequently was not appreciated because both sides believed the worst of their opponents and could not accept the fact than neither side had evil designs on the welfare of America. In a letter to John Lamb, George Clinton described the Antifederalist group at the Poughkeepsie Convention as "Gentlemen opposed to the Adoption of the New Constitution without previous Amendment." In the same letter he ref-

[23] "An American," *New-York Journal*, 12 February 1788.

[24] Cf. Hockett, *Constitutional History*, I, 222; Louise Irby Trenholme, *The Ratification of the Federal Constitution in North Carolina* (New York, 1932), p. 144; Henry Noble MacCracken, *Old Dutchess Forever! The Story of an American County* (New York, 1956), p. 430.

erred to the Federalist group as "the Advocates of Despotism." [25] A more accurate phrase would have been that used during the campaign by the Federalists of Dutchess County: gentlemen in favor of "subsequent amendments." [26]

The question of when amendments should be added may seem trivial, and the Antis may be judged unreasonable for insisting that amendments be added before ratification. But it must be remembered that the Antifederalists were, characteristically, deeply suspicious men, and they did not expect the Federalists to permit any amendment whatever once they had the Constitution safely adopted. "The freemen of America will remember," an Anti wrote, "that it is very easy to change a free government into an arbitrary, despotic, or military one; but it is very difficult, almost impossible to reverse the matter—very difficult to regain freedom once lost." The Federalist argument that subsequent amendments were a practical possibility, he dismissed as "fairy tails" which "cannot deceive the people of any understanding," and "must only be invented to amuse the weak and foolish among themselves." [27]

Tucked away among the inflammatory pieces that filled the newspapers, a mild and reasonable essay occasionally appeared, giving support to the belief that the narrowness of the division betweeen the parties was recognized by those contemporaries who resisted the temptation to view the opposition as instruments of the devil. Early in the campaign, an Antifederalist, that is, a man who wished to offer amendments to the Philadelphia plan, wrote in this amiable style:

As perfection is not the lot of human nature, we are not to expect it in the New Foederal Constitution.—Candour must confess, however, that it is a well wrought piece of stuff, and claims, upon

[25] George Clinton to John Lamb, 21 June 1788, John Lamb Papers, New-York Historical Society.

[26] *Country Journal*, 18 March 1788.

[27] *New-York Morning Post*, 11 March 1788. See also, *New-York Journal*, 20 March 1788; "Algernon Sidney," II, *New-York Journal*, 23 February 1788.

the whole the approbation of all the States. . . . The following strictures on the proposed Constitution, are submitted with diffidence.—Excepting a single instance, they regard points of an inferior magnitude only.[28]

The first letter of the "Cato" series was almost as restrained in its criticism.[29] It is conceivable that many, if not most, Antifederalists began with only mild reservations or even mere hesitation, but dug in their heels once they were attacked with what seemed disproportionate viciousness by the Federalists, "those who are for *cramming down the New Constitution* by *force, fraud and falsehood*." [30]

Jackson Turner Main estimates that not more than one-sixth of the Antifederalists were moderates,[31] but his estimate, based on a selection of campaign documents that must be extreme by their nature, is too conservative. A man's personal beliefs are not necessarily so extreme as his propaganda. Abraham Yates's "Sidney" essays, for example, condemn the Constitution without reservation, although Yates personally favored ratification after amendment.[32] Significant, too, is the speed and enthusiasm with which New York Antifederalists accepted the Constitution once they were sure that amendments would be promptly considered.[33]

The moderates of the campaign for the Constitution are too rarely heard, although, in the long run, they had the clearest view of the political situation. It seems proper, therefore, to quote from an essay by a writer appropriately signing himself "Medium":

[28] *New-York Morning Post*, 2 October 1787.

[29] "Cato," I, *New-York Journal*, 27 September 1787.

[30] "A Lover of Truth," *New-York Packet*, 30 October 1787.

[31] Main, *Antifederalists*, p. 177.

[32] *Country Journal*, 5 February 1788, 4 March 1788, 11 March 1788; *Albany Gazette*, 13 March 1788; *New-York Journal*, 13 June 1788, 14 June 1788; Abraham Yates to Abraham G. Lansing, 25 June 1788, Abraham Yates, Jr., Papers, New York Public Library.

[33] See below, Chap. XX.

My candid opinion is, that most of the anonymous publications which have lately come forth on both sides . . . are well intended . . . I find that all are clearly agreed in the truth of this position: that an energetic Foederal Government is essential to our happiness and existence as a nation. Now, sir, I presume no one has yet called in question the sufficiency of the new constitution in point of energy. The only thing, therefore, remaining to be decided is, whether under this constitution our essential freedom can be maintained. An hot brained Foederalist will tell you, that it must be adopted, hastily adopted, without limitation or reserve; and I have known some go so far, as to call in the assistance of *tar* and *feathers* against such as were of different sentiment. The Anti-Foederalists, in general, are more moderate, but equally obstinate . . . Persons of the above description are swayed by passion, not by reason, and should not be regarded by the honest and sensible part of the community . . . I really think, sir, that if a bill of rights had accompanied our new constitution, little or no opposition would have been made to it . . . Let those, therefore, who call themselves Foederalists, lay aside a little of their arrogance, and instead of abusing, endeavour to convince their fellow citizens of the necessity of embracing the constitution as it stands, the impracticability of securing a better one; and that anarchy will be the consequence of its rejection. Let them unite with their brethren in recommending a bill of rights, which is, in fact, the best security we can have against the encroachments of despotism, and I dare flatter myself, that our state will not be the last that shall accede to it.[34]

[34] *New-York Journal,* 21 November 1787; cf. "Conciliator," John Lamb Papers, New-York Historical Society.

PART IV

The Eleventh Pillar

XIII

A Convention of Delegates

BEFORE the New York election, predictions of its result ranged from that of a Philadelphia man who declared that only New York City would send a Federalist delegation to Poughkeepsie [1] to that of Samuel B. Webb who, though he conceded that the Antis would carry several counties, expected that there would be "at least an equal number of Foederalists" in the Convention.[2] It took almost a full month for the county supervisors to count the ballots, and while they worked, the politicians continued to speculate. Hamilton, cautious as always, wrote to Madison that "all depends upon Albany, where both sides claim the victory." The doubts of the Federalists, he said, would "not be removed till the latter end of the month." [3] Samuel B. Webb, still optimistic in the middle of May, wrote to a Boston friend that "from all the information yet obtained we judge about 37

[1] "An Anti-foederal Tale," *New-York Morning Post,* 11 March 1788.

[2] S. B. Webb to Joseph Barrell, 27 April 1788, W. C. Ford, ed., *Correspondence and Journals of Samuel Blanchley Webb* (New York, 1893–1894), III, 99.

[3] Alexander Hamilton to James Madison, 11 May 1788, Harold C. Syrett, ed., and Jacob E. Cooke, assoc. ed., *The Papers of Alexander Hamilton* (New York, 1961–), IV, 647.

Foederal Members of Convention." [4] As there were to be sixty-five delegates in all, that would have been a Federal majority. At the beginning of June when some hard facts were becoming available, the *Country Journal* reported, "From the most accurate calculations to be made with respect to the late election for members of Convention, it is thought there will be a majority of about 20 against the adoption of the proposed federal government." [5]

The full magnitude of the Antifederalist victory was revealed when the supervisors had completed their canvass of votes. New Yorkers had given the Antifederalists more than two-thirds of the seats in the ratifying convention. In Albany, where the election had been so fiercely contested, a full slate of Antifederalists was elected to the Poughkeepsie Convention, and the Yates faction won all the Assembly seats as well. "Our antagonists are much Crest fallen and have very Little to say," crowed Abraham G. Lansing.[6] The Federalists won the seats of only four counties. They had, as had been expected, nine seats from New York City, two from Kings, and two from Richmond. In a surprise victory [7] they took the six Westchester seats as well. "Westchester," fretted Abraham Yates, "has been most Shamefully . . . taken in." [8]

The Federalists took their defeat philosophically. Peter Van Schaack, who had lost the close Columbia election in which 60 per cent of the qualified voters had gone to the polls, wrote, "I have lost my election without being much mortified. The popular tide was against us, that is (to be sure,) against what was

[4] S. B. Webb to Joseph Barrell, 11 May 1788, Ford, ed., *Correspondence of S. B. Webb*, III, 103.

[5] *Country Journal* (Poughkeepsie), 3 June 1788.

[6] Abraham G. Lansing to Abraham Yates, [28] May 1788, Abraham Yates, Jr., Papers, New York Public Library.

[7] R. R. Livingston to Philip Schuyler, 9 May 1788, Philip Schuyler Papers, Vol. XXXVI, New York Public Library; Leonard Gansevoort to Stephen Van Rensselaer, 6 April 1788, #4069, New York State Library.

[8] Abraham Yates to Abraham G. Lansing, 1 June 1788, Abraham Yates, Jr., Papers, New York Public Library.

right and *good*." [9] Federalists even found reason for satisfaction in the Dutchess County election, which the Antifederalists had carried by a higher percentage of the popular vote than they achieved in any other county except Ulster and Orange.[10] "A correspondent remarks," reported the *Country Journal*, "that it is a circumstance highly favorable to the Federal cause, that in this County there should be at least one third of the votes for members in favor of the Constitution. It is what the most sanguine could scarcely have expected, had they calculated on probable grounds—at the beginning of the year it was the better opinion that there were hardly one twentieth of the Electors inclined to the Federal side; so sudden and so great a change in the public sentiment . . . is almost without parallel." [11]

A drift of public sentiment toward the Constitution was remarked by Hamilton some weeks before the votes were counted [12] and draws attention to the disparity between the overwhelming victory for the Antis as reflected by the relative numbers of convention seats won by the two parties and the comparatively close margin in the popular vote. Although it is frequently assumed that the popular vote was a "smashing defeat for the Federalists," [13] the statistical evidence shows that the supporters of the Constitution won 9,741 out of 22,088 known votes. The Antifederalist margin of victory was less than 2,500 votes, 56 per cent of the known ballots.[14] Since election statistics are available for all but four small counties, it is unlikely that the percentage would be altered significantly if complete returns

[9] Peter Van Schaack to Henry Walton, 3 June 1788, Henry C. Van Schaack, *The Life of Peter Van Schaack* (New York, 1842), p. 425.

[10] See Table 3, p. 167. [11] *Country Journal*, 3 June 1788.

[12] Alexander Hamilton to James Madison, 19 May 1788, Syrett, ed., *Papers of Alexander Hamilton*, IV, 649.

[13] Forrest McDonald, *We the People: The Economic Origins of the Constitution* (Chicago, 1958), p. 286; Charles A. Beard, *An Economic Interpretation of the Constitution of the United States* (New York, 1913), p. 245.

[14] McDonald's figures (*We the People*, p. 286) are in error. See Table 3, p. 167, which is based on the same materials cited by McDonald.

were at hand.[15] In only three counties, New York, Orange, and Ulster, did either party win a landslide victory, and in all but the first of those, voter participation was well below the average for the state. In every other county the minority party won at least one-third of the votes cast.

The sixty-five delegates who attended the Poughkeepsie Convention had probably been chosen mainly because of their known views on the Constitution, but their votes were not pledged in advance. Their constituents expected them to deliberate, to listen to the arguments of the opposition, and then to decide the issue according to their best judgments. For this reason, the Poughkeepsie delegates are important as individuals, and it is unfortunate that, for most of them, the only information available is a few sterile facts about their economic interests and legislative experience.[16]

The Federalist delegation from New York City was the most distinguished in the convention. John Jay, the American secretary for foreign affairs since 1783, led the ticket in the City. Alexander Hamilton held a seat from New York as did R. R. Livingston, the state chancellor, who wisely chose not to run in his own county of Columbia, but was elected on the Federalist ticket in the City. Richard Morris, chief justice of the supreme court and James Duane, mayor of New York City added to the dignity of the New York delegation. The only man of comparable prestige on the Antifederalist side in the convention was Governor George Clinton. The other Antifederalist delegates were mostly country lawyers who had no greater distinction than a few terms in the state legislature.

[15] This calculation agrees very closely with Hamilton's estimate. Hamilton judged the Antifederalist victory at approximately four-sevenths of the popular vote—58 per cent (Alexander Hamilton to James Madison, 8 June 1788, Syrett, ed., *Papers of Alexander Hamilton*, IV, 3, 4).

[16] E. Wilder Spaulding, *New York in the Critical Period, 1783–1789* (New York, 1932), pp. 232–248. Gozen Ryerss and Peter Lefferts, Federalist delegates from Richmond County whom Spaulding fails to identify, were both judges (*Daily Advertiser* [New York], 15 July 1788).

There can be no doubt that the Federalist group in the Poughkeepsie Convention held the balance of wealth, education, and "Shineing Abilities." [17] John Jay wrote with some complacency that "the opposition to the proposed Constitution appears formidable, though more so from numbers than other considerations." [18] The distinguished nature of the Federalist group is principally due to the election of the Federalist ticket in New York City. The Federalists in any other part of the state could not have chosen nearly so brilliant a list. The City, then as now, tended to attract the brightest talents and that fact as well as party preference is reflected in the City list. Had the Federalists succeeded in electing a few more men like Lott W. Sarls and Thaddeus Crane in the country counties, the proportion of wealth and brilliance in the Federalist delegation at the convention would not have been so high. Furthermore, it would be improper to infer from the contrast between the two parties at Poughkeepsie that a similar contrast of wealth and ability existed among Federalists and Antifederalists at large. There is no reason to assume that the electors resembled the elected.

The New York Legislature's resolution calling for the meeting of the ratifying convention stipulated that the convention convene at the court house at Poughkeepsie on 17 June 1788. Poughkeepsie had been the capital of New York State during the Revolution, after the occupation of New York City and the destruction of Kingston. It was a village with a population of less than 3,000,[19] conveniently located on a plain one mile east of the Hudson River, seventy-five miles upriver from New York City and eighty-five miles down the river from Albany. The court house, which had been designated as the place of meeting, was a brand-new building that had been completed late in

[17] John Jay to Mrs. Jay, 21 June 1788, H. P. Johnston, ed., *The Correspondence and Public Papers of John Jay* (New York, 1891), III, 340.

[18] *Ibid.*

[19] United States Bureau of the Census, *Heads of Families at the First Census of the United States Taken in the year 1790: New York* (Washington, 1908), p. 9.

1787 and was used for the meetings of the state legislature in January 1788.[20] It was a large, two-story stone structure, topped by a cupola and containing a vaulted dungeon in its foundations appropriately equipped with manacles and iron rings on the floor and walls.[21] The more comfortable quarters on the first floor were large enough for the sixty-five delegates and as many as two hundred spectators.[22]

With a promptness astonishing for an eighteenth-century gathering, sixty-one delegates appeared in the Poughkeepsie court house at eleven o'clock on Tuesday, 17 June 1788, and the four absentees arrived within a few days. George Clinton was unanimously elected president of the convention. John McKesson and Abraham G. Bancker, both men of Antifederalist sympathies, were appointed secretaries; the publisher of the *Country Journal*, Nicholas Powers, became the official printer; and a messenger and a doorkeeper were appointed. The convention decreed that its meetings would be open at all times and directed James Duane and Gilbert Livingston to make arrangements with the local clergy to have each day's meetings opened with prayer. Then three Federalists and two Antifederalists were appointed to draw up a set of rules for the convention, and the house adjourned. On the following day, twelve rules of parliamentary procedure were adopted and it was decided that debate would begin at ten o'clock Thursday morning.[23]

When the convention adjourned, the Antifederalists returned to their lodgings at Poole's Inn and the Federalists to theirs at Hendrickson's Inn.[24] The Antifederalists were understandably

[20] Edmund Platt, *The Eagle's History of Poughkeepsie* (Poughkeepsie, 1905), p. 56.

[21] Broadus Mitchell, *Alexander Hamilton* (New York, 1957, 1962), I, 436.

[22] *Country Journal*, 31 June 1788.

[23] New York State, *Journal of the Convention of the State of New York* (Poughkeepsie, 1788), p. 5.

[24] Henry Noble MacCracken, *Old Dutchess Forever! The Story of an American County* (New York, 1956), p. 436.

jubilant. "Notwithstanding the Eclat with which the Federalists left the City," crowed a happy observer, "and the Impressions on their Minds of their Weight and Importance, yet I believe there has not been a time since the Revolution in which the *Well Born*, who are the Leaders of that Party, have felt and appeared so uninfluential, as they feel and appear at this Time and Place." Everything seemed to favor the Antifederalists. "Unanimity and Harmony reigns among the Anties—the Promptitude with which they assembled—their Concurrence in Sentiment and their Determination to bend their Force to the same Point are the highest Evidences thereof—and shut out the Shadow of Hope, in the Federalists, of creating Divisions." [25]

Divisions—that was the only thing the Antifederalists feared. Their numbers were overwhelming, and nothing but "Federal Chicanery" [26] could prevent them from obtaining ratification with conditional amendments. Their single worry was that the smooth-talking Federalists might dull the suspicions of some Antis and enable the Federalists to carry a form of ratification that would purport to guarantee amendments, but which, in reality, could not be trusted. That the "well born" intended to exert their influence was never doubted. An Albany Antifederalist divined the Federalist plan early in June: "They pretend to bouy themselves up with an Idea that our Members will on hearing the Arguments which will be offered in favor of the System—and the Consideration that the other States will agree to it—be perswaded [*sic*] that it is necessary first to adopt the Constitution and then strongly recommend amendments." He had learned that "Schuyler, Gansevoort, Cuyler and several others from this City and from New York will attend the Convention." At the time he could laugh off the fear of their influence: "If the Impressions which the interference of those Gentlemen

[25] James M. Hughes to John Lamb, 18 June 1788, John Lamb Papers, New-York Historical Society.

[26] Abraham G. Lansing to Abraham Yates, 22 June 1788, Abraham Yates, Jr., Papers, New York Public Library.

will make on the minds of the Northern Members are not more pernicious to us than their Exertions in the Election we have no reason to wish them to stay at home." [27] But after some of the Albany "grandees" had actually left for Poughkeepsie, concern deepened, and some of the prominent Antifederalists from Albany and New York City considered going to Poughkeepsie themselves to "counteract their views." [28]

The Federalist delegation at Poughkeepsie was quite as dangerous as any visiting "grandees." The gentle manners of the thin, sickly secretary of foreign affairs, the elegant diction of the tall, aristocratic chancellor, and the well-known charm of Schuyler's handsome son-in-law, were forces to be feared. The convention had barely begun before Charles Tillinghast was informing John Lamb that John Jay, R. R. Livingston, and Alexander Hamilton were "continually singling out the members in Opposition (when out of Convention) and conversing with them on the subject." Tillinghast believed that Jay was particularly dangerous, remarking that his "manners and mode of address would probably do much mischief, were the members not as firm as they are." [29] On the other hand, Tillinghast pointed out that Hamilton's monarchical prejudices were so well-known that he would be unable to cajole any Antifederalist into trusting him. Hamilton had a fond confidence in his persuasivve powers. He had even invited Abraham Yates to his home for Sunday dinner late in May, hoping to crack the old man's suspicion,[30] but the Antis were on their guard against him. "You would be surprised, did you not know the Man," wrote Tillinghast, "what an *amazing Republican* Hamilton wishes to make himself be considered. *But he is known*." [31]

[27] Abraham G. Lansing to Abraham Yates, 1 June 1788, Abraham Yates, Jr., Papers, New York Public Library.

[28] Abraham G. Lansing to Abraham Yates, 22 June 1788, *ibid.*

[29] Charles Tillinghast to John Lamb, 21 June 1788, John Lamb Papers, New-York Historical Society.

[30] Abraham Yates to Abraham G. Lansing, 28 May 1788, Abraham Yates, Jr., Papers, New York Public Library.

[31] Charles Tillinghast to John Lamb, 21 June 1788, John Lamb Papers, New-York Historical Society.

The Antifederalists took defensive measures against the Federalist attempts at personal persuasion. These consisted chiefly in segregating themselves strictly from the Federalist members of the convention. At the beginning of July, Issac Roosevelt reported sadly that "our opponents keep themselves at much distance from us, and we cannot collect any of their sentiments, either out or in doors, by any means whatever." [32] A Federalist visitor to Poughkeepsie scornfully wrote a few days later, "The anti's here are easily distinguished by their walking in bodies & by their confused countenances." [33] These measures may have been undignified, but they were effective; for many days, the Antifederalists avoided divisions.

[32] Issac Roosevelt to Richard Varick, 1 July 1788, quoted in Platt, *Eagle's History of Poughkeepsie*, p. 58.

[33] David S. Bogart to S. B. Webb, 8 [July] 1788, Ford, ed., *Correspondence of S. B. Webb*, III, 103.

XIV

Debates at Poughkeepsie

THE Poughkeepsie Convention began to debate at ten o'clock on the morning of 19 June 1788. The convention resolved itself into a committee of the whole, and Governor Clinton surrendered the chair to Henry Oothoudt of Albany County. After the proposed Constitution was formally read, Chancellor R. R. Livingston made the opening oration. He addressed his remarks, the chancellor said, to the gentlemen present "who have yet formed no decided opinion on the important question before us, and who (like myself) bring with them dispositions to examine whatever shall be offered, and not to determine till after the maturest deliberation." Then the chancellor proceeded to the body of his oration: "Ever since a pure and perfect religion has lent her mild lights to philosophy, and extended her influence over the sentiments of men, it has been a received opinion that the happiness of nations, as well as of individuals, depends on peace, and that intimate connection which mutual wants occasion." He spoke in this elevated tone for several hours. Livingston's primary theme was New York's need for Union and the insufficiency of the Articles of Confederation. "As, on the one hand, sir, our situation admits of a union," he pronounced in a classically balanced phrase, "our distresses point out its necessity.

I will not, at this time, touch on the declining state of our commerce; nor will I remind you of our national bankruptcy, of the effect it has upon our public measures, and the private misery that it causes; nor will I wound your feelings by a recapitulation of the insults we daily receive from nations whose injuries we are compelled to repay by the advantages of our commerce." His audience doubtless thanked him much for his restraint. Instead, Livingston made a minute examination of the benefits New York would derive from a strong and efficient federal government. Then, finally, he came to the point and handed a resolution to the chair.[1]

The slip of paper on which the resolution was written out in accordance with the rules of the convention is in the handwriting of Livingston and Hamilton.[2] It reads, "Resolved that no Question general or particular shall be put in this Committee upon the proposed Constitution of Government for the United States, or upon any Clause or Article thereof, nor upon any Amendment which may be proposed thereto, until after the said Constitution and Amendments shall have been considered Clause by Clause." In other words, the Federalists wanted to be sure that the Antifederalists would not force through a rejection or a conditional ratification without giving the minority an opportunity to argue. The Antis had the numbers to do exactly as they pleased, and, had they wished to, they could have rejected or ratified in any form they chose and have returned to their homes in a week. The Federalists were anxious that the convention remain at Poughkeepsie until news came that the ninth pillar had been erected in the "Grand Foederal Edifice" by the convention of New Hampshire or Virginia, both of which were then sitting. When the ninth state had ratified and the old Confederation was dissolved, the Federalists believed they would hold the ad-

[1] Jonathan Elliot, ed., *The Debates in the Several State Conventions on the Adoption of the Federal Constitution* (Philadelphia, 1876), II, 208–216.

[2] John McKesson Papers, New-York Historical Society.

vantage at Poughkeepsie and could easily persuade the Antifederalists to ratify the Constitution unconditionally.

The Livingston resolution was discussed briefly, and then it was agreed to by the unanimous vote of the convention.[3] The Federalists were pleased and surprised. "You see what a figure our antis make," chuckled Peter Van Schaack, "discussing the constitution by paragraphs and so dispassionately after all their clamor against it as RADICALLY wrong." [4] But some Antifederalists outside the convention were worried. Three days after the resolution had been adopted, Abraham Lansing, John Lansing's brother, wrote anxiously to Abraham Yates, "From some expressions in my Brother's Letters I am inclined to believe that our Friends *have* or *are* ready to consent to debate the Constitution by Paragraphs.—If this is determined on, the Business will unavoidably be retarded to the disappointment of our Country Friends with whom it is now the Busy Season. This Circumstance the Federal Gentlemen will no doubt avail themselves of and procrastinate the Business as long as they possibly can. . . . The decision of the other States may also have a Tendency to influence the Conduct of some of the Members—A Friend returned from Poughkeepsie last evening, informed us that he was apprehensive that the Federalists would operate upon the Hopes or Fears of some. I hope my fears may be ill founded—but I am apprehensive we will eventually be injured by delay—notwithstanding the decided majority." [5]

Inside the convention, however, the Antifederalists had no

[3] John C. Hamilton wrote (*History of the Republic of the United States as Traced in the Writings of Alexander Hamilton and his Contemporaries* [Philadelphia, 1864], III, 484, 484n.) that Clinton opposed Livingston's resolution and was furious when it passed. That cannot be true, for Clinton cast his vote in favor of the resolution (Elliot, ed., *Debates,* II, 216; *Daily Advertiser* [New York], 25 June 1788).

[4] Peter Van Schaack to Henry Van Schaack, 22 June 1788, Henry C. Van Schaack, ed., *Memoirs of Henry Van Schaack, Embracing Sections of his Correspondence* (Chicago, 1892), p. 159.

[5] Abraham G. Lansing to Abraham Yates, 22 June 1788, Abraham Yates, Jr., Papers, New York Public Library.

qualms about having accepted the Livingston resolution. Writing to George Mason of Virginia, Robert Yates, who had been elected chairman of the Antifederalist committee at the convention, explained, "We yeilded [*sic*] to a Proposal made by our Opponents to discuss the Constitution in a Committee of the whole, without putting a Question on any part, provided that in the Course of this Discussion, we should suggest the Amendments or Explanations, which we deemed necessary to the exceptional Parts—Fully relying on the Steadiness of our Friends, we see no Danger in this Mode and we came into it to prevent the Opposition from charging us with Precipitation." [6]

The many visitors to the Poughkeepsie Convention were doubtless relieved to learn that they would not be deprived of the pleasure of witnessing a display of the greatest oratorical talents in the state. The debaters gave a splendid performance. The *Country Journal* reported two weeks after the Convention had opened, "The spectators who seldom make a number less than a hundred and oftentimes are twice so many, enjoy a mental feast exquisite as uncommon. The first geniuses of the country have here a field on which their powers have ample room." [7] The debates ran from ten o'clock in the morning until two o'clock in the afternoon, and after 28 June, the convention held a late afternoon session as well.[8] The spectators seemed to have an insatiable appetite for addresses that would quickly cloy the modern taste. They enthused over the speakers of both parties indiscriminately in terms as grandiloquent as those used by the debaters themselves:

Under the federal banner Col. H[amilton] stands the political porcupine, armed at all points, and brandishes a shaft to every opposer: A shaft, powerful to repel and keen to wound. The

[6] Robert Yates to George Mason, 25 June 1788, Emmet Collection, #9528, New York Public Library.

[7] Charles Tillinghast to John Lamb, 21 June 1788, John Lamb Papers, New-York Historical Society.

[8] *New-York Packet*, 4 July 1788.

C[hancellor] pours a stream of eloquence deep as the Ganges, and irrefutable as the Cadaraqui. Mr. Jay's reasoning is weighty as gold, polished as silver, and strong as steel. Mr. H[ariso]n's harangues combine the poignancy of vinegar with the smoothness of oil: His manner wins attention—his matter proselytes the judgment.

Mr. S[mit]h, the Anti champion, adds the subtilty of Locke to the candour of Sydney. If his elocution is hesitating, it is still eloquent; and the exertions of his mind exhibit a man formed for investigations and debate. G[overno]r C[linto]n has spoken but seldom; but his silence does not proceed from a consciousness that he has not powers to persuade or arguments to convince.

Mr. Lansing is often upon the floor, and has that respect paid him by his auditors, which none but men of abilities can obtain: He is heard with attention.[9]

As might have been expected, the distinguished Federalist delegation gathered more debater's points than did their opponents. While the formal debate of the Constitution was in progress, men who were not accustomed to speaking in public were necessarily silent. On 30 June, Melancton Smith pointed out in debate that the Federalists had "the advantage of Abilities and habit of public speaking." [10] George Clinton remarked on another occasion that the representatives of the country counties "were men of sound Judgment, but not used to public speaking." [11]

Consequently, the Federalists carried a much larger share of the debate than their numbers alone warranted. During the formal debate, six Federalist delegates and seven Antifederalists took the floor at one time or another. None of the speakers was an obscure man. Hamilton, Livingston, Jay, Duane, Harison, and Richard Morris—the delegation from New York City—spoke for the Federalists. Melancton Smith, John Lansing, Gov-

[9] *Country Journal* (Poughkeepsie), 31 June 1788.

[10] John McKesson Papers, New-York Historical Society.

[11] "Subject of a Conversation with Gov. Clinton," 12 June 1789, Charles A. King, *Life and Correspondence of Rufus King* (New York, 1894), I, 357.

ernor Clinton, Samuel Jones, Gilbert Livingston, John Williams, and Robert Yates spoke for the majority.[12] The rest of the delegates, both Federalists and Antifederalists, sat silent and listened to those practiced in the art of debate. And yet, although fewer than one-fifth of the Antifederalist members ever took the floor, Charles Tillinghast reported that the Federalists were "greatly disappointed in finding that there are more speakers in the opposition than they counted on." [13]

George Clinton and Robert Yates, both men who might have been expected to lead the debate for their party, actually spoke very little in the convention. Although Yates was the official Antifederalist leader at Poughkeepsie,[14] his sole contribution to the formal debate was made when he was called on by John Lansing to attest to some statements made by Hamilton at the Philadelphia Convention.[15] His remarks then were so brief that Francis Childs, who was printing the debates in his *Daily Advertiser*, did not bother to note them. Samuel Jones's remarks were also too brief to qualify as orations.[16] Governor Clinton took an actual part, though a small part, in the debate. He was president of the convention, but he was free to speak as frequently as he wished while the convention was in committee and Henry

[12] A speech by Thomas Tredwell is printed in Elliot, ed., *Debates*, II, 396–406, but this speech was not actually delivered in the convention. It first appears at the end of the third volume of the 1830 edition of Elliot, pages "1*" to "8*," where Elliot explains that it was sent to him by Tredwell after the first volumes of the *Debates* had gone to press. "*Mr. Tredwell* states to us," Elliot continued, "that these remarks were intended to be delivered to the Convention, but some circumstances, not worth mentioning at this time, prevented him from doing so." I am indebted to Mr. Leonard Rapport of the National Archives for bringing this information to my attention.

[13] Charles Tillinghast to John Lamb, 21 June 1788, John Lamb Papers, New-York Historical Society.

[14] Robert Yates to George Mason, 25 June 1788, Emmet Collection, #9528, New York Public Library.

[15] Christopher P. Yates to Abraham Yates, 30 June 1788, Abraham Yates, Jr., Papers, New York Public Library.

[16] Elliot, ed., *Debates*, II, 325, 376.

Oothoudt in the chair. He availed himself of the right on several occasions, and, as usual, succeeded in impressing the audience even more by what he was than by what he said. James Kent, a regular visitor to the convention, wrote:

> Though I felt strong political prejudices against Governor Clinton, as the leader of the Anti-Federal party, yet during the course of that Convention, I became very favorably struck with the dignity with which he presided, and with his unassuming and modest pretentions as a speaker. It was impossible not to feel respect for such a man, and for a young person not to be somewhat over-awed in his presence, when it was apparent in all his actions and deportment that he possessed great decision of character and a stern inflexibility of purpose.[17]

Two speakers carried more than half the debate between them, Alexander Hamilton for the Federalists and Melancton Smith for the Antifederalists. As the leader of the Schuyler faction in the New York Assembly and the man who had signed the Constitution for the state, it was natural that Hamilton should lead the debate for the Federalists. Furthermore, he was a practiced orator. "He generally spoke with much animation and energy and with considerable gesture. His language was clear, nervous, and classical. His investigations penetrated to the foundation and reason of every doctrine and principle which he examined, and he brought to the debate a mind filled with all the learning and precedents applicable to the subject." [18] The men sympathetic to Hamilton's politics enthused over his ability as a speaker. "What a noble field this young man had for his ebullient parts!" wrote one whose political ideas were much in harmony with the New Yorker's. "It would almost persuade me to be in love with a Republick against my better judgment." [19]

[17] William Kent, ed., *Memoirs and Letters of James Kent, Late Chancellor of the State of New York* (Boston, 1898), p. 306.

[18] Kent, ed., *Memoirs of James Kent*, p. 305.

[19] Patterson to Duane, 22 September 1788, James Duane Papers, New-York Historical Society.

Hamilton was very much the star of the show at Poughkeepsie, but he did not impress the opposition in the convention. As Tillinghast had said, he was known to have monarchical sympathies,[20] and the Antifederalists were not about to change their votes merely to honor their opponents' skill in debate.

The chief of the Antifederalist debaters, Melancton Smith, was a plain man and unimpressed by any of the Federalist histrionics. He dismissed the polished performer R. R. Livingston as "a wretched reasoner," and of Hamilton himself he wrote, "he speaks frequently, very long and very vehemently—has, like publius, much to say not very applicable to the subject." [21] Melancton Smith was in every way a contrast to Alexander Hamilton. He was not handsome. His hair was unpowdered and curled down the back of a thick neck; his head was large and his features irregular.[22] While Hamiton dressed like a courtier, Smith was known for his "prepossessing plainness." [23] And while Hamilton was disliked even by some members of his own party because of the haughtiness that occasionally crept into his manner, Smith was held in warm regard even by men who abhorred his politics. One such wrote of him as "this good and able man and true republican," who was "seduced into antifederalism and eventually declined into democracy." [24] James Kent described Melancton Smith as "a man of remarkable simplicity, and of the most gentle, liberal, and amiable disposition." [25] Smith's influence, like Governor Clinton's, was the sort "which arises from the experienced confidence of an intelligent

[20] Charles Tillinghast to John Lamb, 21 June 1788, John Lamb Papers, New-York Historical Society.

[21] Melancton Smith to Nathan Dane, 28 June 1788, Edmund C. Burnett, ed., *Letters of Members of the Continental Congress* (Washington, 1921–1936), VIII, 757n.

[22] Broadus Mitchell, *Alexander Hamilton* (New York, 1957, 1962), I, 641.

[23] Kent, ed., *Memoirs of James Kent*, p. 304.

[24] William Alexander Duer, *Reminscences of an Old New Yorker* (New York, 1867), p. 8.

[25] Kent, ed., *Memoirs of James Kent*, p. 306.

people in the integrity of their representatives." [26] Smith particularly prided himself on his sound logic, and his manner in debate was "dry, plain, and syllogistic." James Kent noted that it was necessary for his "adversary to examine well the ground on which they [*sic*] started, and not to concede too much at the beginning, or he would find it somewhat embarrassing to extricate himself from a subtle web of sophistry." [27]

The battle between Smith and Hamilton amused the spectators, but it had no appreciable effect on the men who were to vote on the Constitution, few of whom can have been so entirely free of prior prejudice as the chancellor had declared he was when opening the debate. The convention had debated about half the clauses of the Constitution when Jay wrote to Washington that "there is no reason to think that either party has made much impression on the other." [28] It was not remarkable that the debate made no converts, for as in the newspaper essays, the participants rarely directed their remarks to meeting the objections of the opposition. The Federalists spoke as if they suspected the Antis of designs against the Union and the Antis spoke as if the Federalists were aristocratic advocates of tyranny —though the language was politer as suited face-to-face discussion.

Melancton Smith made his opening oration on 20 June. "He was as strongly impressed with the necessity of a union as any one could be," Smith told the convention. "He would seek it with as much ardor. In the discussion of this question, he was disposed to make every reasonable concession, and, indeed, to sacrifice every thing for a union, except the liberties of his country." As far as he was concerned, Smith continued, "the defects of the old confederation needed as little proof as the necessity of

[26] Duer, *Reminscences,* p. 7.

[27] Kent, ed., *Memoirs of James Kent,* p. 306.

[28] John Jay to George Washington, [30] June 1788, H. P. Johnston, ed., *The Correspondence and Public Papers of John Jay* (New York, 1891), III, 346.

a union." Yet that in itself was no argument for adopting the proposed Constitution. "Defective as the old Confederation is, he said, no one could deny but it was possible we might have a worse government. But the question was not whether the present Confederation be a bad one, but whether the proposed Constitution be a good one." [29]

When Hamilton took the floor, he objected to the dismissal of Chancellor Livingston's long oration on the necessity of the Union as irrelevant to the subject under discussion. "I will not agree with gentlemen who trifle with the weaknesses of our country, and suppose they are enumerated to answer a party purpose, and to terrify with ideal dangers. No. I believe these weaknesses to be real, and pregnant with destruction." [30] Then Hamilton entered into what Governor Clinton described as "a second Edition of Publius well delivered." [31] Hamilton was quite unable to accept the fact that the Antifederalists honestly and sincerely favored the preservation and strengthening of the central government, although almost every Antifederalist speaker made a point of affirming a deep devotion to the federal Union. On Saturday, 21 June, Hamilton so badly misconstrued some of Clinton's remarks that the governor protested. "The gentleman has attempted to give an unjust and unnatural coloring to my observations. I am really at a loss to determine whence he draws his inference. I declare that the dissolution of the Union is, of all events, the remotest from my wishes. That gentleman may wish for a consolidated, I wish for a federal republic. The object of both of us is a firm, energetic government; and we may both have the good of our country in view, though we disagree as to the means of procuring it." [32] But Hamilton could never conceive of George Clinton being concerned for the good of his country, and so he continued "repeating over Parts of

[29] Elliot, ed., *Debates*, II, 223, 224. [30] *Ibid.*, 230.

[31] George Clinton to John Lamb, 21 June 1788, John Lamb Papers, New-York Historical Society.

[32] Elliot, ed., *Debates*, II, 263.

Publius" [33] to the convention, annoying his opponents rather than converting them.

A pleasing contrast to Hamilton's polished but irrelevant orations was the single recorded speech that John Jay made during the formal debate, in which he expressed pleasure at the general agreement "that a strong, energetic federal government is necessary for the United States." Jay had given a more sympathetic hearing to the Antifederalists than had Hamilton, and he dwelt on the points of accord. In contrast to Hamilton and Livingston, who enjoyed twisting the remarks of the opposition whenever an ill-phrased comment gave them the opportunity, Jay politely turned to Melancton Smith to ask whether he was stating his views properly.[34] A spectator wrote that Jay had "the most peculiar knack of expressing himself I ever heard. Fancy, passion, in short everything that makes an orator, he is a stranger to; and yet none who hear but are pleased with him, and captivated beyond expression." [35]

The other Federalist speakers were neither pleasing nor captivating. Although the audience found them entertaining and those who supported the Constitution were delighted by the embarrassment that the unskilled speakers on the Antifederalist side suffered at the hands of the men from the City, the men whose words were twisted and who winced under the cleverness of their opponents were not put in a frame of mind favorable to the Federalist cause. Whenever a question was put to the house, the Antifederalists continued to vote in a bloc.

The formal debate lasted until 2 July, when the Federalists had received news of ratification by both New Hampshire and Virginia. Then they suddenly halted their oratory and bent their efforts to employing these new developments as levers to force a ratification on their terms. It was not until that point that the convention began to make serious progress. The debate was

[33] George Clinton to John Lamb, [27?] June 1788, John Lamb Papers, New-York Historical Society.

[34] Elliot, ed., *Debates*, II, 282. [35] *Daily Advertiser*, 28 June 1788.

brilliant, but it had achieved nothing. On the last day of June a writer in the *Country Journal* reported, "Upon the whole I believe, that in no state in America has the new constitution been fairer canvassed, abler defended, more powerfully opposed. What will be the result I dare not divine." [36]

[36] *Country Journal*, 31 June 1788 [*sic*].

XV

Collapse of the Old Roof

THE Antifederalist position grew weaker with each new state that ratified the Constitution. Once nine states had accepted the new instrument, the old Confederation would automatically be dissolved, and the Antifederalists would have to choose between ratifying the Constitution as it stood or running the risk of being left out of the Union. In order to avoid this unpalatable dilemma, the Antifederalists ought to have sought the support of sympathizers in other states early in the campaign. The Federalists recognized the need to organize across state lines, and all of the prominent Federalists in the Confederation kept up political correspondences with the like-minded in other states. The Antifederalists were, by contrast, extraordinarily tardy. Although John Lamb was suspected of sending copies of "Centinel" and the "Federal Farmer" to Connecticut in December of 1787,[1] most of the pieces arriving in that state fell into the hands of Federalists,[2] and had obviously not been distributed according to an Antifederalist master plan. There is no evidence that New

[1] *Daily Advertiser* (New York), 5 December 1787; *ibid.*, 19 December 1787; Hugh Ledlie to John Lamb, 15 January 1788, John Lamb Papers, New-York Historical Society.

[2] *Daily Advertiser*, 4 December 1787; Hugh Ledlie to John Lamb, 15 January 1788, John Lamb Papers, New-York Historical Society.

York Antifederalists attempted to establish a connection outside their own state until the middle of May 1788, after seven states had already ratified the Constitution.

In May, letters signed by John Lamb "in behalf of the federal Republican Committee" were sent to North Carolina, New Hampshire, Virginia, South Carolina, and Maryland.[3] Maryland had already ratified before the letter was sent, but it was probably hoped that the Maryland Antifederalists would support a movement for a second convention. The letter to Peabody of New Hampshire was typical of the lot. It mentions that copies of the "Federal Farmer" are enclosed, and continues:

> While we see in common with our Brethren of the other States, the Necessity of making alterations in our present existing federal Government: We cannot but apprehend that the one proposed in its room, contains in it principles dangerous to public Liberty and Safety. . . . We are anxious to form a Union with our Friends in other States, and to manifest to the Continent, and to the World, that our Opposition to this Constitution does not arise from an impatience under the restraint of good government, from local or state attachments, from interested motives, or party Spirit—But from the purer sentiments of the love of Liberty, an Attachment to republican Principles, and an adherence to those Ideas which prevailed at the commencement of the late revolution.[4]

Replies came back to New York City in June and July, approving the sentiments expressed by the Federal Republican Committee. Only in Virginia and North Carolina, however, did the materials forwarded by the Committee arrive before the state had ratified the Constitution.[5]

Early in June, the Federal Republican Committee wrote letters to the Antifederalists of New Hampshire and Virginia in-

[3] John Lamb Papers, box 5, New-York Historical Society.

[4] John Lamb to Nathaniel Peabody, 18 May 1788, John Lamb Papers, New-York Historical Society.

[5] Aedanus Burke to John Lamb, 23 June 1788; Joshua Atherton to John Lamb, 23 June 1788, *ibid.*

forming them of the sweeping Antifederalist victory in New York State and requesting that they "take measures to bring about a communication between your Convention and ours on the subject of amendments." Melancton Smith, who wrote these letters, was optimistic that cooperation among the Antifederalist groups in the three states would make amendment of the Constitution certain. "There cannot be a doubt," he wrote, "but that the necessary alterations can be effected, and all the apprehensions of danger from the new government removed, if your State and ours could unite in sentiments respecting amendments, and act in concert in measures to bring them about." [6]

The state of New Hampshire ratified the Constitution before there was any opportunity to begin a correspondence with the Antifederalists of New York. Communication between New York and New Hampshire was poor. It was not safe to travel through the rebellious New Hampshire Grants, and letters were frequently lost or otherwise delayed even when sent through Massachusetts. Early in June an Albany Antifederalist speculated on the possibility of making special arrangements for informing the "Republicans" in New Hampshire of the Antifederalist success in the New York election.[7] What arrangements were made, however, were made by the other party.

On 6 June, Alexander Hamilton wrote to John Sullivan, the president of New Hampshire (as the governor was called) and president of the state ratifying convention:

> You will no doubt have understood that the Antifederal party has prevailed in this State by a large majority. It is therefore of the utmost importance that all external circumstances should be made use of to influence their conduct. This will suggest to you the *great advantage* of a speedy decision in your State, if you can be sure of the question, and a prompt communication of the event to

[6] [Melancton Smith], Draft letters to New Hampshire and Virginia, 6 June 1788, *ibid.*

[7] Abraham G. Lansing to Abraham Yates, 1 June 1788, Abraham Yates, Jr., Papers, New York Public Library.

us. With this in view, permit me to request that the instant you have taken a decisive vote in favor of the Constitution, you send an express to me at Poughkeepsie. Let him take the *shortest route* to that place, change horses on the road, and use all possible diligence. I shall with pleasure defray all expenses, and give a liberal reward to the person.[8]

Four days later, Rufus King, in Boston, made arrangements with John Langdon in New Hampshire to send the information of the New Hampshire ratification to Poughkeepsie. He specified that the rider should travel cross-country to Springfield in Massachusetts where Henry Knox had made arrangements with a rider to have the news sent on to Hamilton at Poughkeepsie.[9] By this means, the fastest mode of communication that human ingenuity could devise, it was hoped that news from the New Hampshire convention at Concord would reach Poughkeepsie within forty hours.[10]

Actually, it took the express riders three days to bring Hamilton the letter he had been anxiously anticipating. John Langdon scratched a note and dispatched it as quickly as he could manage: "I have the great pleasure and satisfaction of informing you that this State, has this day Adopted the federal Constitution; this al-important Question, was Carried by a Majority of Eleven 57 Yeas 46 Nays. Excuse hast;" [11] and the rider was on his way.

On the afternoon of 25 June, Abraham Yates was seated at his mahogany desk in the Congress Chamber in New York City

[8] Alexander Hamilton to John Sullivan, 6 June 1788, Harold C. Syrett, ed., and Jacob E. Cooke, assoc. ed., *The Papers of Alexander Hamilton* (New York, 1961–), V, 2.

[9] Rufus King to John Langdon, 10 June 1788, Charles A. King, *Life and Correspondence of Rufus King,* (New York, 1894), I, 331; Rufus King to Alexander Hamilton, 12 June 1788, Syrett, ed., *Papers of Alexander Hamilton,* V, 5.

[10] Hugh Williamson to John Gray Blount, 3 June 1788, Edmund C. Burnett, ed., *Letters of Members of the Continental Congress* (Washington, 1921–1936), VIII, 747.

[11] John Langdon to Alexander Hamilton, 21 June 1788, Syrett, ed., *Papers of Alexander Hamilton,* V, 34.

writing letters, when the news was brought in that New Hampshire had ratified the new Constitution. The affairs of the old Confederation suddenly became uninteresting. The news, Yates reported, "bread such an inattention to the Business[,] the Southern Members to write letters to Verginia . . . and Others talking the Matter over (it being the Ninth State) that we adjourned." Members from other states clustered around Yates and asked what effect the news would have on the New York convention. What would the men at Poughkeepsie do now? Yates calmly replied that they would do "the same they would have done if New Hampshire had not adopted it[.] they will adopt but I hoped not without previous amendments—That my mind was made up, that if all the twelve States were to come in that New York ought not and I trusted they would not." While he reported this conversation to his friends in Albany, the City bells began to ring,[12] and the joyful clangor continued for five hours.[13]

In the Poughkeepsie Convention, the article of the Constitution dealing with the Senate had been under consideration when the message from Concord arrived. The news was not mentioned on the floor of the convention until the following day when Chancellor Livingston prefaced his remarks on the Senate with a few offensive words:

> It would not, perhaps, be altogether impertinent to remind the committee, that, since the intelligence of yesterday, it had become evident that the circumstances of the country were greatly altered, and the ground of the present debate changed. . . . He presumed the Convention would consider the situation of their country. He supposed, however, that some might contemplate disunion without pain.[14]

[12] Abraham Yates to Abraham G. Lansing, 25 June 1788, Abraham Yates, Jr., Papers, New York Public Library.

[13] *New-York Journal*, 26 June 1788.

[14] Jonathan Elliot, ed., *The Debates in the Several State Conventions on the Adoption of the Federal Constitution* (Philadelphia, 1876), II, 322.

Melancton Smith, who spoke next, passed lightly over the Chancellor's remarks, merely observing that "with respect to the change of circumstances which had such a solemn effect upon the honorable gentleman, he confessed it had not altered his feelings or wishes on the subject. He had long been convinced that nine states would receive the Constitution." [15]

But John Lansing rose to answer the taunt. He spoke emphatically and with some heat:

> Mr. Chairman, I do not rise to speak to the paragraph under consideration, but to make some remarks on the sentiments of the honorable gentleman from New York, respecting the change in our situation. That our particular circumstances are in fact altered since yesterday, I cannot agree . . . I presume I shall not be charged with rashness, if I continue to insist that it is still our duty to maintain our rights.

Understandably, Lansing was outraged that Livingston still slurred the patriotism of the Antifederalists by questioning their devotion to the Union. "It has been said that some might contemplate disunion without terror," he said. "I have heard no sentiment from any gentleman that can warrant such an insinuation. . . . The suggestion first came from the other side of the house. It was nothing more than a false construction of our argument." "Sir," he continued, "I know not any gentleman who wishes for a dissolution of the Union. I make this remark because an idea has been circulated that there are certain persons in this body who are disposed to dissolve the Union, which I am persuaded is utterly false." [16]

Since the Antifederalists had every intention of ratifying the Constitution and coming into the new Union, the news that the ninth state had ratified did not upset them. They still saw no barrier to ratifying the document on their own terms—with previous amendments. Moreover, they were still hopeful that the powerful state of Virginia would insist on coming in with

[15] Elliot, ed., *Debates*, II, 324.

[16] *Ibid.*, 324, 325.

the same reservations. The Antifederalists at Poughkeepsie radiated confidence. "I steal this Moment while the Convention is in Committee and the little Great Man employed in repeating over Parts of Publius to us, to drop you a line," Governor Clinton wrote to John Lamb while Hamilton held the floor. "The News from New Hampshire has not had the least Effect on our Friends at this Place." [17] Other members agreed with the governor that the information that New Hampshire had erected the ninth pillar, which the Federalists had gone to such pains and expense to bring promptly to Poughkeepsie, had had no effect on the men who had come to the convention determined to ratify with previous amendments. "Among our Friends," an Anti delegate wrote, "I observe no change in the countenance, the opinion or the resolution of any." [18]

Meanwhile, Virginia, too, had ratified the Constitution. The tenth state ratified on the very day that Robert Yates directed a letter on behalf of the Antifederalists at Poughkeepsie to the Antifederalists in the Virginia Convention.[19] He posted it on 25 June 1788; it was another letter sent too late. The slowness and uncertainty of communication with the state of Virginia worked to the disadvantage of the Antifederalists throughout the ratification campaign. Antifederalism was strong in both states with support from prominent, capable men as well as from the bulk of the population. Both states were so situated in the Union that confederation without them was inconceivable, since they broke the remaining territory into three disjoined chunks. Effective cooperation between the Antifederalists of the two states would have enabled them to force the acceptance of any form of ratifi-

[17] George Clinton to John Lamb [27?] June 1788, John Lamb Papers, New-York Historical Society.

[18] Christopher P. Yates, Jr., to Abraham Yates, 27 June 1788, Abraham Yates, Jr., Papers, New-York Public Library. Cf. Henry Oothoudt to Abraham Yates, 27 June 1788; Abraham Yates to George Clinton, 27 June 1788; George Clinton to Abraham Yates, 28 June 1788, *ibid.*

[19] Robert Yates to George Mason, 25 June 1788, Emmet Collection, #9528, New York Public Library.

cation they chose to adopt. But a series of remarkable coincidences prevented cooperation between the previous-amendment men of the two states.

The unusually poor mail service during 1788 and the delayed organization of the New York Federal Republican Committee frustrated the formation of an unofficial liason between Antifederalists of New York and Virginia. A letter sent from New York City in May did not reach Richard Henry Lee in Virginia until 27 June.[20] The Virginia Convention had been in session a week when some pamphlets and letters from the New York Antifederalists were brought to the Antifederalists at Richmond by Eleazer Oswald, editor of the Philadelphia *Independent Gazeteer*.[21] The material came too late to influence the Virginia election and too early to have included either definite information of the Antifederalist victory in New York or a draft of the amendments favored by the New York Antifederalists.[22] Oswald did not remain in Richmond very long, and his brief conferences with Patrick Henry and George Mason [23] were no substitute for direct communication between Antifederalist leaders of New York and Virginia.

The attempts to form an official connection between the Antifederalist legislatures and conventions of the two states also failed. On 30 November 1787, George Mason and Patrick Henry supported a resolution in the Virginia legislature inviting the other states to confer on previous amendments to the Consti-

[20] Richard Henry Lee to [John Lamb], 27 June 1788, John Lamb Papers, New-York Historical Society.

[21] Kate Mason Rowland, *The Life of George Mason* (New York, 1892), II, 233.

[22] Oswald probably arrived in Richmond on 7 June (*ibid*). The results of New York's election were not known until 5 June and the proposed amendments were sent to Virginia on 25 June (Robert Yates to George Mason, 25 June 1788, Emmet Collection, #9528, New York Public Library).

[23] James Madison to George Washington, 13 June 1788, Gaillard Hunt, ed., *Writings of James Madison, Comprising His Public Papers and His Private Correspondence* (New York, 1900–1910), V, 179.

tution. Governor Randolph sent copies of the resolution to the governors of the other states on 27 December 1787, requesting that it "be submitted to the Legislature of your State." [24] By some mischance the letter addressed to Governor Clinton did not reach its destination until 7 March 1788, a delay of two months and eleven days. When it reached New York, the state legislature had already adjourned and could not consider Virginia's invitation. Clinton, however, wrote an unofficial reply, which was forwarded to Governor Randolph on 8 May. Clinton explained that he had no directions from the legislature, but that he believed that the New York Convention would, "with great cordiality, hold a communication with any sister State on the important subject, and especially with one so respectable in point of importance, ability, and patriotism as Virginia." He presumed that the overtures would come from the Virginia Convention, since it would begin its meetings several weeks before the New York Convention.[25]

The Virginia Convention, however, made no overtures, since they knew nothing of Clinton's letter until the day after they had ratified the Constitution. Governor Randolph called a special session of the legislature to meet on 23 June, two days before the state ratified, and Clinton's letter was among the papers that were sent in on the first day. But the legislature could not assemble a quorum. Patrick Henry, the greatest orator in America, held the floor in the ratifying convention, and the legislators abandoned their chamber to witness the performance.[26]

Henry no longer presented the fine figure of his earlier years when his eloquence had stirred the Virginia House of Burgesses. At fifty-three his shoulders sagged, his weak vision forced him

[24] Edward P. Smith, "The Movement for a Second Convention in 1788," in J. Franklin Jameson, ed., *Essays in the Constitutional History of the United States in the Formative Period, 1775–1789* (Boston, 1889), pp. 60, 61; Moncure Daniel Conway, *Omitted Chapters of History Disclosed in the Life and Papers of Edmund Randolph*, (2nd ed., New York, 1889), p. 110.

[25] Conway, *Omitted Chapters*, p. 111. [26] *Ibid.*

to wear spectacles, and his bald head was covered by a brown wig. When debate grew heated the aging orator would slap his hand to his head and twirl his wig about.[27] Yet while he had lost his physical attractiveness, Henry retained all of his oratorical powers, and his orations at the Richmond ratifying convention have been called the finest of his career.[28] When he spoke for the Antifederalists, his opponents felt his eloquence to be a real threat to ratification. "I fear that overwhelming torrent, Patrick Henry," wrote Henry Knox. "I would it were well over and the parchment lodged in the Secretary's office." [29]

On 24 June, while Clinton's letter waited the attention of the absent legislators, Henry wove his spell in the convention hall. He spoke of the threat to liberty in the new Constitution:

> I see the awful immensity of the dangers with which it is pregnant. I see it. I feel it. I see beings of a higher order anxious concerning our decision. When I see beyond the horizon that bounds human vision, and look at the final consummation of all things, and see those intelligent beings which inhabit the ethereal mansions reviewing the political decisions and resolutions which, in the progress of time, will happen in America, and the consequent happiness or misery of mankind, I am led to believe that much of the account, on one side or the other, will depend on what we now decide.[30]

At this point the sky suddenly darkened and a summer thunder storm added its voice to Henry's. The doors of the hall slammed shut, the windows rattled, and lightning and thunder accompanied the powerful voice of the orator. The audience was stunned, and men leaped from their seats. As Henry concluded, the sun returned, and the storm passed.[31] Despite this magnificent display, Henry's party lost the final vote the following day.

[27] Hugh Blair Grigsby, *History of the Virginia Federal Convention* (Richmond, 1890–1891), I, 76, 76n.

[28] *Ibid.*, p. 76.

[29] Henry Knox to Rufus King, 19 June 1788, King, *Life and Correspondence of Rufus King*, I, 335.

[30] Elliot, ed., *Debates*, III, 625.

[31] Grigsby, *History of the Virginia Federal Convention*, I, 316, 317.

Clinton's letter, hinting of help from New York, was not read to the Virginia legislature until the day after that, much to the disgust of the Antifederalists.

Early on the morning of 2 July 1788, the same gentleman who had ridden express from Poughkeepsie with the news of New Hampshire's ratification a week earlier[32] galloped into New York City from the other direction with the news that Virginia, too, had come into the new Union. The rider, Colonel Henley, had been on his way to Richmond with the information that New Hampshire had ratified, when he met an express coming in the opposite direction carrying the announcement of Virginia's action. He immediately turned about "to bring the tidings to the anxious expectants in New York." It was three in the morning when he arrived in the City and no one slept much later. The bells were set to ringing at once and did not stop for four hours, and at sunrise a salute of ten twenty-four pounders was fired in honor of the ten states that had ratified the new Constitution.[33]

As soon as he could saddle a horse, William Livingston set out along the main post road for Poughkeepsie with the packet that Henley had brought from Virginia.[34] He arrived about noon the same day, in a little more than nine hours.[35] He galloped up to the court house on his sweating bay horse, threw the reins into the hands of a boy standing outside, and handed his precious

[32] *New-York Journal*, 26 June 1788.

[33] *New-York Journal*, 3 July 1788; S. B. Webb to Joseph Barrell, [2] July 1788, W. C. Ford, ed., *Correspondence and Journals of Samuel Blanchley Webb* (New York, 1893–1894), III, 109; S. B. Webb to Catherine Hogeborn, 2 July 1788, *ibid.*, 110.

[34] *New-York Journal*, 3 July 1788.

[35] *New-York Morning Post*, 9 July 1788; De Witt Clinton to Charles Tillinghast, 2 July 1788, De Witt Clinton Papers, Special Collection, Columbia University; Benson J. Lossing's interview with eye-witness, *Poughkeepsie Daily Eagle*, 18 February 1888, quoted in Edmund Platt, *The Eagle's History of Poughkeepsie* (Poughkeepsie, N.Y., 1905), p. 59. The *Country Journal* (Poughkeepsie) probably made a typographical error when it reported the time as seven-and-a-half hours (8 July 1788).

packet to the doorkeeper of the convention.[36] Inside the court house, Governor Clinton had the floor, but when Colonel Livingston made his appearance at the door with the news of Virginia's ratification, there was "such a buz though the House, that little of his Excellency's Speech was heard." [37] The Federalists who were present cheered, and a crowd gathered outside formed a procession and marched around the building several times to the music of a fife and drum.[38]

Within a few hours the elation of the Federalists faded as they observed with horror that the Antis were wholly unaffected by the news from Virginia and continued to debate clauses and propose amendments as calmly as if nothing had occurred.[39] The failure of the Virginia Antifederalists to adopt conditional amendments had been anticipated by the New York party,[40] and the majority still intended to demand previous amendments in New York's ratification. After all, the votes in the Virginia convention had been very evenly balanced, while the New York Antifederalists had an enormous majority.

One of the Federalist delegates, overwhelmed by disappointment, wrote to New York City the following day, "We fondly (but in vain) expected that the ratification of Virginia would have a very serious effect on the minds of the antifederal party, and would have constituted so forcible an appeal to their apprehensions, that it would have compelled them to adopt a system different from that destructive one they seem intent on pur-

[36] Benson J. Lossing's interview with eye-witness, *Poughkeepsie Daily Eagle*, 18 February 1888, quoted in Platt, *Eagle's History of Poughkeepsie*, p. 59.

[37] *New-York Morning Post*, 9 July 1788.

[38] Benson J. Lossing's interview with an eye-witness, *Poughkeepsie Daily Eagle*, 18 February 1888, quoted in Platt, *Eagle's History of Poughkeepsie*, p. 59.

[39] De Witt Clinton to Charles Tillinghast, 2 July 1788, De Witt Clinton Papers, Special Collections, Columbia University; Nathaniel Lawrence to John Lamb, 3 July 1788, John Lamb Papers, New-York Historical Society.

[40] Robert Yates to George Mason, 25 June 1788, Emmet Collection, #9528, New York Public Library.

suing." Since the Federalists had found "the powers of eloquence and argument are unavailing," they would "refrain from any further exertions in defence of the Constitution." [41] Formal debate ended on 2 July, the day the news of Virginia's ratification was received. The Federalists stopped displaying their cleverness and began to negotiate with their opponents. But before they could do that, they had to learn precisely what it was that the Antifederalists wanted.

During the afternoon of 2 July and during the sessions of 3 July, the Antifederalists observed with curiosity the "somewhat singular" silence of the usually loquacious Federalists.[42] "The information from Virginia seems to have no effect on *us*," Nathaniel Lawrence wrote to John Lamb, "tho' it has on the other party which they have discovered to day by changing their plan of defence. You have heard no doubt that they have disputed every inch of ground but to day they have quietly suffered us to propose our amendments without a word in opposition to them. What their object is I know not." [43]

There was no concealed object to the new Federalist tactic. The party was astonished and confused when ratification by ten states failed to create a schism in the Antifederalist ranks. Now they had no reason to delay action by the convention, so they allowed the majority to move as quickly as it chose. "We now permit our opponents to go on with their objections and propose their amendments without interruption," Issac Roosevelt wrote. "When they have gone through we may more fully learn their intentions." [44]

[41] *Daily Advertiser*, 7 July 1788.

[42] De Witt Clinton to Charles Tillinghast, 2 July 1788, De Witt Clinton Papers, Special Collections, Columbia University.

[43] Nathaniel Lawrence to John Lamb, 3 July 1788, John Lamb Papers, New-York Historical Society.

[44] Issac Roosevelt to Richard Varick, 5 July 1788, quoted in Platt, *Eagle's History of Poughkeepsie*, p. 59.

XVI

Progress at Poughkeepsie

ON 4 July 1788, the twelfth anniversary of American independence, the Poughkeepsie Convention recessed while delegates and visitors forgot their current divisions and joined to celebrate the occasion. Both Federalists and Antifederalists gave dinners, and members of both parties mingled at the tables and drank the same toasts simultaneously, the proper moment for draining the glass being "communicated by the sound of drum and accompanied by the discharge of cannon." [1] After the Fourth of July recess, the atmosphere at the convention changed. A gentleman who left the village a few days later reported to the men of New York City that "the spirit of warm contention had in great measure subsided between the parties in Convention, and that cool reasoning instead of angry debate had taken place in that honorable body, and that matters were likely to take a *favorable turn*." [2]

Once the Federalists had decided to allow the majority to proceed to whatever object it had in mind, the Antifederalists

[1] John Jay to Mrs. Jay, 5 July 1788, H. P. Johnston, ed., *Correspondence and Public Papers of John Jay* (New York, 1891), III, 347, 348; *Daily Advertiser* (New York), 9 July 1788; *Country Journal* (Poughkeepsie), 8 July 1788.

[2] *New-York Packet,* 8 July 1788.

made rapid progress through their amendments and began to consider the precise form that ratification should take. The issue became the dull one of legal phraseology, and the lively debates of the previous weeks were followed by what James Madison described as "a very tedious discussion." [3] Francis Childs, possibly believing that the debate would be of scant interest to his readers, stopped making short-hand notes of the speeches after 2 July and reported only summaries of the daily proceedings. But while the discussion during the last three weeks of the Poughkeepsie Convention makes difficult reading, it was through the day-to-day debate of technical questions that the delegates at Poughkeepsie finally worked out a form of ratification that could command a majority vote. The form of ratification—not the question of ratification itself or even of the content of amendments—became the crucial issue in the New York convention.

The Federalists soon discovered that when the Antifederalists were left to pursue their own purposes, they displayed far less hostility toward the Constitution. One Federalist visitor to the convention observed that "since the news from Virginia, notwithstanding the proposition of amendments . . . there appears to be a disposition in the opposition rather friendly to the Constitution." [4] The Antifederalists began to speak of the excellence that the proposed government would possess once it had been properly reformed. After listening for a day while the Antis proposed amendments one after another, a Federalist observer wrote with a sneer, "They have just finished their amendments, which, if inserted, these wise antifederalists think will render it very nearly a perfect system." [5]

[3] James Madison, Jr., to Col. James Madison, 27 July 1788, United States Bureau of Rolls and Library, *Documentary History of the Constitution of the United States* (Washington, 1894–1903), IV, 821.

[4] *Daily Advertiser* 9 July 1788.

[5] David S. Bogart to S. B. Webb, 8 [July] 1788, W. C. Ford, ed., *Correspondence and Journals of Samuel Blanchley Webb* (New York, 1893–1894), III, 103.

The last amendments were proposed on Monday, 7 July. There were fifty-five of them altogether.[6] The problem now was how to write the amendments into the ratification, and that question was the subject of a number of meetings held by the Antifederalists during the following week.[7] All of the Antifederalists agreed that amendments must be made a condition of ratification, but they were not altogether agreed whether they should be a previous or a subsequent condition. Should New York declare that she would not come into the Union until after the amendments had been acted on, or should she come in at once while stipulating that the amendments must be considered within a specified time and reserving the right to withdraw from the Union if the condition was not met?[8] The disagreement on this question among the Antifederalists did not reflect a difference of opinion on the propriety of ratifying the Constitution or on the value of the various amendments proposed. Indeed, the division was essentially insignificant, for the unity of the Antifederalists in regard to the ultimate ends desired was unbroken. Nevertheless, the appearance of a split of any sort in the ranks of the majority party was viewed as a hopeful sign by the Federalists, and it alarmed Antis outside the Convention.[9]

On Tuesday and Wednesday, the eighth and ninth of July, the convention met and adjourned without doing any business in order to give the Antifederalists time to decide on the form of ratification they would introduce.[10] By Thursday, the majority had agreed, and John Lansing introduced the list of amendments arranged under three headings: explanatory, conditional, and

[6] See Appendix B. [7] *Daily Advertiser,* 16 July 1788.

[8] John Jay to George Washington, 8 July 1788, *Documentary History,* IV, 467; Alexander Hamilton to James Madison, 8 July 1788, Harold C. Syrett, ed., and Jacob E. Cooke, assoc. ed., *The Papers of Alexander Hamilton* (New York, 1961–), V, 147.

[9] John Jay to George Washington, 8 July 1788, *Documentary History,* IV, 467; Abraham G. Lansing to Abraham Yates, 9 July 1788, Abraham Yates, Jr., Papers, New York Public Library.

[10] *Daily Advertiser,* 15 July 1788.

recommendatory. Then he proposed that an informal committee composed of members of both parties be appointed "to make such an accomodation, and so to arrange the amendments as to bring the business to a quick and friendly decision." [11]

Fourteen men, seven Federalists and seven Antifederalists, were appointed to the informal committee. Robert Yates, John Lansing, Melancton Smith, Thomas Tredwell, John Haring, Samuel Jones, and Gilbert Livingston were the Antifederalist representatives, while the Federalists sent John Jay, James Duane, Richard Morris, John Sloss Hobart, Gozen Ryerss, Peter Lefferts, and Richard Hatfield.[12] Significantly, Alexander Hamilton and R. R. Livingston did not attend the meetings of the informal committee. These men had made themselves so obnoxious during the debate that they would have been liabilities in a situation that called for conciliation. The Federalists wisely selected John Jay to direct their strategy in the new phase of persuasive activity. Jay had spoken infrequently during the formal debate, and when he had spoken he had shown a flattering courtesy toward his opponents that contrasted sharply with the sneering sarcasm that marked some of his colleagues.

Nevertheless, the informal committee failed to achieve a compromise since Jay insisted that the Federalists could never agree to any form of ratification that included the word "condition." [13] The Antifederalists, on the other hand, considered the proposition presented by Lansing, by which only the most important amendments were labeled conditional, to be "the ne plus ultra" of their concession. The party had united on the Lansing plan with some difficulty, and De Witt Clinton remarked that "if the feds had been friendly instead of being inimical to the proposal I have no doubts whether a majority of antis would not have voted against it." The rigidity of the Federalists, however, assured the unity of the Antifederalists. "The opposition of their political adversaries has reconciled them," wrote De Witt Clinton. He believed that any danger of division in the majority

[11] *Ibid.* [12] *Ibid.* [13] *Ibid.*

party was over, and that all Antifederalists were united in support of the Lansing plan.[14]

Despite its failure to agree on a compromise, the informal committee dissolved on a friendly note. Although some of the Antifederalists were angered by Jay's insistence that no conditions would be accepted, Melancton Smith and Samuel Jones were said to have "discovered a disposition somewhat moderate." [15] Another Federalist reported that the Antifederalists "seem to have been influenced by our arguments, but they are too proud to confess it." [16]

On the following day, Friday, 11 July, John Jay moved two resolutions on the floor of the convention:

Resolved, as the opinion of this committee, that the Constitution under consideration ought to be *ratified* by this Convention.
Resolved, further, as the opinion of this committee, that such parts of the said Constitution as may be thought doubtful ought to be explained, and that whatever amendment may be deemed useful, or expedient, ought to be recommended.[17]

Thus, the Federalists agreed to Lansing's explanatory and recommendatory amendments, but refused to approve the conditional. For several days the Convention debated the propriety of conditional amendments. The Federalists argued that Congress would not accept New York into the new Union if the state ratified conditionally, while the Antifederalists insisted that the state would be accepted.

John Jay argued that Congress had no power to accept New York on special terms and pointed out that the other states had ratified unconditionally. Furthermore, if New York decided to withhold ratification until amendments were considered, the state might be out of the Union for as long as two years and

[14] De Witt Clinton to [Charles Tillinghast], 12 July 1788, De Witt Clinton Papers, Special Collections, Columbia University.

[15] *Daily Advertiser*, 15 July 1788. [16] *Ibid.*, 14 July 1788.

[17] Jonathan Elliot, ed., *The Debates in the Several State Conventions on the Adoption of the Federal Constitution* (Philadelphia, 1876), II, 410.

would have no part in organizing the new government. "These are not threats," he said. "This is prudence." [18] He begged the majority to agree to a form of ratification similar to that used by other states. "Let us join with our Neighbors to obtain the same Ends in the same Way," he said. "Let us agree and be unanimous. . . . We will have our Constitution you will have your A[men]dments." [19] R. R. Livingston and Richard Morris seconded Jay's arguments,[20] while John Lansing, Governor Clinton, and Melancton Smith took the floor to oppose Jay's resolutions. Smith criticized the Federalists for speaking of compromise and then talking as if "nothing can be done but *Adopt* or *reject* the Constitution." The arguments the Federalists advanced, he complained, went "only to Shew the evil Tendency of Rejecting the Constitution," and a conditional ratification was not a rejection.[21]

"The business of the Convention is now wound up to a Crisis," [22] De Witt Clinton wrote after the sessions of Saturday, 12 July. The Antifederalists were ready to vote, and unless the final vote could be put off, they would pass a form of conditional ratification over the opposition of the nineteen Federalist delegates. Still, the Antifederalists disliked the prospect of overwhelming the minority by force of numbers, and during the following week the Federalists managed to persuade them to delay the final vote from day to day. On Tuesday, 15 July, the Federalists made a fresh effort to reach a compromise. Hamilton read a form of ratification including amendments and declared that the Federalists "were ready to go as far as they thought safe in recommendatory and explanitory Amend [ments]s," and that he and the other Federalist delegates were willing to pledge themselves to obtain them once the new government was estab-

[18] [11] July 1788, John McKesson Papers, New-York Historical Society.

[19] *Ibid.* [20] Elliot, ed., *Debates*, II, 411.

[21] Reports of the Poughkeepsie Convention, [12] July 1788, John McKesson Papers, New-York Historical Society.

[22] De Witt Clinton to [Charles Tillinghast], 12 July 1788, De Witt Clinton Papers, Special Collection, Columbia University.

lished.[23] Then Jay stood up and begged the Antifederalists to be patient a little longer. "Cannot the Conditional Amendments be paired [*sic*] down so that we may agree," he asked. "We honestly think Congress must reject such an Adoption." The Antifederalists had made concessions, now the Federalists had made a concession. The parties might yet agree.[24] "Each appear to have a disposition to advance—had we not better wait, and endeavor to meet." [25]

By way of further concession, Melancton Smith introduced an amendment to Jay's resolution. He observed that if the Federalists were correct in believing that Congress would not accept New York's ratification in the form proposed by Lansing on 10 July, it was clearly necessary for the Antifederalists to offer another plan. Smith's amendment to Jay's resolution began, "*Resolved,* as the opinion of this committee, that the Constutition under consideration ought to be ratified by this Convention: *upon condition, nevertheless,* That until a convention shall be called and convened for proposing amendments to the said Constitution. . . ." Then the amendment provided that certain powers of the new Congress would be temporarily restricted: the power to send the militia out of the state for more than six weeks, the power to alter the place and time of elections, the power to lay excises, and the power to lay direct taxes.[26]

To the Antifederalists, the Smith amendment appeared an enormous concession. But to the Federalists, the concession did not seem great enough. The word "condition" was still there. On Wednesday, 16 July, they made another attempt to delay taking the final question by introducing a motion to adjourn the convention until the beginning of September. The motion was

[23] Gilbert Livingston Reports of the Poughkeepsie Convention, 13 July 1788, New York Public Library.

[24] Reports of the Poughkeepsie Convention, 15 July 1788, John McKesson Papers, New-York Historical Society.

[25] Gilbert Livingston Reports of the Poughkeepsie Convention, 15 July 1788, New York Public Library.

[26] Elliot, ed., *Debates,* II, 411.

introduced by John Sloss Hobart, one of the City delegation. He argued that if the delegates went home and consulted with their constituents, the men from New York City "may devise a mode to meet their Northern brethren." [27] Or, thought the Antifederalists, there was the more likely possibility that the uncertain position of the state would operate to arouse the public desire for immediate ratification on any terms, resulting in total victory for the Federalists.

The Antifederalists had always feared adjournment for just this reason.[28] In June, Abraham Yates had written, "The principle [*sic*] object the other side have in view is to get an adjournment which I confess is the only apprehension I have For if they can obtain an adjournment the members During that time will be Seperated and open to their management both in the Newspapers—and the state the whole time in Convulsions." [29] When the vote was taken on Hobart's motion, it was defeated forty to twenty-two. Only Samuel Jones, John Schenck, and Jonathan N. Havens voted with the nineteen Federalists.[30] Hobart then admitted that he had introduced the motion merely to delay taking the final question. He still wished something could be proposed that would satisfy both sides.[31]

After the defeat of the Hobart resolution, the question before the house was once again the Jay resolutions of 11 July as they

[27] Gilbert Livingston Reports of the Poughkeepsie Convention, 16 July 1788, New York Public Library.

[28] Curiously enough, the Federalists at one time suspected that the Antifederalists wished an adjournment (John Jay to George Washington, [30] June 1788, John Jay Papers, Monaghan Collection, Columbia University; Philip Schuyler to J. B. Schuyler, 26 June 1788, quoted in Broadus Mitchell, *Alexander Hamilton* [New York, 1957, 1962], I, 438).

[29] Abraham Yates to Abraham G. Lansing, 29 June 1788. Also, Abraham Yates to George Clinton, 27 June 1788; Abraham G. Lansing to Abraham Yates, 20 July 1788, Abraham Yates, Jr., Papers, New York Public Library.

[30] Reports of the Poughkeepsie Convention, 17 July 1788, John McKesson Papers, New-York Historical Society.

[31] Gilbert Livingston Reports of the Poughkeepsie Convention, 17 July 1788, New York Public Library.

had been amended by Smith on 15 July. Governor Clinton delivered a long address urging that this compromise be accepted. The governor declared that if Smith's amendment were not accepted, Jay's resolution calling for unconditional ratification would certainly be voted down. And would not such a vote constitute a rejection of the Constitution? All were agreed that a rejection would be disastrous for New York State. "I entreat Gentlemen to reflect what will be the consequences if this proposal should be rejected and question taken upon the original motion," said Clinton. "We have been told of the necessity there is for a spirit of conciliation and unanimity upon this important point," he continued. "I think the proposition is a reasonable one, that it contains nothing that can give offence or that can prevent its being accepted [by Congress]." The object of Smith's amendment "is barely to prevent the immediate operation of powers the most odious to our Constituents until they have been considered by the people of America to whose decision we declare our willingness to submit." He thought the Antifederalists made the greater concession by agreeing to the Smith amendment. He would vote for it although he had "heard nothing in the Committee to change my opinion of the Constitution," and although he believed his constitutents would not have been willing to concede so much. "I could only be induced to this from a strong attachment to the union," he declared, "from a spirit of conciliation and an earnest desire to promote peace and harmony among the Citizens of the states to forward the interest and happiness of whom I am bound by ties uncommonly strong." [32]

The Federalists remained adamant. They would not accept conditional ratification. A motion was put to postpone consideration of the Smith amendment, but the Antifederalists over-

[32] "Remarks made in the N.Y. State Convention on the question as to the mode in which the State should express its acceptance of the new Constitution" [17 July 1788], George Clinton Papers, New York Public Library.

whelmed it, forty-one to twenty.[33] Still, the Antifederalists did not turn the weight of their numbers against the opposition to crush them on the final vote. Melancton Smith proposed yet another compromise. Smith was convinced that it was senseless to pass a form of ratification that Congress would not accept, and the Federalist certainty that the forms which the Antifederalists had so far proposed would not be accepted, had begun to weigh on him. He now considered it "very doubtful" whether Congress would accept New York under the form of ratification he himself had suggested two days earlier. His aim, however, remained the same as it had been all along: "to propose a mode which would bring us into the Union—next to have our objections considered by a convention." Smith proposed a new plan which he believed "will avoid the objections on both sides." Although he might not be supported by either party, he declared that "duty obliges him to bring them—& risk them." His proposal was to ratify unconditionally but reserving the right to secede from the Union if amendments were not considered by the new government within a specified time.[34]

Smith's sudden desertion of his own amendment took the Antifederalists by surprise, and they were not pleased with his new proposal.[35] They immediately voted to adjourn, hoping to agree among themselves before the following day. That they had failed was obvious as soon as the convention reassembled on the morning of 18 July. Instead of beginning debate or formally proposing that consideration of Smith's amendment to Jay's resolutions be postponed in order to consider the new Smith resolution, there was an extended silence. John Jay observed that the Antifederalists "seemed embarassed—fearful to divide among themselves, and yet many of them very averse to the new

[33] Gilbert Livingston Reports of the Poughkeepsie Convention, 17 July 1788, New York Public Library.

[34] *Ibid.*

[35] John Jay to George Washington, 17 [*sic*] July 1788, *Documentary History*, IV, 799.

Plan." [36] There was very little debate that morning. John Lansing spoke against Smith's new proposal, pointing out that once the new government had been in operation for several years it could not be dissolved, and John Jay spoke encouragingly of the proposition. He thought it was "less evil than the former," and declared that he would "vote for making it the basis—to proceed on." [37] Then the house adjourned. The majority party could do nothing until the division that had suddenly appeared was repaired, and they spent most of the day discussing the problem among themselves.

When the convention met again on Saturday morning, 19 July, the Antifederalists had the situation under control. They had decided temporarily to avoid consideration of the issue that divided them. Lansing proposed instead discussion of the bill of rights and amendments that were to be attached to ratification. So for the next three days the convention occupied itself with a rather desultory review of the Antifederalist revisions. Meanwhile, the essential business of "arranging the amendments" was assigned, at Governor Clinton's suggestion, to a new informal committee of four: Harison and Duane representing the Federalists and Yates and Smith the Antis.[38]

All of this parliamentary maneuvering was highly bewildering to observers. "What will become of all these propositions I cannot determine," wrote De Witt Clinton after attempting to follow the action for a week. "The political ship is so frequently overcast and so variable that I am oftentimes at a loss what to think or what to say." [39] Said another reporter, "We cannot discover the least feature in these momentous debates by which

[36] *Ibid.*

[37] Gilbert Livingston Reports of the Poughkeepsie Convention, 18 July 1788, New York Public Library.

[38] *Country Journal,* 22 July 1788; Gilbert Livingston Reports of the Poughkeepsie Convention, 19 July 1788; New York Public Library.

[39] De Witt Clinton to Charles Tillinghast, 28 [*sic*] July 1788, De Witt Clinton Papers, Special Collections, Columbia University.

an adequate idea can be formed of its final result."[40] The convention's conclusion was clearly imminent, but no one could guess what the conclusion would be. "I think by tomorrow the House must come to something decisive," wrote an observer on 22 July, "it is impossible to tell what that final decision will be: I cannot even conjecture with plausibility."[41] Even Hamilton would not venture to predict the outcome, but his report to James Madison written on 22 July was faintly optimistic: "We are debating on amendments without having decided what is to be done with them. There is so great a diversity in the views of our opponents that it is impossible to predict any thing. Upon the whole, however, our fears diminish."[42] Whatever the convention did, the uncertainty would not last much longer.

40 *New-York Journal,* 21 July 1788.

41 *Daily Advertiser,* 24 July 1788.

42 Alexander Hamilton to James Madison, 22 July 1788, Harold C. Syrett, ed., and Jacob E. Cooke, assoc. ed., *The Papers of Alexander Hamilton,* (New York, 1961–), V, 187.

XVII

Encouragement from the City

THE men of New York City were enthusiastic Federalists, and although their party composed only a small minority in the Poughkeepsie Convention, the majority treated it with respect and was reluctant to carry the final vote against its wishes. "The decided opinion of the Metropolis of the State, of a part rated in all its contributions *at one-fourth of the whole,* and which is the great seat of the commerce, that supplies its *wants,* and furnishes its *revenues,* cannot fail to make a serious impression on all considerate men in every other part of it," a writer had observed in the *Independent Journal.*[1] Were the Antifederalist majority to force its will on the minority at Poughkeepsie, the political harmony essential to any state would be severely strained. The large voter turn-out and the decisive Federalist victory in the City election testified to intense feeling, which the Antifederalists in the ratifying convention were obliged to respect.

After the old Confederation was dissolved, the City people had an additional motive for Federalism. For many years New York had profited from the presence of the Continental Congress in the City. John Jay estimated that Congress was worth

[1] "One of Yourselves," *Independent Journal* (New York), 30 April 1788.

£100,000 a year. Indeed, he told the convention, "All the Hard Money in the City of New York arise from the Sitting of Congress there."[2] If New York rejected the Constitution or if Congress refused to accept the form of ratification adopted by the state, the City would lose a valuable source of income.[3] The fear of losing Congress was shared by City Feds and Antis alike,[4] and as the weeks passed without any decisive action by the Poughkeepsie Convention, Antifederalists in the City grew concerned that their party would be blamed if Congress decided to make its residence elsewhere when the new government went into operation. "The Anxiety of the Citizens, is probably greater than you would imagine," Samuel Osgood wrote to Melancton Smith and Samuel Jones in mid-July. "If New York should hold out, the Opposition will have all the Blame laid at their Door for forcing Congress to leave this City," and when Smith and Jones returned to Manhattan, "it needs not the Spirit of Prophecy to foretell that your Reception will not be very cordial." Although Osgood insisted that he did not "suggest this in Order to operate upon your Decisions," Smith and Jones must certainly have felt some pressure.[5]

While the Poughkeepsie Convention was struggling to work out a form of ratification that would be acceptable to both sides, the Federalists made occasional references to the City they represented. If the New York ratification were rejected by Congress, they argued, the state would be out of the Union, and

[2] Reports of the Poughkeepsie Convention [12 July 1788], John McKesson Papers, New-York Historical Society.

[3] *Daily Advertiser* (New York), 25 June 1788; Otto to Montmorin, 2 August 1788, Edmund C. Burnett, ed., *Letters of Members of the Continental Congress* (Washington, 1921–1936), VIII, 768n.; S. B. Webb to Catherine Hogeborn, 11 September 1788, W. C. Ford, ed., *Correspondence and Journals of Samuel Blanchley Webb* (New York, 1893–1894), III, 116.

[4] Samuel Osgood to M[elancton] Smith and S[amuel] Jones, 11 July 1788, National Park Service, Collections of Federal Hall National Memorial, New York City.

[5] *Ibid.*

among the misfortunes that would attend such a development, the Federalists named the alienation of the counties that had elected Federalists to the convention. Certainly, the outraged feelings of the men in the City were among the less fearsome consquences of isolation, but they were worth mentioning and were mentioned twice.

R. R. Livingston touched the matter in a speech of 12 July. "I dread to mention perhaps the Southern part of the State may Separate," he said. "It is pain to me to mention it—but Truth must come out." [6] Apparently, Livingston did not labor the point, for no one replied to it, and when the debate was printed in the *Daily Advertiser* the remark was omitted.[7] But a few days later, Hamilton returned to the subject. He pointed out that the southern district of the state was "warmly attachd" to the new government and expressed his conviction that the sentiment would grow stronger as time passed. He added that while "the election of separation will never be made," a separation would, nevertheless, inevitably take place if New York rejected the Constitution.[8]

The only reaction to Hamilton's remarks was a sharp reprimand from George Clinton. Clinton declared that Hamilton's observations "were highly indiscreet and improper." He hoped they would never be repeated. "I verily believe," said the governor, "they will tend to occasion the evil which I hope they were intended to prevent." Clinton was aware that the passions of the population had been involved in the debate on the Constitution and that a decisive defeat for either party would arouse its supporters and threaten the peace of the state. "Gentlemen ought to consider . . . that from the most conclusive testimony a large majority of the people are opposed to the unconditional adoption of the system—some respect ought surely to be paid to

[6] Reports of the Poughkeepsie Convention, 12 July 1788, John McKesson Papers, New-York Historical Society.

[7] *Daily Advertiser*, 16 July 1788.

[8] Gilbert Livingston Reports of the Poughkeepsie Convention, 17 July 1788, New York Public Library.

their opinions." The convention should take care not to go too far out of consideration for the minority, for "if we reason rightly I believe we will be convinced that the danger will chiefly be in a deviation from the will of a majority." [9]

The possible secession of the southern counties was not mentioned again in the convention.[10] Nevertheless, a number of historians believe that the threat was made frequently off the floor of the convention and had such weight with the Antifederalists as to force them to the final compromise with the Federalists.[11] Since there is no direct evidence of such informal conversations, evaluation of the hypothesis involves two logically independent questions: Was there a serious secession movement in the southern counties? Did the threat of secession impress the Antifederalist delegates at Poughkeepsie? The Antifederalists may have feared secession even if there was no active movement, or they may have been indifferent to the threat despite the existence of an organized revolt.

Curiously enough, the first mention of secession came not in New York City, but in Philadelphia, the birthplace of a number of the more interesting rumors of the ratification campaign. In mid-May, an essayist speculating on the consequences of a New York rejection of the Constitution predicted that Staten Island,

[9] Notes on the Poughkeepsie Debates [17 July 1788], George Clinton Papers, New York Public Library.

[10] In his speech of 23 July, Melancton Smith was chiefly concerned with convulsions in the *northern* part of the state (cf. George Dangerfield, *Chancellor Robert R. Livingston of New York, 1746–1813* [New York, 1960], p. 231).

[11] Paul Leicester Ford, ed., *The Federalist* (New York, 1898), p. 38; E. Wilder Spaulding, *New York in the Critical Period, 1783–1789* (New York, 1932), p. 255; Forrest McDonald, *We the People: The Economic Origins of the Constitution* (Chicago, 1958), pp. 287, 288; Dangerfield, *Chancellor Robert R. Livingston*, pp. 231, 232; Jackson Turner Main, *The Antifederalists, Critics of the Constitution, 1781–1788* (Chapel Hill, N.C., 1961), pp. 238, 239. On the other hand, Lee Benson (*Turner and Beard: American Historical Writing Reconsidered* [Glencoe, Ill., 1960], p. 212n.) and Staughton Lynd (*Anti-Federalism in Dutchess County, New York* [Chicago, 1962], p. 89) are dissatisfied with that explanation.

"from its federalism and contiguity to New-Jersey, will abandon New York, and cling to the confederacy . . . to which New Jersey belongs." [12] Shortly after the republication of this essay in New York, "An American" sent a piece to the *New-York Packet.* He did not advocate secession, but expressed a fear that not merely Staten Island, but all of New York south of West Point might be forced to separate from the state if failure to ratify the Constitution resulted in war with Connecticut and New Jersey.[13] About two weeks later, a third essay on the subject, clipped from the *Philadelphia Gazette,* appeared in the *Daily Advertiser.* The writer, who called himself "A Pennsylvanian," boasted that he was "totally unknown" to every citizen of New York State, and one wonders how much he could have known about affairs in New York City. "A Pennsylvanian" addressed himself to the members of the Poughkeepsie Convention, pointing out that if New York failed to enter the new Union the commerce of the state with New Jersey and Connecticut would be disrupted, and concluding, "These things will be most seriously felt throughout your whole commonwealth, but to the islands of New York, Long Island and Staten Island, they will be almost runious. . . . Should these considerations induce the honest opponents of the constitution among them to adhere to the new confederacy, what can prevent their secession?" [14] The only other mention of secession in the New York press was a sarcastic article purporting to discourage New York City from forming itself into an independent nation.[15]

If there was a serious secession movement in New York City

[12] *Daily Advertiser,* 16 May 1788.

[13] *New-York Packet,* 27 May 1788.

[14] *Pennsylvania Gazette* (Philadelphia), 11 June 1788; *Daily Advertiser,* 14 June, 17 June 1788; McDonald writes (*We the People,* p. 288n.), "Rumors of the City's threatened secession were published . . . several times in the Philadelphia *Pennsylvania Gazette* in June and July." A careful examination of the files of the newspaper for those months revealed only the single article cited above.

[15] *Daily Advertiser,* 14 June 1788.

it was a remarkably quiet one. Over a period of three months only four articles appeared on the subject, none of them openly advocating secession and only two of them written by New Yorkers. Moreover, the writers did not agree on what sort of secession movement would develop in the event New York did not join the new Union. One writer said that Staten Island would secede and join New Jersey. A second writer speculated on the secession of all the territory south of West Point. A third writer predicted the secession of the six island counties—including Queens and Suffolk, which had sent Antifederalists to Poughkeepsie. And the last article, with tongue in cheek, warned against Manhattan Island seceding from New York State and forming a political unit independent of both the state and the Union. Surely, a serious secession movement would have been better agreed on its objects.

Talk of secession was not confined to the newspapers. Several New York Federalists mention that the secession rumor was circulating in the City. John Jay wrote to George Washington late in May, after the first two newspaper references had appeared, "An idea has taken the air that the southern part of the State will, at all events, adhere to the Union; and, if necessary to that end, seek a separation from the northern." [16] About a week later Hamilton wrote to Madison about the possible conduct of the Antifederalists in the convention. He remarked in passing that the Antis believed the Federalists would join with New Jersey and Connecticut to bring the southern district of New York into the Union, if the Poughkeepsie Convention rejected the Constitution without debate.[17] The rumor was still alive in July, for S. B. Webb wrote on the sixth of that month that if the

[16] John Jay to George Washington, 29 May 1788, William Jay, *Life of John Jay* (New York, 1833), I, 265.

[17] Alexander Hamilton to James Madison, 8 June 1788, Harold C. Syrett, ed., and Jacob E. Cooke, assoc. ed., *The Papers of Alexander Hamilton* (New York, 1961–), V, 3.

Constitution were rejected, " 'tis more than probable there will be a separation of the State;"[18] and a week later he declared, "The Southern District are determined on a Separation to join the union."[19]

For all of these men, every one an active Federalist, the secession movement was something he believed was threatening, but which he, personally, had no part in. None had been to a meeting or knew anything of definite political action. In fact, when Hamilton mentioned a possible division of the state on the floor of the convention, he spoke of it as an event that would take place despite the fact that no one would desire it.[20] The conclusion is inescapable that there was no organized secession movement in existence at the time of the Poughkeepsie Convention. Rather, a division of the state was listed among the other disasters that would probably befall New York if she refused to come into the new Union. A secession movement was not yet a reality, although it might become one in the future.

Since the Antifederalists had every intention of coming into the Union, they were no more affected by the secession rumor than they were by descriptions of the other terrifying consequences of disunion. Some weeks before the convention met, Jay and Hamilton expressed opinions that the idea of secession was operating on the fears of Antifederalist leaders,[21] but there is no direct evidence to support the belief. If the Antis had ever taken the rumor seriously, they had got over their fears by the end of June, for at that time Abraham Yates judged the heated Federalism of the City to be cooling down. "It appears to me the

[18] S. B. Webb to Catherine Hogeborn, 6 July 1788, Ford, ed., *Correspondence of S. B. Webb*, III, 111.

[19] S. B. Webb to Catherine Hogeborn, 13 July 1788, *ibid.*

[20] Gilbert Livingston Reports of the Poughkeepsie Convention, 17 July 1788, New York Public Library.

[21] John Jay to George Washington, 29 May 1788, Jay, *Life of John Jay*, I, 265; Alexander Hamilton to James Madison, 8 June 1788, Syrett, ed., *Papers of Alexander Hamilton*, V, 3.

Fire Edge in this place is wearing off very fast," he told Abraham Lansing.[22]

There is no reason to suppose that the secession rumor that had been circulating for two months should suddenly, near the end of July, have struck the Antifederalist delegates at Poughkeepsie with such force that they capitulated to the Federalists. While Congress might conceivably support a secession movement if New York State rejected the Constitution, they would be most reluctant to support the movement if the state adopted conditionally—even if such ratification was unacceptable to the Congress. The new Union needed the state of New York, and Congress would do nothing to antagonize the state unnecessarily. In addition, there was a conviction that the division of states on any grounds would set an undesirable precedent.[23]

The most conclusive evidence that the threat of secession did not affect the votes cast in the Poughkeepsie Convention is that, except for Clinton's rebuke of Hamilton on 17 July, there is not a single reference to the possible secession of part of the state in the letters or recorded remarks of any Antifederalist.[24] It is inconceivable that the Antifederalist delegates should have remained silent on the subject if it had been the true reason for the change of votes at the end of the convention. The Antifederalists who finally voted with the Federalists were hard pressed to explain their apparent apostacy, and if they voted as they did in order to prevent civil war, there is no reason why they should not have said so.

The City Federalists were so much occupied during the month of July 1788 that they cannot have given much thought

[22] Abraham Yates to Abraham G. Lansing, 29 June 1788, Abraham Yates Jr. Papers, New York Public Library.

[23] William Grayson to Edmund Randolph, 12 June 1787, quoted in Charles Warren, *The Making of the Constitution* (Boston, 1928), p. 212.

[24] Main cites a letter from Abraham Yates dated 28 May 1787 as proof that Yates was aware of the secession rumor (*Antifederalists*, p. 238). This letter, however, refers to possible division of the *Union*, not of the state.

to the chance that they might soon be obliged to secede from the state. July was the month of the "Grand Foederal Procession," which involved more than 5,000 persons in its preparation [25] and cost almost £10,000. [26] Since the preceding December, New Yorkers had been reading newspaper reports of the federal processions held in other states as they came under the "New Roof." Philadelphia, Boston, Charleston, and Portsmouth had arranged splendid celebrations in which the butchers, bakers, tallow chandlers, and other "mechaniks" marched through the town carrying symbolic banners and displaying the tools of their trades. Antifederalists, of course, scoffed at the demonstrations. They described the Massachusetts affair thus:

> There they went up, up, up,
> And there they went down, down, downy,
> There they went backwards and forwards,
> And poop for Boston towny! [27]

According to Abraham Yates, the more serious New Yorkers were soon "tyred of the furer and Noise" connected with repeated Federalist celebrations,[28] and a Congressman resident in the City thought there was "danger of running into excess in regard to processions," but he added that "the Yorkers are determined . . . to have their frolic." [29]

The New York procession was planned to celebrate the ratification of the Constitution by nine states,[30] with, perhaps, some hope that the display of metropolitan Federalism would have

[25] William Alexander Duer, *Reminiscences of an Old New Yorker* (New York, 1867), p. 64.

[26] S. B. Webb to Catherine Hogeborn, 20 July 1788, Ford, ed., *Correspondence of S. B. Webb,* III, 112.

[27] "The Grand Federal Edifice," *New-York Journal,* 25 February 1788.

[28] Abraham Yates to Abraham G. Lansing, 29 June 1788, Abraham Yates, Jr., Papers, New York Public Library.

[29] Samuel Alleyne Otis to George Thatcher, 17 July 1788, Burnett, ed., *Letters of Members of the Continental Congress,* VIII, 763.

[30] S. B. Webb to Joseph Barrell, 1 July 1788, Ford, ed., *Correspondence of S. B. Webb,* III, 109; *Independent Journal,* 2 August 1788.

some influence on the delegates at Poughkeepsie or on the Congressmen who would decide on the location of the new capital city.[31] The date of the celebration was originally set for the Fourth of July,[32] but was postponed in order not to interfere with the regular Independence Day celebration and to permit the construction of a "Federal Ship." [33] Later it was postponed several times more "in the interesting hope, that this state . . . would likewise accede to the union." [34] Wednesday, 23 July, was the date finally set.

It was drizzling in New York City on 23 July 1788. "We congratulate the procession gentry upon the agreeableness of this day," chuckled an amused Anti, "just rain enough to lay the dust." [35] Despite the dampness, several thousand New Yorkers watched the mile and a half long procession.[36] "As this splendid, novel, and interesting exhibition moved along," the Federalist report runs, "an unexpected silence reigned throughout the city, which gave solemnity to the whole transaction suited to the singular importance of the cause. No noise was heard but the deep rumbling of carriage-wheels, with the necessary salutes and signals. A glad serenity enlivened every countenance, while the joyous expectation of national prosperity triumphed in every bosom." [37] Thomas Greenleaf had a different impression of the spectators. "It was really laughable to see the variety of phizzes

[31] Duer, *Remininscences*, p. 50; Louis G. Otto to Armand Marc Montmorin, 23 July 1788, Burnett, ed., *Letters of Members of the Continental Congress*, VIII, 768n.

[32] S. B. Webb to Joseph Barrell, 1 July 1788, Ford, ed., *Correspondence of S. B. Webb*, III, 109; Abraham Yates to George Clinton, 27 June 1788, Abraham Yates, Jr., Papers, New York Public Library.

[33] S. B. Webb to Joseph Barrell, 1 July 1788, Ford, ed. *Correspondence of S. B. Webb*, III, 109.

[34] *Independent Journal*, 2 August 1788; *New-York Journal*, 7 July, 10 July, 18 July 1788.

[35] *New-York Journal*, 23 July 1788.

[36] Duer, *Reminiscences*, p. 64; John Randolph to St. George Tucker, 30 July 1788, Emmet Collection, #9582, New York Public Library; *New-York Journal*, 24 July 1788.

[37] *Independent Journal*, 2 August 1788.

on this occasion," he told the *New-York Journal* readers the following morning. "The poar *antis* generally minded their own business at home: others, who were spectators at an *awful* distance, looked as sour as the Devil. As for the *feds*, they rejoiced in different degrees—there was the ha, ha, ha! and the he, he, he!" [38]

The finest part of the procession was the ship *Hamilton*, named in honor of the man who had signed the Constitution for New York and who was the Federalist champion of the Poughkeepsie debates. She sailed "with flowing sheets, and full sails, down Broadway, the canvass waves dashing against her sides, the wheels of the carriage concealed." [39] Unfortunately the flag at the masthead was of painted cloth, and its colors ran in the rain so that it came to resemble the modern French tricolor.[40] As the ship rumbled along the procession route, shifting its sails and signaling as appropriate, it arrived at Great Dock Street where a Spanish packet was anchored. The packet saluted the *Hamilton*, and the federal ship began to return the compliment, but after five shots had been fired, the gunner fell into convulsions and could not continue. The *Hamilton*'s commander, however, apologized to the commander of the packet, and the "apology was politely received." [41]

At the end of the procession route a banquet was served. The seats were canopied with canvass that protected the diners from the rain, and their spirits were high as they feasted on roasted bullocks, mutton, and ham.[42] Although New York was not yet a member of the new Union, there was reason to hope that "the Convention will adopt the Constitution in such a manner that Congress will receive us into the Union." [43] When the meal was

[38] *New-York Journal*, 24 July 1788. [39] *Ibid.*

[40] Thomas E. V. Smith, *The City of New York in the Year of Washington's Inauguration, 1789* (New York, 1889), p. 48.

[41] *New-York Journal*, 24 July 1788.

[42] *New-York Journal*, 24 July 1788.

[43] S. B. Webb to Catherine Hogeborn, 20 July 1788, Ford, ed., *Correspondence of S. B. Webb*, III, 112.

over the toasts were drunk, and no doubt the glass drained with the most enthusiasm was that pledged to "The Convention of the State of New York; may they soon add an eleventh pillar to the Federal Edifice." [44]

[44] *Independent Journal*, 6 August 1788.

XVIII

The Eleventh Pillar

WHILE the New York Federalists were parading through the streets of the City, the Poughkeepsie Convention finally passed a compromise resolution, and three days later the delegates had ratified the Constitution and gone home. The end came so suddenly that it was difficult to understand what had occurred. On Tuesday, 22 July, an overwhelming Antifederalist majority faced nineteen Federalists. On Wednesday, 23 July, the Federalists passed a crucial motion. The minority, it appeared, had persuaded the majority.

When the convention met on Wednesday morning, John Lansing proposed ratification in the form originally suggested by Smith on 15 July. At that point Samuel Jones, the prominent Queens County Antifederalist, proposed as an amendment that the words "upon Condition" be struck out and the phrase "in full confidence" be inserted.[1] For more than a week Jones had been tormented by his fear that conditional ratification would be rejected by Congress. On 14 July, when he was absent from the convention, there was speculation about his "political sickness." [2]

[1] Jonathan Elliot, ed., *The Debates in the Several State Conventions on the Adoption of the Federal Constitution* (Philadelphia, 1876), II, 412.

[2] John Bogart to S. B. Webb, 14 [July] 1788, W. C. Ford, ed., *Correspondence and Journals of Samuel Blanchley Webb* (New York, 1893–1894), III, 105.

By 20 July it was said that Jones was "so much intimidated by the Threats of the Federalists that he does not any more take an active part." [3] Most of the other Antifederalists were confident that Congress would accept a conditional ratification, but Jones, fearing that they might not do so, was torn by the conflict between his desire for amendments and his equally strong desire to keep New York in the Union. His solution was to drop the word "condition" and substitute the ambiguous phrase, "in full confidence." [4]

Melancton Smith supported Jones's amendment. Smith, too, had been sufficiently persuaded by the Federalist assertion that Congress would not accept conditional ratification to believe that disunion would indeed be the consequence of leaving the offensive word "condition" in the official instrument, and he urged his Antifederalist friends to agree to the new phraseology. Realizing that many Antifederalists believed the concession Jones proposed was quite unnecessary and a capitulation to the Federalists, Smith reaffirmed his loyalty to the Antifederalist aims and candidly explained his motives for supporting the Jones amendment.

He was still firmly convinced, Smith said, that "the Constitution was radically defective." His aim was still amendments. But he no longer believed that amendments could be obtained before the new government went into operation, and it was consequently necessary to amend in the way prescribed by the Constitution itself. The Federalists in the convention insisted that Congress would not receive New York under the form of ratification that had been proposed, and the Federalist delegates were men of so much prestige that their opinions alone would have "vast weight in the national councils." If New York's ratifica-

[3] Abraham G. Lansing to Abraham Yates, 20 July 1788, Abraham Yates, Jr., Papers, New York Public Library.

[4] This phrase, first used by John Hancock in the Massachusetts Convention (Elliot, ed., *Debates*, II, 175), was deliberately equivocal. It could be interpreted as implying a condition.

tion was rejected, the strength of the Antifederalists "would be dissipated, their Union lost, their object probably defeated, and they would, to use the simple figurative language of Scripture, be dispersed like sheep on a mountain." Therefore, Smith concluded, "it was no more than a proper discharge of his public duty as well as the most advisable way of obtaining the great end of his opposition to vote against any proposition which would not be received as a ratification of the Constitution." [5] Two of Smith's colleagues from Dutchess County, Gilbert Livingston and Zephaniah Platt, also spoke in support of Jones's amendment, and when the vote was taken the amendment passed by a majority of two.[6]

Never had the convention been so near complete accord. John Jay spoke the following morning expressing an ardent hope that the convention might come to an unanimous agreement so that both parties might "go hand in hand" to get a second convention and procure amendments. The Antifederalists were equally optimistic and John Lansing, speaking for the majority, expected that ratification would now pass unanimously if accompanied by the reservation of a right to withdraw from the Union if amendments were not submitted to a second convention within a specified number of years.[7] He and other Antifederalists had earlier opposed the reservation as insufficient while Jay and Hamilton had spoken sympathetically of the proposal when Smith had introduced it some days previously.[8] The Federalists, however, were no longer friendly to the reservation of a right to secede. Upon consideration, they had concluded that the reservation would actually be a condition on ratification and as such would be unacceptable to Congress. Jay spoke for his party, explaining why the Federalists would not agree to the reservation. He thought all could agree on ratification without it. The Antifed-

[5] *Independent Journal* (New York) supp. extraordinary, 28 July 1788.

[6] *Ibid.*

[7] Gilbert Livingston Reports of the Poughkeepsie Convention, 24 July 1788, New York Public Library.

[8] 18 July 1788.

eralists should be pleased "because they have carried all their amendments"; the Federalists should be pleased "because we have adopted such measures as will bring us into the union." Both parties should be gratified "because we have the highest possible prospect of a convention for amendments—we are now one people all pledged for amend[ment]s." [9]

The same morning, Alexander Hamilton read a letter from James Madison to the convention.[10] Madison gave his opinion that "a reservation of a right to withdraw, if amendments be not decided on under the form of the Constitution within a certain time is a *conditional* ratification, that it does not make N. York a member of the New Union, and consequently that she could not be received on that plan." [11] The opinion of the Virginian had its effect on the Antifederalists, who appreciated his influence in Congress.[12] Hamilton continued with a plea for unanimity. "Is it not of importance that we Join—unanimously to procure a convention," he asked. He suggested that the Poughkeepsie Convention prepare a circular letter for all the states, requesting support for a second convention.[13] The Antifederalists approved the idea, but a few men were irrritated by Hamilton's insistence on unanimity. Matthew Adgate of Columbia County thought the Federalists should think of those parts of the state which had voted against the Constitution and make greater concessions to the majority. But what more could the Federalists concede? asked John Jay. "We come in with them in everything but a rejection—& that they themselves do not want." [14] He,

[9] Gilbert Livingston Reports of the Poughkeepsie Convention, 24 July 1788, New York Public Library.

[10] *Ibid.*

[11] James Madison to Alexander Hamilton [20 July 1788], Harold C. Syrett, ed., and Jacob E. Cooke, assoc. ed., *The Papers of Alexander Hamilton* (New York, 1961–), V, 184.

[12] William Kent, ed., *Memoirs and Letters of James Kent, Late Chancellor of the State of New York* (Boston, 1898), p. 310.

[13] Gilbert Livingston Reports of the Poughkeepsie Convention, 24 July 1788, New York Public Library.

[14] *Ibid.*

Hamilton, Duane, and R. R. Livingston "all concurred in expressing an anxious wish, that, since the House had succeeded so far to an accomodation, they might now conclude the business with harmony, and to the satisfaction of both parties." [15]

The final question was voted on Friday, 25 July. Still seeking unanimity, John Jay opened the proceedings by reading the circular letter that he, John Lansing, and Melancton Smith had composed.[16] The draft was chiefly Jay's work, and the fair copy presented to the convention was penned by his hand.[17] The convention agreed to the circular letter unanimously, but when the final votes on ratification were taken, there was a smaller majority in the New York Convention than there had been in any other state. Lansing's motion to reserve the right to secede was defeated by a vote of 31 to 28, and the committee of the whole then voted to ratify "in full confidence" by the same margin. At five o'clock the convention met for its evening session and formally voted to accept the committee report; this time ratification passed by a vote of 30 to 25. "There were several members out of doors," a Federalist wrote, "but they were all for us." [18] When, on the following morning, the official vote was taken on the engrossed ratification, it carried 30 to 27—a margin of three votes.

Despite the narrowness of the final vote, the session of the Poughkeepsie Convention closed in an atmosphere of good feeling.[19] Both sides had made concessions in the hope of achieving unanimity, and although they had not attained complete agreement, the distance between them had all but closed. Many Antifederalists felt bound to vote against any form of ratification that did not include the word "condition" and yet were not greatly displeased with the form of ratification adopted. Henry Wisner of Orange County actually voted for ratification on the

[15] *Independent Journal*, supp. extraordinary, 28 July 1788.
[16] John McKesson Papers, New-York Historical Society. [17] *Ibid.*
[18] *Independent Journal*, supp. extraordinary, 28 July 1788.
[19] Kent, ed., *Memoirs of James Kent*, p. 311.

two votes taken 25 July, but when it came to voting on the engrossed ratification, he changed his mind. He had come to the convention "determined to reject it," he told the convention, but with the other Antifederalists had "gone from one step to another." Now, at the crucial moment, he felt he could not vote for an unamended Constitution, but he promised that if it was carried he would "aid it all he can." [20]

George Clinton voted against ratification in the committee of the whole, observing that "whatever his opinion might be, he stood there as a representative of the County of Ulster; that he should therefore pursue what he believed to be the sense of that County." [21] As president of the convention, Clinton did not cast a vote on Friday evening or Saturday morning, but he stressed his intention to support the Constitution if it was ratified. After the vote on the engrossed ratification, one observer reports, Clinton "addressed the Convention very politely," remarking "that until a Convention was called to consider the amendments now recommended by this Convention, the probability was, that the body of the people who are opposed to the Constitution, would not be satisfied; he would however, as far as his power and influence would extend, endeavour to keep up peace and good order among them." It was noted that "the members and spectators were very attentive" to the governor's remarks, "and more than a common pleasantness appeared in their countenance." [22]

When the final votes were taken, some men who had been elected to the convention as Antifederalists voted with the Federalists. It is not strictly accurate to describe these men as apostates, for although they voted with their former adversaries, the motions for which they cast affirmative votes had been proposed by leaders of their own party and were designed to

[20] Gilbert Livingston Reports of the Poughkeepsie Convention, 26 July 1788, New York Public Library.

[21] *Independent Journal*, supp. extraordinary, 28 July 1788.

[22] *Daily Advertiser* (New York), 1 August 1788.

achieve the original aim of the Antifederalists: amendments. Those men who were persuaded that conditional ratification would mean expulsion from the Union, followed Smith and Jones in the alternative form of ratification they believed would keep New York in the Union while retaining every possible guarantee of future amendment.

The schism in the Antifederalist party first appeared on the vote to substitute the phrase "in full confidence" for the words "on Condition," and was also reflected in the three final votes on ratification as indicated in Table 4.

Four Antifederalists, Dirck Swart and Peter Vrooman of Albany, Ezra Thompson of Dutchess, and David Hedges of Suffolk, did not vote on any of these questions. Ezra Thompson became ill and left the convention early,[23] and it seems likely that the other three had also left Poughkeepsie. As members of the majority party they would have had reason to believe their presence would not be needed, and if they had been in town at the time they would surely have voted. The Poughkeepsie Convention delegates were elected specifically to vote on the Constitution, and no man in the convention could have neglected his duty to express an opinion on the final question. The crucial vote was that taken during the morning session on 25 July by which the committee of the whole decided to ratify "in full confidence" without reserving the right to secede—the second vote illustrated in Table 4. Except for the four men named above, only two delegates failed to vote at that time. Henry Oothoudt was presiding, and John Smith of Suffolk was probably absent on that day. Smith also failed to vote in the evening although his affirmative vote on 23 July suggests that he had already decided to vote with the Federalists as he actually did on 26 July.[24]

The Antifederalists who joined the Federalists on the final

[23] Henry Noble MacCracken, *Old Dutchess Forever! The Story of an American County* (New York, 1956), p. 445.

[24] Only one man, John Williams of Washington County, voted for the Jones amendment on 23 July and yet failed to vote yes on 26 July.

Table 4. Division on the final votes at the Poughkeepsie Convention

Delegates	Party	"In full confi- dence" amend- ment	No right of seces- sion	Commit- tee rati- fication	Final ratifi- cation
Albany					
John Lansing	Anti	no	no	no	no
Henry Oothoudt	Anti			no	no
Dirck Swart	Anti				
Anthony Ten Eyck	Anti	no	no	no	
Israel Thompson	Anti	no	no	no	no
Peter Vrooman	Anti				
Robert Yates	Anti	no	no		no
Columbia					
Matthew Adgate	Anti	no	no	no	no
John Bay	Anti	no	no	no	no
Peter Van Ness	Anti	no	no	no	no
Dutchess					
Jonathan Akins	Anti	no	no		no
John De Witt	Anti		yes	yes	yes
Gilbert Livingston	Anti	yes	yes	yes	yes
Zephaniah Platt	Anti	yes	yes	yes	yes
Melancton Smith	Anti	yes	yes	yes	yes
Jacobus Swartwout	Anti	no	no	no	no
Ezra Thompson	Anti				
Kings					
Peter Lefferts	Fed	yes	yes	yes	yes
Peter Vandervoort	Fed	yes	yes	yes	yes
Montgomery					
John Frey	Anti	no	no	no	no
William Harper	Anti	no	no	no	no
Henry Staring	Anti	no	no	no	no
Volkert Veeder	Anti	no	no	no	no
John Winn	Anti	no	no	no	no
Christopher P. Yates	Anti	no	no	no	
New York					
James Duane	Fed	yes	yes	yes	yes
Alexander Hamilton	Fed	yes	yes	yes	yes
Richard Harison	Fed	yes	yes	yes	yes
John Sloss Hobart	Fed	yes	yes	yes	yes
John Jay	Fed	yes	yes	yes	yes
R. R. Livingston	Fed	yes	yes	yes	yes
Nicholas Low	Fed	yes	yes	yes	yes
Richard Morris	Fed	yes	yes	yes	
Isaac Roosevelt	Fed	yes	yes	yes	yes

Table 4 (cont.)

Delegates	Party	"In full confi- dence" amend- ment	No right of seces- sion	Commit- tee rati- fication	Final ratifi- cation
Orange					
John Haring	Anti	no	no	no	no
Henry Wisner	Anti	no	yes	yes	no
John Wood	Anti	no	no	no	no
Jesse Woodhull	Anti	no	yes	yes	yes
Queens					
Stephen Carman	Anti	yes	yes	yes	yes
Samuel Jones	Anti	yes	yes	yes	yes
Nathaniel Lawrence	Anti	yes	yes	yes	yes
John Schenck	Anti	yes	yes	yes	yes
Richmond					
Abraham Bancker	Fed	yes	yes	yes	yes
Gozen Ryerss	Fed	yes	yes	yes	yes
Suffolk					
Jonathan N. Havens	Anti	yes	yes	yes	yes
David Hedges	Anti				
Henry Scudder	Anti	yes	yes		yes
John Smith	Anti	yes			yes
Thomas Tredwell	Anti	no	no	no	no
Ulster					
John Cantine	Anti	no	no		no
Ebenezer Clark	Anti	no	no	no	no
George Clinton	Anti	no	no		
James Clinton	Anti	no	no	no	no
Cornelius Schoonmaker	Anti	no	no	no	no
Dirck Wyncoop	Anti	no	no	no	no
Washington & Clinton					
Albert Baker	Anti	no	no	no	no
David Hopkins	Anti	no	no	no	no
Ichabod Parker	Anti	no	no	no	no
John Williams	Anti	yes	no	no	no
Westchester					
Thaddeus Crane	Fed	yes	yes	yes	yes
Richard Hatfield	Fed	yes	yes	yes	yes
Philip Livingston	Fed	yes	yes	yes	yes
Lewis Morris	Fed	yes	yes	yes	yes
Lott W. Sarls	Fed	yes	yes	yes	yes
Philip Van Cortlandt	Fed	yes	yes	yes	yes

votes came from Queens, Suffolk, Dutchess, and Orange counties. All four men in the Queens County delegation, of which Samuel Jones was a member, changed their votes, and in neighboring Suffolk County, where Jones's influence was also strong, only Thomas Tredwell persisted in voting no. In Dutchess County Melancton Smith's influence persuaded all but Jonathan Akins and Jacobus Swartwout. Only Jesse Woodhull of the Orange County delegation voted yes on the engrossed ratification, but his colleague, Henry Wisner, had voted yes on the two previous votes and had been sorely tempted to join the Federalists.[25] On the final vote, a dozen Antifederalists voted yes and there were others who might have cast an affirmative vote had the issue rested on their action.[26]

There was so little hard feeling displayed between the Antifederalists who voted with the Federalists and those who continued to oppose them, that some writers have suggested that George Clinton advised some members of his party to change their votes in order to give a majority to the ratificationists while emphasizing the strength of those who remained in opposition.[27] Other writers have described a caucus which is said to have taken place on the evening of 24 or 25 July, *after* the first divided vote, in which the party leaders deliberately selected the Antifederalists who should vote for ratification.[28] There is,

[25] Gilbert Livingston Reports on the Poughkeepsie Convention, 26 July 1788, New York Public Library.

[26] *Memoirs of James Kent*, p. 311.

[27] [Franklin Ellis], *History of Columbia County, New York* (Philadelphia, 1878), p. 47; Jabez Delano Hammond, *History of Political Parties in the State of New York* (Cooperstown, N.Y., 1846), p. 25; James J. Heslin, "Amendents are Necessary," *New-York Historical Society Quarterly*, XLIII (1959), 438; John Stilwell Jenkins, *Lives of the Governors of the State of New York* (Auburn, N.Y., 1851), p. 57.

[28] Forrest McDonald, *We the People; The Economic Origins of the Constitution* (Chicago, 1958), pp. 284, 288n.; George Dangerfield, *Chancellor Robert R. Livingston of New York, 1746–1813* (New York, 1960), p. 231.

however, no substantial evidence to support either hypothesis.[29] The changed votes reflected a true division of opinion among the Antifederalists, and for many months the party leaders worried lest the division between "adopting and non-adopting antis" [30] endure and deepen to the detriment of the movement for a second convention.[31]

What precisely caused the rift? How were twelve Antifederalists persuaded to change their votes? Charles Beard admitted that analysis of the delegates' economic interests does not solve the problem.[32] Nor is it likely that a sectional factor was involved. The four counties that cast one or more Antifederalist votes for ratification—Dutchess, Orange, Queens, and Suffolk—appear to have nothing in common that would account for the voting behavior of their delegates. Dutchess and Orange counties elected their Antifederalist delegations by a higher percentage of the popular vote than was received by the delegates of any other Antifederalist county. In Queens, on the other hand, the Antifederalists had their narrowest victory.[33] A sectional influence that operated on individual delegates, but not on the voting population, would have to be subtle indeed. It seems more likely that the influence of Melancton Smith and Samuel Jones, men who early recognized the need for compromise, ac-

[29] The only basis for the belief that the Antifederalists may have caucused sometime near the end of the convention is an imprecise statement made some fifty years later by one George F. Hopkins, based on his childhood recollections (William Dunlap, *A History of the New Netherlands, Province of New York, and the State of New York* [New York, 1840], II, 281n).

[30] De Witt Clinton to James Clinton, 23 November 1788, De Witt Clinton Papers, Library of Congress.

[31] *Ibid.;* The Federal Republican Society to the Republican Committee of Ulster County, 4 November 1788, John Lamb Papers, New-York Historical Society; Melancton Smith to Gilbert Livingston, 14 January 1789, New York State Library.

[32] Charles A. Beard, *An Economic Interpretation of the Constitution of the United States* (New York, 1913), p. 245.

[33] Table 3, p. 167. No figures are available for Suffolk County.

counts for the change of votes among their close connections in Dutchess County and Long Island.

There should never have been any mystery about the votes that were changed in the New York Convention,[34] for the men who changed were understandably concerned to justify their conduct, and they explained their motives at length, both on the floor of the convention and later in letters. Quite simply, the twelve delegates changed their votes because it seemed expedient to do so.[35] Many writers speak as though the change in votes amounted to a conversion brought about by Alexander Hamilton's debating skill. "He won the New York convention to his views by the sheer force of his arguments," one historian

[34] There has, however, been considerable puzzlement (Max Farrand, *The Fathers of the Constitution* [New Haven, Conn., 1921], p. 156; Edward Channing, *A History of the United States* [New York, 1905–1925], III, 552; Nathan Schachner, *Alexander Hamilton* [New York, 1946], p. 226; Lee Benson, *Turner and Beard: American Historical Writing Reconsidered* [Glencoe, Ill., 1960], p. 212n.).

[35] Samuel Osgood, an Antifederalist living in New York City, clearly stated the argument from expediency in a letter directed to Melancton Smith and Samuel Jones—the leaders of the twelve who changed their votes—in the middle of July: "I know very well your Situation is extremely delicate & that I cannot help you out of it. . . . I believe those who have been deemed antifederal, have done a great Deal of good—It appears to me they have very nearly accomplished their Views—In all the States where Amendments have been recommended—The Members in the general Convention, who were of the State Conventions also, have not dared to disagree to such Amendments; They are therefore compleately [*sic*] committed; as to their own inspired Works—In the present State of the Business, I am well convinced that those who have had, & still have well founded Objections to some Parts of the Plan, will succeed in their laudable Endeavors of getting those Objections fairly removed—And I must confess that it appears to me there is so little Danger in assenting to the Plan now, that it has become a Matter of no small Expediency—Indeed the Danger of not obtaining Amendments such as we would wish for, will in my Opinion be greatly enhanced by the Absence of New York" (Samuel Osgood to M[elancton] Smith and S[amuel] Jones, 11 July 1788, National Park Service, Collections of Federal Hall National Memorial, New York City).

writes.[36] Actually, Hamilton's clever speeches and his well-known sympathy with monarchy were ill-suited to persuading the Antifederalists, and the records of the final weeks of the convention indicate that the words of John Jay had far more weight with the men who opposed unconditional ratification.[37] The fundamental beliefs of the Antifederalists who voted with the Federalists remained unchanged even after they were convinced that it was expedient to vote yes.

Gilbert Livingston was one of the Antifederalists who voted with the Federalists on the final question. These are the words he addressed to the convention in explanation. They might have been spoken by any of the twelve:

Mr. President . . . Permit me sir again to say, that I have had a severe struggle in my mind between *duty* and *prejudice*.

I entered this house, as fully determined on previous amendments (I sincerely believe) as any one member in it. Nothing sir, but a conviction that I am serving the most essential interests of my country, could ever induce me to take another ground, and differ from so many of my friends on this floor. . . . With respect to the constitution itself, I have the same idea of it I ever had—that is, that there is not safety under it, unless amended. Some time after we first met sir, a majority of those in this house who oppose it, did determine not to reject it. Only one question then remained—which was the most eligible mode, to ensure a general convention of the States, to reconsider it, to have the essential amendments ingrafted into it? . . . [O]n the most mature and deliberate consideration . . . the result of my judgment is—that the adoption on the table, with the bill of rights and amendments contained in it, and the circular letter to the different States accompanying it, is,

[36] Esmond Wright, *Fabric of Freedom* (New York, 1961), p. 175. Also, Broadus Mitchell, *Alexander Hamilton* (New York, 1957, 1962), I, 431; Carl Van Doren, *The Great Rehearsal* (New York, 1948), p. 234.

[37] Gilbert Livingston Reports of the Poughkeepsie Convention, New York Public Library. Cf. MacCracken, *Old Dutchess Forever!*, pp. 439, 440; Jackson Turner Main, *The Antifederalists, Critics of the Constitution*, 1781–1788 (Chapel Hill, N.C., 1961), p. 238.

considering our *present* situation with respect to our sister States, the wisest and best measure, we can possibly pursue. I shall therefore vote for it . . . I will steadily persevere, in every possible means to procure this desirable object, a revision of the Constitution.

For a consistency in conduct, to this *honorable house*, to *my constituents*, and to *my country* . . . I do submit myself.[38]

For the men who thought like Gilbert Livingston, the vote that brought New York State under the "New Roof" was not the end of the war; it was merely a tactical retreat. In the following months they planned to continue the campaign for amendments, supported by the more sceptical members of the party, who still questioned whether amendments could be obtained when the Constitution had been solemnly ratified by every state in the Confederation except North Carolina and Rhode Island.

[38] *Country Journal* (Poughkeepsie), 29 July 1788; cf. Federal Republican Society to Republican Committee of Ulster County, 4 November 1788, John Lamb Papers, New-York Historical Society.

PART V

The Grand Federal Edifice

XIX

Antifederalist Victory

THE instrument of ratification adopted by the Poughkeepsie Convention on 26 July 1788 [1] did not contain the word "condition," but in every other respect it was a conditional ratification. The document opened with a declaration of rights—the amendments the Poughkeepsie delegates had classified as "explanatory." [2] Then followed the formal statement by which the Convention ratified the Constitution "under these impressions and declaring that the rights aforesaid cannot be abridged or violated . . . and are consistent with the said Constitution." In other words, ratification was given on the assumption that the "explanatory" amendments were already binding, and New Yorkers believed that they would be protected by this bill of rights even before the Constitution was officially amended.[3] New York's form of ratification was unique in this respect. Other

[1] See Appendix B.

[2] The "explanatory" amendments came to be referred to as a bill of rights (Gilbert Livingston Reports of the Poughkeepsie Convention, New York Public Library; Abraham G. Lansing to Abraham Yates, 3 August 1788, Abraham Yates, Jr., Papers, New York Public Library).

[3] Abraham G. Lansing to Abraham Yates, 3 August 1788, and Abraham Yates, "Pub. 15 & 22 March 1790," Abraham Yates, Jr., Papers, New York Public Library.

states had proposed amendments, but no other state had bound them into the act of ratification so tightly.

New York's ratification was qualified still further. The state accepted the Constitution "in confidence" that a list of "recommendatory" amendments appended to the act of ratification would "receive an early and mature Consideration," and "in full confidence" that four specified restrictions on Congressional power would be observed "until a Convention shall be called and convened for proposing amendments."

There were twenty-three "explanatory" amendments. Seventeen of these dealt with matters that were eventually covered by Madison's Bill of Rights. But that should by no means be taken to imply that the other six were rejected. The first two of the neglected six consist of declarations that "all Power is originally vested in and consequently derived from the People, and that Government is instituted by them for their common Interest Protection and Security," and "that the enjoyment of Life, Liberty and the pursuit of Happiness are essential rights which every Government ought to respect and preserve." These echoes of the Declaration of Independence are so much a part of the American tradition that many people today would probably be surprised to learn that they are not actually written into the law of the land. Two other amendments advance interpretations of the Constitution that have never been challenged since they involve questions that have never come into dispute. And a fifth amendment, which attempted to guarantee the right of a state to apportion its representatives among legislative districts at its discretion, touches a point that has only recently become controversial. The sixth amendment neglected by Madison, involving the suability of states, was partially enacted by the Eleventh Amendment in 1794.

The "explanatory" amendments were the ones most important to the Antifederalists at Poughkeepsie and were considered a condition on adoption in all but name. The thirty-two "recommendatory" amendments dealt with matters that one or more of the delegates to the New York Convention thought would be desirable improvements in the Constitution, but which they did not believe were vital. Several of the suggestions sought to meet contingencies that have never arisen, such as the President wishing to lead an army in the field despite Congressional objections, and others proposed alterations in the Constitution that were enacted as soon as the need for them became clear—for instance, the provision that a President may serve only two terms. Most of the "recommendatory" amendments had been introduced by Antifederalist members of the Poughkeepsie Convention after the Federalists had stopped debating. The Federalists actually encouraged the opposition to introduce as many amendments as they could think of and promised to support them—so long as the amendments were merely recommendations and not condition on ratification.[4]

The Antifederalists were willing to submit to the decisions of a general convention on this second list of amendments. They merely insisted that such a convention meet and that amendments be considered. It was to insure the meeting of a second convention that the four "restrictions" were imposed. Strictly speaking, these restrictions should not be counted as additional amendments, since they were not intended to impose permanent limitations on federal power, but were to apply only until a general convention met.[5]

Antifederalist support for the list of recommendatory amendments was probably prompted more by a desire to assert the right of the ratifying convention to amend what it was called on to approve than by enthusiasm for the particular amendments put forward. The list was not an Antifederalist "package" as

[4] Note, for instance, Jay's resolutions of 11 July 1788, Jonathan Elliot, ed., *The Debates in the Several Conventions on the Adoption of the Federal Constitution* (Philadelphia, 1876), II, 410.

[5] All four restrictions also appear as recommendatory amendments, so that counting the restrictions as amendments would result in duplication.

most of the explanatory amendments were,[6] and the exhausting caucuses held by the Antis in July debated how to attach amendments to the Constitution, not what amendments should be attached.[7] The important amendments, on which all Antifederalists agreed, were classed as explanatory and became a condition of ratification. The recommendatory amendments, on the other hand, deal with subjects that had rarely or never been discussed in the press or in Antifederalist correspondence, and after the Poughkeepsie Convention adjourned no one was sufficiently concerned about any one of these amendments to plead for it in the papers or in private letters or to lament its absence from Madison's list. In fact, when one of the recommendatory amendments, that concerning changes in Congressional salaries, was proposed by Madison as Amendment II of the twelve sent to the states, it was actually voted down by the members of New York's Antifederalist Assembly by a vote of fifty-two to five.[8] Apparently no substantive alteration in the Constitution seemed worth insisting on once a bill of rights guaranteed that those powers of the central government that had been judged potentially dangerous could not be used to violate the essential rights of citizens.

One historian has referred to the New York act of ratification as "little more than a jingle of words." [9] Abraham Yates always insisted that the state's ratification was far from an absolute

[6] The Antifederalist delegates had prepared notes for amendments even before the Convention met (Abraham Yates to Abraham G. Lansing, 15 June 1788, Abraham Yates, Jr., Papers, New York Public Library). These notes have not been located, but the explanatory amendments are so similar even in wording to amendments proposed by conventions which had met earlier that the fact cannot be coincidental.

[7] De Witt Clinton to [Charles Tillinghast], 12 July 1788, De Witt Clinton Papers, Special Collections, Columbia University; *Daily Advertiser* (New York), 15 July 1788.

[8] *Journal of the Assembly of the State of New York* (New York, 1790), 26 January 1790.

[9] John Bach McMaster, *A History of the People of the United States from the Revolution to the Civil War* (New York, 1885), I, 449.

adoption of the Constitution. "Those that advance this opinion [that New York's ratification was unconditional]," he wrote, "must not be very scrupulous what they say and not probably much how they act. The absurdity of it appears to me too glaring to need refutation." [10] Certainly it was an equivocal victory for the Constitution's supporters, but it was enough to bring the state into the Union. As late as 22 July, Madison had doubted whether New York would adopt a form of ratification that "can make New York immediately a member of the new Union," and it was his opinion that the Antifederalists at Poughkeepsie could not "come to that point without yielding a complete victory to the Federalists." [11] In fact, the New York ratification was an honest compromise, which left both sides faintly dissatisfied.

The extreme concession of the Antifederalists had been to surrender the word "condition." The extreme concession of the Federalists had been the circular letter to the states. The suggestion that Federalist support for such a letter might persuade the Antifederalists to forgo the security of conditional ratification was first made on the floor of the convention by Hamilton, and the letter adopted was mainly the work of John Jay.[12] It was a powerful instrument, directed as it was by the unanimous voice of the New York Convention. "We, the members of the Convention of this state," it began, "have deliberately and maturely considered the Constitution proposed for the United States. Several articles in it appear so exceptionable to a majority of us, that nothing but the fullest confidence of obtaining a revision of them by a general convention, and an invincible reluctance to separating from our sister states, could have prevailed upon a sufficient number to ratify it without stipulating for previous amendments. We all unite in opinion, that such a revision will be necessary to recommend it to the approbation and support of a

[10] Abraham Yates, "Pub. 15 & 22 March 1790," Abraham Yates, Jr., Papers, New York Public Library.

[11] James Madison to Edward Randolph, 22 July 1788, Henry D. Gilpin, ed., *The Papers of James Madison*, (New York, 1841), II, 673.

[12] See above, pp. 244, 245.

numerous body of our constituents." The letter then requested the other states to support the movement for a second convention, pointing out that other states had also indicated a desire to see the Constitution amended, so that "motives of mutual affection and conciliation will conspire with the obvious dictates of sound policy to induce even such of the states as may be content with every article in the Constitution to gratify the reasonable desires of that numerous class of American citizens who are anxious to obtain amendments of some of them." In concluding, the letter again emphasized the devotion to the Union that had outweighed all other considerations in bringing New York under the "New Roof." "Our attachment to our sister states, and the confidence we repose in them, cannot be more forcibly demonstrated than by acceding to a government which many of us think very imperfect, and devolving the power of determining whether that government shall be rendered perpetual in its present form, or altered agreeably to our wishes, and [*sic*] a minority of the states with whom we unite." [13] The Antifederalists had reason to expect that these words would be sympathetically received in the legislatures of other states.

By giving their votes for the circular letter, the Federalists at Poughkeepsie gained an unconditional ratification of the Constitution. Most Federalists believed that congratulations were in order for the men who had brought about that conclusion in the New York Convention. George Washingon wrote to John Jay, "Although I could hardly conceive it possible, after ten States had adopted the constitution, that New-York . . . would withdraw herself from the union, yet considering the great majority which appeared to cling together in the Convention . . . I did not, I confess, see the means by which it was to be avoided. The exertion of those who were able to effect this great work, must have been equally arduous and meritorious." [14]

[13] Elliot, ed., *Debates,* II, 413, 414.

[14] George Washington to John Jay, 3 August 1788, William Jay, *Life of John Jay* (New York, 1833), II, 194, 195.

On the other hand, when James Madison learned the details of New York's ratification, he had no urge to congratulate the Federalist delegation to Poughkeepsie. On the contrary, Madison was gravely concerned that the circular letter would result in total victory for the Antifederalists. He believed the letter had "a most pestilent tendency," for if it succeeded in forcing Congress to call a second convention in the near future, "it is seriously to be feared, that the system, which has resisted so many direct attacks, may be at last undermined by its enemies." [15]

Before a month had passed, Madison and numerous other Federalists, some of whom had previously seen no danger in New York's action, were convinced that "the circumstances involved in the ratification of New York will prove more injurious than a rejection would have done." Rejection, said Madison, "would have alarmed the well-meaning anti-Federalists everywhere; would have had no ill effect on the other party; would have excited the indignation of the neighboring States; and would have been necessarily followed by a speedy reconsideration of the subject." The Virginian could see no worthy motive for the New York Federalist support of the worse-than-nothing ratification. "I am not able to account for the concurrence of the Federal part of the convention in the circular address on any other principle than a determination to purchase an immediate ratification in any form and at any price, rather than disappoint this city of a chance for the new Congress." [16]

The City delegates had certainly been interested in retaining the federal capital in New York,[17] but that was not the most

[15] James Madison to George Washington, 15 August 1788, Jared Sparks, ed., *Writings of George Washington* (Boston, 1834), IX, 420.

[16] James Madison to George Washington, 24 August 1788, quoted in W. C. Rives, *History of the Life and Times of James Madison* (Boston, 1866), II, 629; George Washington to General Lincoln, 28 August 1788, *ibid.*, 630.

[17] Gilbert Livingston Reports of the Poughkeepsie Convention, New York Public Library; Reports of the Poughkeepsie Convention [12 July 1788], John McKesson Papers, New-York Historical Society.

important reason for compromising with the Antifederalists. Although Madison and others might think New York's ratification worse than a rejection, they could not think it worse than conditional ratification. No one at Poughkeepsie would have voted for rejection, but defeat of the compromise proposal would have resulted in the adoption of a conditional ratification. The Federalists claimed to be certain that such a ratification would not be accepted by Congress, but Congress might well have been reluctant to reject New York. North Carolina and Rhode Island both had votes in Congress, although those states had not ratified, and other states with large Antifederalist minorities would most likely have hesitated before voting against accepting New York's ratification. Moreover, the New York Federalists may be assumed to have had sufficient loyalty to their state to have gone to considerable lengths before subjecting New York to the painful consequences of disunion, which they so graphically depicted in the Poughkeepsie debates. Both parties at Poughkeepsie agreed that almost every consideration could be subordinated to the need to keep the state in the Union. The compromises made by both parties had been motivated by that necessity.

In addition, the New York Federalists soon discovered that party spirit cooled rapidly after ratification and that there was little likelihood that their opponents would insist that a second convention meet immediately. By October, John Jay, who was a fairly shrewd political observer, believed that the Antifederalists could now be satisfied merely by the prompt passage of a resolution summoning a new convention, even if the date for the meeting were set three years in the future.[18] There was no need for the Federalists to fear a second convention movement because by the fall of 1788 there was no longer a vigorous opposition to the Constitution in New York State.

[18] John Jay to Edward Rutledge, 15 October 1788, H. P. Johnston, ed., *The Correspondence and Public Papers of John Jay* (New York, 1891), III, 362.

XX

Antifederalism Vanishes

DURING the ratification campaign, the chasm separating Federalists and Antifederalists in New York had been deep—there was real suspicion, fear, and sometimes even hatred between members of the opposing factions—but it had been very narrow. The issue, when to amend the Constitution, that divided the parties was almost trivial, and there were wide areas of agreement. Both parties wanted stronger government, and both parties valued individual rights. The Antifederalists wished the adoption of a properly amended Constitution, and few Federalists had serious objection to the addition of a bill of rights if it could be added without damaging the Constitution itself. The war between Feds and Antis was a contest in which both sides could win, and political hostility was bound to fade quickly once that truth was apparent.

Shortly after the Poughkeepsie Convention met it was clear that the Antifederalists would not reject the Constitution and that the Federalists would be willing to support all of the most important Antifederalist amendments. The gradual cooling of passion in the convention, and the harmony displayed during the bipartisan celebration of the Fourth of July in Poughkeepsie, was complemented by a new calm among the politically minded population of the state. Early in July a report from Hudson in Columbia County stated, "The spirit of amity and conciliation which prevails in the convention is equally prevalent among the people at large, and all parties show a return of good humor, and a desire of once more becoming a united people." [1] Ten days earlier, Abraham Yates had observed a similar tendency in New York City.[2]

Today it seems quite banal to remark on the speed and good nature with which Americans forget their political differences after a question has been decided by an approved procedure. It has become the "American Way," and is so much accepted that it is difficult to realize that it is an extraordinary phenomenon, not at all the usual aftermath of hotly fought political campaigns in other countries. Furthermore, the ratification campaign of 1788 was the first occasion on which a serious political dispute was so quickly forgotten by Americans. The most recent occasion prior to 1788 on which Americans disagreed on a political issue had culminated in a civil war between patriots and loyalists. Consequently, New York's politicians were seriously worried that dissatisfaction with the decision of the Poughkeepsie Convention would lead to violence in the state, and few men noticed the signs of growing harmony.

Revolt seemed most probable in the northern parts of the state,[3] where the Antifederalist majority might well view the formally unconditional ratification as capitulation to the Federalists of New York City. Violence seemed especially likely in Albany County, where the election had been bitterly contested and where partisans of both sides were numerous and fond of rioting. On 4 July, the very day that witnessed the friendly, bipartisan celebration at Poughkeepsie, a serious clash occurred

[1] *New-York Journal*, 21 July 1788.

[2] Abraham Yates to Abraham G. Lansing, 29 June 1788, Abraham Yates, Jr., Papers, New York Public Library.

[3] *Independent Journal* (New York), supp. extraordinary, 28 July 1788; Notes on the Poughkeepsie Debates, 17 July 1788, George Clinton Papers, New York Public Library.

between the Feds and Antis at Albany. The day began peacefully enough, with a joint procession by both parties to celebrate Independence, but in the afternoon the Federalists organized a second procession in which all the Federalist members of the militia paraded under arms, carrying a field piece and firing salutes as they stopped at different parts of the town. The procession was ambushed by the Antifederalists as it passed the tavern where those who opposed ratification had met for their Fourth of July dinner, and bricks, clubs, and stones were used against the parading militiamen. The Federalists defended themselves with bayonets, forced the Antis to retreat into the tavern, and then smashed the windows and broke up the furniture. More than a dozen men were wounded, and the property damage exceeded £70.[4]

The Fourth of July disturbance in Albany was actually no more than a street brawl that could easily have been controlled by a municipal police force. But since there were no police, the incident was potentially extremely dangerous. A street brawl with political overtones has set off more than one revolution. Three days after the fracas at Hilton's Tavern, the Federalists learned that the Antis were "trying to raise an armed force in the country, to ransack the city." [5] Fortunately, the members of the Albany Anti-Federal Committee were responsible men and were able to discourage further violence. When the Antis from outside the town came to see them, the Antifederalist leaders "recommended them to be peaceable and quiet" and explained that something more potent than politics had been the cause of the Independence Day disturbance. "The quarrel which we had in this City was unintentional on our side," they told their country friends, "and would not have happened had our Friends and their Antagonists not been heated with Liquor." [6] There was no

[4] *New-York Journal*, 14 July, 11 July 1788; *New-York Packet*, 15 July 1788.

[5] *New-York Packet*, 15 July 1788.

[6] Abraham G. Lansing to Abraham Yates, 9 July 1788, Abraham Yates, Jr., Papers, New York Public Library.

further bloodshed, but feeling continued to run high for many days,[7] and there seemed good reason to fear further violence if the Albany Antifederalists should be dissatisfied with the action of the Poughkeepsie Convention.

After the final vote on ratification was taken, the Antifederalist leaders pledged themselves to support the Constitution and to exert all their influence to maintain order among those Antifederalists who were not content with the Convention's action.[8] Robert Yates, the formal leader of the Antifederalists at Poughkeepsie, a former delegate to the Philadelphia Convention, and a delegate from Albany County at the New York ratifying convention, promptly called on the people of Albany to support the Constitution. "Before the Constitution was ratified, I had been opposed to it," he declared; 'it is now mine and every other man's duty to support it." [9]

The form of ratification adopted at Poughkeepsie was accepted by the men of Albany more readily than many had feared. "The News of the adoption [has] been in Town some days past," Abraham G. Lansing wrote to Abraham Yates on 3 August, "and our Friends are much better pleased with it than we had reason to expect." The explanatory amendments that had been interwoven with the ratification were interpreted as an effective condition on adoption and were widely approved as "security against the Encroachments of the Gen[era]l Government." Lansing himself was more reserved in his approval of the Poughkeepsie ratification than many Albany Antifederalists, but even he was satisfied with it. "Upon the whole," he wrote to Abraham Yates, "I believe or *endeavour* to believe that it is best so both in a political and private light—for had the Constitution

[7] De Witt Clinton to Charles Tillinghast, 12 July 1788, John Lamb Papers, New-York Historical Society.

[8] *Country Journal* (Poughkeepsie), 29 July 1788.

[9] Quoted in B. J. Lossing, *Life and Times of Philip Schuyler* (New York, 1873), II, 447.

been so adopted as that Congress would not accept it—yourself and our Friends would have incurred blame & Censure if any serious commotions had ensued—as we stand our Friends in this quarter are firmly united—and I trust we shall be able to send such Members [to the Congress] as will assist in bringing about the reformation we wish." [10]

Meanwhile, the Federalists at Albany exerted themselves to end the quarrel with the Antis. They tried to bring the Antifederalists into the preparations for a celebration and procession in honor of New York's ratification,[11] telling the Antis that "we were all to rejoice together and that all animosity would then subside." But the Anti-Federal Committee refused to sanction cooperation with "a Body of Men who Stile themselves the Federal Committee while we have a Committee and Chairman of our own," and they remained "quiet at Home" on the day of the celebration.[12]

Despite the boycott, the day was a huge success. Albany even managed to produce a "Federal ship" of sorts:

> A Batteau: elegantly painted and decorated; on a carriage drawn by two grey horses, neatly caparisoned, loaded with goods proper for the Indian trade, navigated by a proper number of batteaumen furnished with setting-poles, paddles, &c., which were used with great skill during the procession. Mr. Gerardus Lansing, in the character of a trader, and an Indian, properly dressed and ornamented, sitting in the stern. During the repast, the batteau made a voyage towards the Mohawk country, and returned with a full cargo of peltry.[13]

There was no violence, and the "Ode written in honor of the day" contained this verse:

[10] Abraham Yates, Jr., Papers, New York Public Library.

[11] *Albany Journal*, 4 August 1788.

[12] Abraham G. Lansing to Abraham Yates, 3 August 1788, Abraham Yates, Jr., Papers, New York Public Library.

[13] Joel Munsell, ed., *The Annals of Albany* (Albany, 1850), I, 331–335.

> YORKERS rejoice! your state is SAV'D FROM BLOOD!
> UNION protects her with a guardian's care;
> DISCORD, that threaten'd like a raging flood,
> Has spent her fruitless breath in empty air.[14]

In October Aaron Burr reported that he found "political strife still high" in Albany, but remarked at the same time that Albany was "the only part of the state where the spirit of party is kept thoroughly alive."[15] Elsewhere, members of both factions had joined to celebrate ratification, and had then forgotten their differences like the men of Red-Hook who, according to reports, celebrated ratification on 6 August, "spending the day in a sociable and harmonious manner, smoaking the Calumet of Peace, and burying in oblivion all distinctions of party."[16] In New York City, the bells rang, cannon were fired, the merchants at the Coffee House huzza'd, and mobs caroused through the streets during the night cheering and toasting the Constitution. Even known Antis "drank freely of the *Federal Bowl*, and declared that they were now perfectly reconciled to the New Constitution."[17] While the boistrous crowds moved through the streets, they took it into their heads to break into Thomas Greenleaf's printing shop where they destroyed his types. The unfortunate editor was obliged to cease publication of his *New-York Journal* as a daily and return to a single weekly edition.[18] The drunken attack on Greenleaf's press is the single act of violence that occurred anywhere in the state.

The jolly-good-fellowship that made drinking companions of political adversaries was not limited to the days when ratification

[14] *Federal Herald* (Albany), 11 August 1788.

[15] Aaron Burr to Theodore Sedgwick, 10 October 1788, Massachusetts Historical Society.

[16] *Country Journal*, 12 August 1788.

[17] *Independent Journal*, supp. extraordinary, 28 July 1788; S. B. Webb to Catherine Hogeborn, 27 July 1788, W. C. Ford, ed., *Correspondence and Journals of Samuel Blanchley Webb* (New York, 1893—1894), III, 113.

[18] *New-York Journal*, 31 July, 7 August 1788.

was celebrated. Stubborn Antifederalism was melting away with astonishing rapidity. Two months after New York had ratified, John Jay remarked how "the opponents in this State to the constitution decrease and grow temperate." Not only did relatively few men continue active agitation for amendments, but those who did seemed willing to be content with far less extensive amendment than the Federalists had formerly supposed. "Many of them," said Jay, "seem to look forward to another Convention, rather as a measure that will justify their opposition, than produce all the effects they pretend to expect from it." [19]

Ironically, it was the New York City Antis who, after sitting out the campaign in the spring and providing the leadership for the forces of compromise at Poughkeepsie, were the most active campaigners for a second convention in the post-ratification months. Jay's observation that they sought a convention mainly to "justify their opposition" has uncomfortable relevance when applied to men like Samuel Jones and Melancton Smith who, after all, had personal reasons for wishing to convince themselves and others that their action at Poughkeepsie had not been a desertion of the cause. On 30 October 1788, ten New York Antifederalists, including Smith, Jones, and John Lamb, met at Fraunces's Tavern and "after some deliberation, determined to form themselves into a Society for the purpose of procuring a general convention, agreeable to the circular letter of the late Convention of this state." [20] The following week, the new Federal Republican Society drafted two letters, one to the New York counties, and one for the Antifederalists in other states, explaining the reasons that had persuaded the New York Antifederalists to vote for the form of ratification that was adopted at Poughkeepsie and urging unity among all those desiring amend-

[19] John Jay to George Washington, 21 September 1788, H. P. Johnston, ed., *The Correspondence and Public Papers of John Jay* (New York, 1891), III, 360.

[20] Minutes of the Federal Republican Society, John Lamb Papers, New-York Historical Society.

ments.[21] No further action followed, however, and by mid-November the committee of ten could not assemble a quorum and the Federal Republican Society apparently dissolved.[22] By January 1789, no trace can be found of Antifederalist activity in New York State except for Melancton Smith's lament to an Antifederalist friend in Albany, "All we hear of you is from the papers—We receive no more letters than if there was not in ye City one person who did not believe the new Constitution was of divine Original." [23]

And there soon was precious little in the papers. An interesting reflection of the disintegration of the Antifederalist movement is the sharp decline in the number of political essays appearing in the New York press after ratification, and the virtual disappearance of pieces expressing dissatisfaction with the Constitution or with Madison's amendments once those had been proposed in Congress. The *Daily Advertiser*, for instance, which had been filled with essays during the ratification campaign, published only four articles dealing with the Constitution between June 1789, when Madison introduced his amendments, and January 1790, when New York acted on them. Two of these articles, both praising Madison's amendments without reservation, were clipped from the newspapers of other states.[24] Then, early in January 1790, "A Customer" requested that the *Daily Advertiser* reprint the letter written in September by the Virginia Senators Richard Henry Lee and William Grayson, which condemned Madison's amendments as "inadequate." And so, the letter was published in New York two months after the Virgin-

[21] Draft letters dated 4 November 1788, *ibid.*

[22] Minutes of the Federal Republican Society, *ibid.*

[23] Melancton Smith to Gilbert Livingston, 14 January 1789, #955, New York State Library. Smith's remark points up the interesting circumstance that the extant correspondence of Antifederalists makes practically no references to the Constitution or possible amendments after the summer of 1788.

[24] "A Pennsylvanian," *Daily Advertiser* (New York), 3 July 1789; "From Fredricksburg, Va.," *ibid*, 14 July 1789.

ians had written it,[25] but it provoked no comment from anyone. The fourth article was an open letter to James Madison from a Federalist using the name "Pacificus," criticizing Madison for having introduced amendments since, "Pacificus" claimed, the people generally did not want amendments and proposing them "may sow seeds of discord from New Hampshire to Georgia." [26]

The letter from "Pacificus" did provoke a response from "A Free Mechanic," defending Madison's action and praising his amendments, which was published in the *New-York Journal.*[27] This article was the only essay on the Constitution to appear in that paper between June 1789 and January 1790. And the *New-York Journal*, it should be remembered, was the newspaper that had been most popular with Antifederalist writers during the ratification campaign. Greenleaf's paper appeared only once a week after the attack on his printing office in July 1788, but there was still ample room in its columns for him to print Antifederalist essays had any been submitted. That Greenleaf printed only one essay on the Constitution and yet made none of his customary apologies for unprinted contributions is strong evidence that no others were handed to him.

Although Antifederalist activity in New York lapsed soon after ratification, the state government was officially committed to obtaining consideration of amendments, and the conviction that the New York Legislature would attend to implementing the Poughkeepsie recommendations probably contributed to the inactivity of private groups. Governor Clinton called a special session of the legislature for early December 1788 so that it might consider "the proceedings of the convention of this state lately held at Poughkeepsie, and the ordinance of Congress for putting into operation the constitution of the United States." [28]

[25] *Daily Advertiser*, 2 January 1790.

[26] *Daily Advertiser*, 17 August 1789.

[27] *New-York Journal*, 20 August 1789.

[28] New York State. *Messages from the Governors*, Charles Z. Lincoln, ed. (Albany, 1909), II, 289, 290.

In his opening address, Clinton called "particular attention" to the amendments and the circular letter, and the legislature duly called on Congress to summon an amending convention as specified by Article V of the new Constitution.[29]

Support from other states came slowly. The Massachusetts legislature, meeting in January, refused to call for a second convention on the grounds that it would be expensive and perhaps dangerous to the Union.[30] Not until May did Virginia petition Congress for a second convention, making the second of a requisite eight states. Had the business of amending the Constitution been left to the initiative of the states, there would have been a long delay before amendments were considered.[31]

In the end, however, a second convention proved unnecessary. The Federalist James Madison, like many others of his party, had pledged himself to work for amendments after ratification, but he was so fearful of the confusion that might result if a second convention were called, that he introduced a list of amendments into Congress himself. Congressional initiative was thus substituted for state initiative, and twelve amendments were offered to the state legislatures for ratification. With the submission of Madison's amendments to the states, the New York movement for a second convention collapsed completely, and what remained of the opposition to the Constitution in the state vanished.

Although Antifederalism had been fading ever since ratification, it did not entirely disappear in New York until the Federalists had proved their good faith by introducing amendments in Congress early in June 1789. A prime article of the Antifederalist faith was that governments once established could not be amended without violence. Such, they pointed out, was "the ex-

[29] *Ibid.; Journal of the Assembly of the State of New York* (New York, 1789), 5 February 1789.

[30] John Hancock to George Clinton, 21 February 1789, quoted in Broadus Mitchell, *Alexander Hamilton* (New York, 1957, 1962), I, 559.

[31] Francis N. Thorpe, *Constitutional History of the United States* (Chicago, 1901), II, 214.

perience of all ages." [32] Even Melancton Smith, who had voted for unconditional ratification, began to have second thoughts a few months later and worried that the Federalists might have deceived him at Poughkeepsie. "The fair promises and pretentions of most of the leading men who were in favour of the new System are mere illusions," he wrote in January 1789. "No reliance can be placed in any of them. We ought therefore to strive to maintain our union firm and immoveable as ye mountains, to pursue [the] object of amendments with unremitting ardour and diligence." [33] Abraham Yates, with his habitual pessimism, thought it too late even for "ardour and diligence," and he began to compose a history of the aristocratic conspiracy by which his country had been duped into surrendering its liberties. He had finished it in June 1789, when Madison submitted his amendments to Congress, and the event so astonished him that he put away his manuscript and decided not to publish it.[34]

Another New York Antifederalist who had given up all hope for amendments happened to be present in the Congress Chamber when the committee considering Madison's bill of rights reported to the House. He expressed warm satisfaction with the amendments and delight at the unexpected success in a letter to a friend in North Carolina: "You know that I was from the first warmly opposed to the new constitution, and principally because the Congress were not expressly prohibited from dangerous exercises of power, which might be attempted, though they could not be fully justified under the constitution. I confess, when the adoption took place, I lost all idea of amendments;

[32] Abraham Yates [Rough Hewer], 8 December 1788, Abraham Yates, Jr., Papers, New York Public Library. See also *New-York Morning Post*, 11 March 1788; *New-York Journal*, 20 March 1788; "Algernon Sidney," II, *New-York Journal*, 23 February 1788.

[33] Melancton Smith to Gilbert Livingston, 14 January 1789, #955, New York State Library.

[34] Staughton Lynd, "Abraham Yates's History of the Movement for the United States Constitution," *William and Mary Quarterly*, third series, XX (1963), 223–245.

supposing that when the Congress were in possession of power, they would not of themselves, take any steps to diminish it, and would be jealous of any other endeavours for that purpose.—You judged more favourably, and concluded that they would propose some material amendments, if with no other view than to give more general satisfaction. I have now the pleasure to acquaint you, that I was yesterday in the house of representatives, when the committee . . . made their report on the subject. It consisted of most satisfactory amendments indeed; the rights of conscience—the liberty of the press—the trial by jury in all common law cases, and other things I do not so particularly remember, are all included, and guarded in the plainest manner. My heart warmed when I heard the report read, and I am assured there is no reason to doubt that these amendments will take place." [35]

In Congress itself, the New York representatives accepted Madison's amendments almost as a matter of course. The state's senators, Rufus King and Philip Schuyler,[36] were both Federalists and, although the debates of the Senate were secret, it is highly unlikely that they would have attacked Madison's amendments for not going far enough in meeting Antifederalist demands. Certainly they wrote no letters comparable to those written by the Virginia senators, Grayson and Lee.[37] In the House, only two of New York's six representatives participated in the August debates on Madison's resolutions. John Lawrence, an Antifederalist, and Egbert Benson, a Federalist, made a few

[35] *Fayetteville Gazette*, 14 September 1789.

[36] A disagreement between the two houses of the New York Legislature over the method by which senators should be chosen delayed the seating of these men until July 1789 (*Journal of the Assembly*, 9 July 1789; United States, *Journal of the First Session of the Senate of the United States of America* [Washington, 1820], pp. 44, 45; Frank Fletcher Stephens, *The Transitional Period, 1788–1789* [Columbia, Mo., 1909], pp. 22–28).

[37] For instance, Richard Henry Lee and William Grayson to the governor of Virginia, 28 September 1789, United States Bureau of Rolls and Library, *Documentary History of the Constitution of the United States* (Washington, 1894–1903), V, 216, 217.

very brief remarks, and both approved Madison's amendments.[38]

"The amendments agreed to in Congress and now offered to the State legislatures . . . ought to be in the hands of every well wisher to freedom," wrote Abraham Yates early in 1790. True, that morose individual added, Madison's proposals were "unimportant or trivial" to the people of New York, since they had had the good sense to incorporate almost all of them in their instrument of ratification, but for "such states . . . as have ratified the new system without explanation or provision" the proposed bill of rights was desirable and would be decidedly useful.[39] Yates then turned his attention from the Constitution and found new occupation for his contentious disposition in the reports of the new Secretary of the Treasury, his old acquaintance Alexander Hamilton.[40]

By the time Yates turned from Antifederalism, most New Yorkers had long since done so. The Madison amendments came before the New York Legislature with no fanfare, Clinton presenting them with his usual detachment.[41] All of Madison's proposals except for the second, the one dealing with alteration of the salaries of Congressmen and Senators, were accepted by both houses without recorded division.[42] And the official action was

[38] [Annals of Congress], Joseph Gales, compiler, *Debates and Proceedings in the Congress of the United States, 1789–1824* (Washington, 1834–1856), I, 703–756.

[39] Abraham Yates, "Pub. 15 & 22 March 1790," Abraham Yates, Jr., Papers, New York Public Library.

[40] *Ibid.*

[41] *Journal of the Senate of the State of New York* (New York, 1790), 13 January 1790.

[42] *Journal of the Senate*, 26 January 1790; *Journal of the Assembly*, 26 January 1790. The Council of Revision gave its official approval on 27 February 1790 (*Journal of the Senate*, 1 March 1790). There is record of only one member of the New York Legislature making remarks critical of Madison's bill of rights. Samuel Jones worried that the first amendment, protecting freedom of the press, might make it impossible to punish libel and that Madison's proposed eighth amendment left the right of trial by jury inadequately protected since it might be taken to repeal the

reported in the newspapers without comment.[43] In January 1790, amending the Constitution was no longer a controversial subject in New York State.

The rapid disappearance of Antifederalism in New York points up the fundamentally insubstantial nature of the division between Feds and Antis in that state. The split had its beginning in the personal animosity and distrust that characteristically underlie political alignments in the pre-party period of "faction politics." The split was deepened and poisoned by hard feelings as a result of Congress's clumsy handling of the impost affair in 1786. While the Philadelphia Convention was meeting, Alexander Hamilton's enemies became potential enemies of the Constitution because of Hamilton's ill-advised attack on Governor Clinton; and after the Constitution was presented to the people, suspicion of the immoderate haste with which the Federalists wished to force the adoption of an unamended Constitution solidified the opposition. Their suspicion drove them stubbornly to insist on their right to amend before they approved, and especially to make adoption of a bill of rights a condition of ratification.

Such were the foundations of New York Antifederalism. Had opposition to the Constitution in that state been rooted in any more substantial question of principle or in any deep and fundamental cleavages—social, economic, or sectional—it certainly would not have vanished so abruptly as it did as a factor in New York politics. With the amendment of the Constitution, Antifederalism died, and, simultaneously, the Constitution was deified. Political antagonisms continued in the nation and in New York State, but after adoption of the bill of rights men no longer divided on the question of support or hostility for the

---

Constitutional guarantees in Article III, Section 2. Neither Jones nor anyone else in the legislature made reference to the amendments proposed by the Poughkeepsie Convention and ignored by Madison (*New-York Gazette*, 27 January 1790).

[43] For instance, *New-York Journal*, 28 January 1790.

Constitution. Although New York State politics were much more heated in the nineties than they had been in the Confederation decade, parties drew new lines that cut across far too many old loyalties to be considered mere continuations of the Federalist-Antifederalist division. Indeed, in 1789 the most fiercely contested gubernatorial election since the Revolution saw two Antifederalists, George Clinton and Robert Yates, opposing each other. Before many years had passed, R. R. Livingston had joined the Republicans and Samuel Jones had broken with his old friends and become a Federalist—these realignments were only two of the most conspicuous changes.

Most Antifederalists, however, are believed to have become Republicans.[44] That Antifederalists should have shown a preference for the Republican party is, on the face of it, very odd, for the Republicans posed as pre-eminently the supporters and defenders of the Constitution. Although both parties became worshippers at the Constitutional shrine, the former Antifederalists were blindest in their adoration. The Federalists believed that the Constitution might be improved by some judicious interpretation of its clauses, but the Republicans would tolerate no tampering and were the champions of strict construction. Early in the ratification campaign, an anonymous essayist had predicted, "The present enemies of the federal government will ere long be its most zealous friends." [45] It was a true prophecy. After the addition of Madison's amendments there were no more enthusiastic supporters of the federal Constitution than the ex-Antifederalists, for they had got what they wanted.

[44] Wiliam Nisbet Chambers, *Political Parties in a New Nation* (New York, 1963), pp. 103, 104.

[45] *Independent Journal*, 10 October 1787.

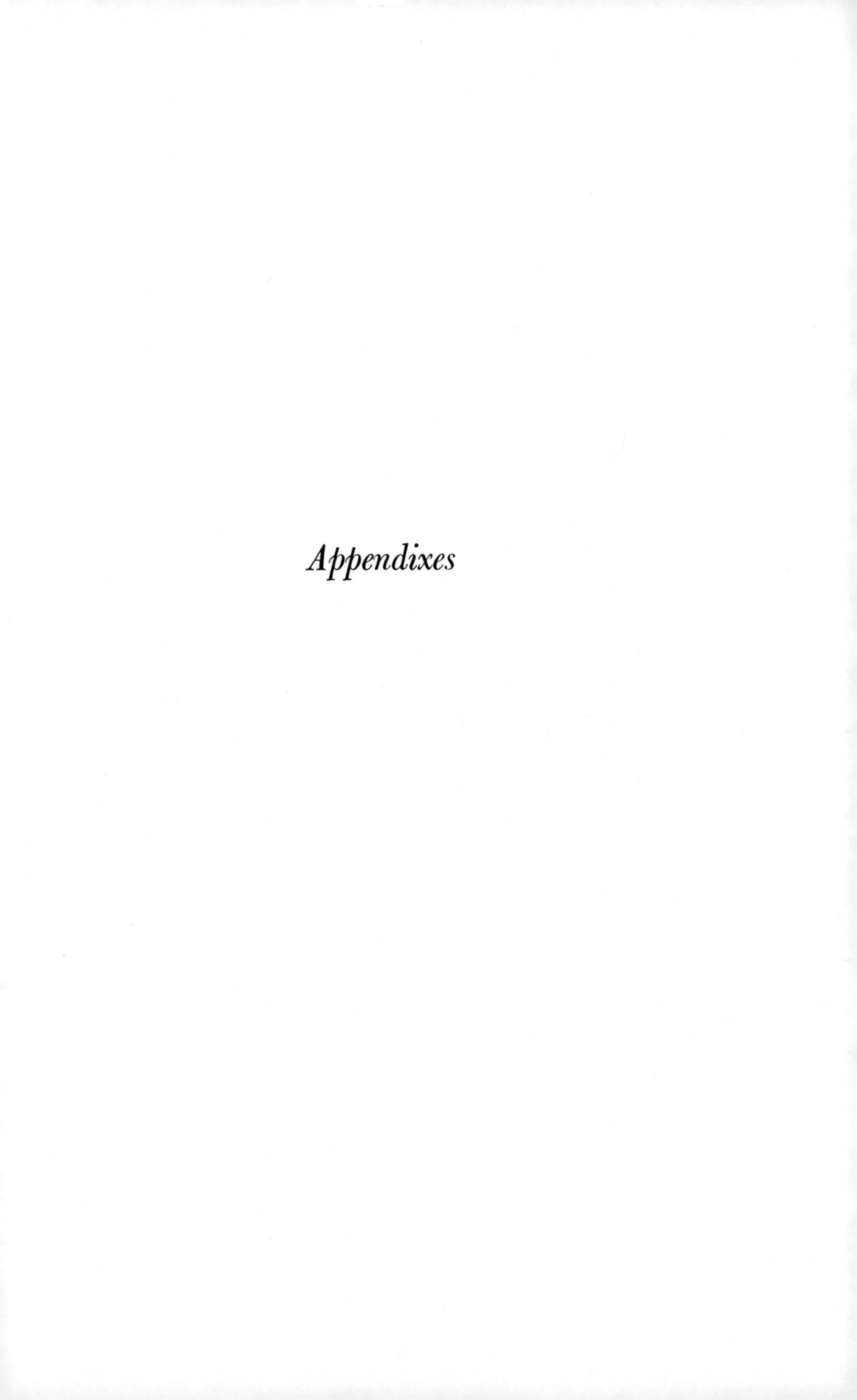

Appendixes

Appendix A

The Authorship of the Cato Letters

THE first "Cato"[1] letter appeared in the *New-York Journal* five days after the publication of the Constitution and a week after the document had been presented to Congress.[2] The essay was not an attack on the Philadelphia plan, but it hinted at future opposition. "Without directly engaging as an advocate for this new form of government, or as an opponent," "Cato" wrote, "let me conjure you to consider this a very important crisis of your safety and character." He advised the people of New York to "deliberate, therefore on this new national government

[1] Cato the younger committed suicide after Caesar's triumph over the liberty of his country. Jackson Turner Main (*The Antifederalists, Critics of the Constitution, 1781–1788* [Chapel Hill, N.C., 1961], p. 8) suggests that those who used the pseudonym Cato were thinking of the volume *Cato's Letters* by Thomas Gordon and John Trenchard as often as of the Roman patriot.

[2] E. Wilder Spaulding (*His Excellency George Clinton, Critic of the Constitution* [New York, 1938], p. 173) states that "Cato," I, and the Constitution were published in New York on the same day, 27 September 1787. Forrest McDonald (*We the People: The Economic Origins of the Constitution* [Chicago, 1958], p. 284) repeats this information and adds that the series of articles must have been written before the Constitution was in existence. Actually the Constitution first appeared as a supplement to the *Independent Journal* (New York) on Saturday, 22 September. "*Cato*," I, was not printed until the following Thursday.

with coolness; analyze it with criticism; and reflect on it with candour," and concluded by promising, "hereafter, and when it will be necessary, I shall make such observations on this new constitution as will tend to promote your welfare and be justified by reason and truth," [3] It was a dull, pedantic article, but it was immediately attacked by a writer who was offensive and obviously outraged: "Caesar." Referring to the suggestion offered by "Cato" that if amendments were desirable the present was the time to secure them, "Caesar" wrote: "O excellent thought, and happily advised! Be clamorous, my friends—be discontented—assert your prerogative—forever assert the power and *majesty of the people*. . . . . Has not the wisdom of America been drawn, as it were, into a focus, and the proferred constitution set forth with a unanimity that is unequalled in ancient or modern story? And shall we now wrangle and find fault with the *excellent* whole because some of its parts *might have been* more perfect?" Obviously, "Caesar" thought not, and he concluded by warning that "Cato in his future marches will very probably be *followed* by Caesar." [4]

"Cato" devoted his second essay to "Caesar." If "Cato" had had doubts before, he was now convinced that certain persons had a sinister interest in forcing the adoption of the Constitution without previous examination. He reproached "Caesar" for treating the people with "passion, insult, and threat," and concluded solemnly, "Hereafter I do not intend to be diverted by Caesar or any other. My object is to take up this new form of national government—compare it with the experience and opinions of the most sensible and approved political authors—and to show that its principles, and the exercise of them, will be dangerous to your liberty and happiness." [5] True to his promise, "Cato" continued his dreary march undaunted by the taunts of "Caesar" or of "Curtius" [6] and "Americanus," [7] the successors

[3] "Cato," I, *New-York Journal*, 27 September 1787.
[4] "Caesar," I, *Daily Advertiser* (New York), 1 October 1787.
[5] "*Cato*," II, *New-York Journal*, 11 October 1787.
[6] "*Curtius*," *Daily Advertiser*, 18 October 1787.
[7] "*Americanus*," *Daily Advertiser*, 23 November 1787.

of "Caesar." He contributed a total of seven articles to the *New-York Journal* before the series ended abruptly early in January.

"Caesar" appeared only once again, replying to the second essay by "Cato." "For my own part," he wrote, "I sincerely esteem it [the Constitution] a system, which, without the finger of *God*, could never have been suggested and agreed upon by such a diversity of interests." Since "Cato" had objected to "Caesar" "anticipating parts of his subject which he intended for future periods," "Caesar" sarcastically agreed to "break in no more upon his arrangements." [8] And "Caesar" did not march again.

The "Cato" essays were among the better pieces produced during the ratification campaign, although hardly good enough to be considered of enduring value or even of particular historical importance. The two "Caesar" essays were in no way outstanding; even as personal insults they were surpassed every week, and they were read chiefly because they attacked "Cato." Antifederalists suspected the author was a man "of little consequence" although he had assumed a grand Roman name.[9] Both sets of essays have received considerably more attention from historians than their intrinsic merits would warrant, because of the belief that Governor George Clinton was the author of the "Cato" series and Alexander Hamilton the author of "Caesar."

In 1892, Paul Leicester Ford made the identification of the authors of "Caesar" and "Cato" as Hamilton and Clinton that was accepted by all historians without question until Jacob E. Cooke published an article in 1960 [10] that presented persuasive evidence that Hamilton did not write the two articles.[11] Cooke also

[8] "*Caesar*," II, *Daily Advertiser*, 17 October 1787.

[9] "Countryman," IV, *New-York Journal*, 10 January 1788.

[10] Jacob E. Cooke, "Alexander Hamilton's Authorship of the 'Caesar' Letters," *William and Mary Quarterly*, third series, XVII (1960), 78–85.

[11] The evidence against Ford's identification of Hamilton as "Caesar" is strengthened by an examination of the *New-York Journal* article quoted by Ford, which Cooke could not locate ("Authorship," p. 83). It appeared in the *New-York Journal* of 4 February 1788. It is an excerpt from a paragraph clipped from a Philadelphia paper and ascribed to "a southern writer." The author of the remarks Ford relies on could have

remarked that Ford's identification of the author of the "Cato" letters was "not altogether convincing," but he accepted the opinion of George Clinton's only biographer that the governor was the author.[12] Yet Clinton's biographer does not give documentary support for his own identification of "Cato" and apparently accepted Ford's conclusion uncritically.[13]

Ford advanced three arguments to support his identification of George Clinton as the author of the "Cato" series. *1.* "These letters," he wrote, "were commonly ascribed to the pen of George Clinton in the press of the day." *2.* This ascription is confirmed by a letter found in the George Clinton Papers in the New York State Library signed by "A. Hamilton," but in the handwriting of John Lamb, the New York City Antifederalist:

18 October 1787.

Dear Sir:

Since my last the chief of the state party has declared his opposition to the government proposed, both in private conversation and in print. That you may judge of the *reason* and *fairness* of his views, I send you the two essays, with a reply by Caesar. On further consideration it was concluded to abandon this personal form, and to take up the principles of the whole subject. These will be sent to you as published, and might with advantage be republished in your gazettes." **** [*sic*]

A. Hamilton

3. Finally, Ford notes that "the last of this series was printed on January 3, 1788, and the New York Assembly met on the 9th of the same month, after which Governor Clinton was probably too occupied to write more. . . ." [14]

Although Ford asserts that the ascription of "Cato" to George

---

had little knowledge of happenings in New York, and, as Cooke suspected, the omitted portion of the article alters the sense.

[12] Cooke, "Authorship," p. 79n.

[13] Spaulding, *His Excellency George Clinton*, p. 173.

[14] Paul Leicester Ford, ed., *Essays on the Constitution of the United States Published During its Discussion by the People, 1787–1788* (Brooklyn, 1888), p. 243.

Clinton was "common" in the contemporary press, I have been able to find no direct ascription of this character nor any certain indirect ascription. "Cato" is once referred to as a "state demagogue," [15] but that could apply to countless individuals including Abraham Yates and John Lamb, who were denounced under the epithet frequently. More likely, "Cato" was called a state demagogue because of the prevalent belief at that period that only state demagogues would oppose the Constitution.[16] Writers need not have known the real author of "Cato" in order to attack him as a "state demagogue." Moreover, the writer who uses that term implies that "Cato" presently holds no office, which would mean the governor could not have been intended. Another writer described "Cato" as "undoubtedly . . . some little State Sovereign," [17] which might be thought to apply to Clinton, but the writer was being facetious and did not intend his identifications to be taken seriously. "Cato" was called a little "State Sovereign" because "State Sovereignty seems to be the burden of the song." And the writer continued in the same tone, "Marcus is so full of his *interest* that I suspect him to be a *usurer*." [18] Incidentally, if one were to describe Clinton as a "State Sovereign," the governor was surely not a "little" one. In the single set of articles that explicitly couples the name of "Cato" with that of "his X–L–N–C" it is implied that the two are separate individuals.[19]

The letter that Ford cites is of doubtful authenticity, as Cooke convincingly demonstrates.

No scholar save Ford, so far as can be determined, has seen the letter; as it no longer exists, it presumably was destroyed by the fire of 1911. . . . The authenticity of the letter is unsupported by

[15] "Cato's Soliloquy," *Daily Advertiser*, 23 October 1787.

[16] See above, Chap. XI.

[17] "A Man of No Party," *Daily Advertiser*, 19 October 1787.

[18] *Ibid.*

[19] "Song First," *Northern Centinel*, 11 December 1787; "Song Second," *ibid.*, 18 December 1787.

> any corroborative evidence. It is not mentioned in any letter to or from Hamilton, and no reference to it has been found among the correspondence of his contemporaries. . . . Was the letter really in Lamb's hand or in that of someone unknown whose integrity might be suspect? Even if the letter were in Lamb's writing, certain difficulties would remain. The last line, for example, indicates that it was addressed to someone outside New York State. Since Hamilton at this time did not keep copies of his letters, Lamb could not have secured a copy of it from Hamilton's files, and it is highly unlikely that any of Hamilton's correspondents would have supplied Lamb with one of his letters.[20]

One also wonders why any contemporary should bother to take a copy of the letter, which appears to have no usefulness except to historians.

Even if the letter were accepted as genuine, it does not prove that Clinton was "Cato." The expression used to describe the author of the series is "chief of the state party," a phrase that applies with more justice to Abraham Yates than to George Clinton.[21] Furthermore, it is certain that Hamilton did not believe the governor was "Cato." [22] Had he believed that those pieces were from Clinton's pen he would surely have exploited the fact by pointing it up in a personal attack. He never hesitated to denounce the governor by name on much slimmer evidence of an antifederal disposition.[23] Indeed, had *any* Federalist suspected that the governor had written the "Cato" series, a barrage of essays would have been directed against him.

If Clinton was "Cato," he hid his identity amazingly well since there is no reference to a connection between the two even in the private correspondence of the Antifederalists, and "Cato" was not among the publications that the Antifederal committees took pains to circulate. Had the party leaders suspected that the

20 Cooke, "Authorship," pp. 81, 82. 21 See above, Chaps. III, IV.

22 Cooke, "Authorship," pp. 79, 80n.

23 See above, Chap. IV; "Letters of H. G.," Harold C. Syrett, ed., and Jacob E. Cooke, assoc. ed., *The Papers of Alexander Hamilton* (New York, 1961–), V, 262, *passim.*

letters came from the pen of the governor, they would surely have made an effort to exploit his prestige. Moreover, Clinton must have been very sure that his authorship of the series would not be uncovered, for he insisted to the end that he had an open mind on the question and he would have appeared a blatant hypocrite had anyone known him as "Cato." [24]

Ford's final argument, the coincidence between the end of the "Cato" series and the opening of the New York Legislature would apply even more strongly to men who were actually members of that body—like Abraham Yates. But there is no necessary connection between the convening of the legislature and the end of the series. "Cato," whoever he was, may have stopped scribbling for innumerable reasons. He may have grown bored. He may have moved to Albany. He may have died.

"But who is Cato," as "Curtius" asked, "[w]hose elegant diction and long-spun argumentation would lead us to suspect him both the scholar and the sophist." [25] George Clinton is not a likely candidate. As far as is known, Clinton never sent a piece to the printers either before or after the "Cato" series, and the pedantry of the essays falls strangely on a man who never made the slightest "pretence to intellectual eminence or scholarship sublime," and who, as his biographer has written, "was never an eager reader." [26] Where did he gather the ponderous references to Sidney, Hume, Locke, and Montesquieu? And how did this man, who seldom spoke in public and wrote no more than he had to,[27] manage to produce his first attempts at scholarly essay writing so quickly? Furthermore, if Clinton was "Cato" he had suddenly grown strangely short-tempered. As governor, Clinton kept silent in the face of Hamilton's attack of 21 July,[28] as si-

[24] Remarks made in the N.Y. State Convention, [17 July 1788], George Clinton Papers, New York Public Library.

[25] "Curtius," II, *Daily Advertiser*, 18 October 1787.

[26] Spaulding, *His Excellency George Clinton*, p. 11.

[27] E. Wilder Spaulding, *New York in the Critical Period, 1783–1789* (New York, 1932), pp. 97, 98.

[28] See above, Chap. IV.

lence was his reply to other attacks both before and later. Yet "Cato" could not ignore "Caesar" but snapped back at once with *ad hominem* retorts.

Since Clinton did not enjoy writing and entertained no illusions concerning his intellectual gifts, he could have had no motive for writing the "Cato" essays unless he intended to make his authorship known for the influence his name would have. Hamilton wrote of Clinton that he "was not a man governed in ordinary cases by sudden impulse . . . he was circumspect and guarded, and seldom acted or spoke without premeditation or design." [29] For Clinton to have written the "Cato" essays would have been quite at variance with this character. Clinton cherished his reputation as a man who reached decisions slowly and deliberately, striving with scrupulous honesty to reach conclusions free from prejudice and passion. Had he felt it imperative that a derogatory mention of the Philadelphia plan appear in the press five days after the document itself had reached the public, he could have delegated the task to a qualified friend. Since the author of "Cato" was unknown, the series did not owe its influence to the governor's prestige, and an identification of Clinton as the author would have destroyed his reputation as a deliberate thinker and his policy of keeping his views on the document to himself until the legislature had acted. Clinton was not the sort of man to run such a risk.

Who, then was "Cato," if he was not George Clinton? The name Abraham Yates has already been mentioned three times in this discussion, and while no positive identification is possible, Yates is a plausible suspect. For what they are worth, the indirect identifications of "Cato" made by contemporaries apply to him with greater force than they do to the governor. He was a member of the New York Legislature that met in Poughkeepsie in January 1788. He was, moreover, a widely read man

[29] Quoted in John C. Hamilton, *History of the Republic of the United States as Traced in the Writings of Alexander Hamilton and his Contemporaries* (Philadelphia, 1864), III, 324.

with quotations from the authorities always at his fingertips, and he was an experienced propagandist. He obviously enjoyed writing political essays, and his "Rough-Hewer" and "Sidney" pieces were well-known. Strangely enough, however, with the exception of a single "Sidney" essay printed in mid-October,[30] Abraham Yates is known to have written no other piece on the Constitution until another essay signed "Sidney" appeared in the *Albany Gazette* more than three months later.[31] But he was frequently attacked in the press. Perhaps Yates was not silent for those three months in the winter of 1787–1788, but wrote the series over the pseudonymn "Cato" in order to protect himself from the personal attacks that showered him as "Sidney" and "Rough-Hewer." A desire for anonymity would also explain the comparatively restrained style of "Cato." Abraham Yates could have delivered the five final numbers of the "Cato" series to Thomas Greenleaf late in October or he might have mailed them from Albany [32] when he was out of the City, requesting that the essays be printed weekly in the Thursday edition of Greenleaf's paper, which was sent to country subscribers as well as to the City readers. A letter from Abraham G. Lansing suggests that Yates was engaged in writing a series of articles in January.[33] Perhaps when the legislature convened he was too engaged with his business as Antifederalist leader in the Senate to contribute any more essays for the City.[34] It is certainly a possibility. Perhaps the wit who wrote the following cryptic verse was hinting at such a connection:

> Much joy to ye printers, ye'll now get your part
> The *law* and *land-jobbers* are losing the start

[30] *New-York Journal,* supp. extraordinary, 18 October 1787.

[31] *Country Journal,* 5 February 1788.

[32] The post ran between Albany and New York City twice a week (Joel Munsell, ed., *The Annals of Albany* [Albany, 1850–1859], II, 203.

[33] Abraham G. Lansing to Abraham Yates, 31 January 1788, Abraham Yates, Jr., Papers, New York Public Library.

[34] Melancton Smith to Abraham Yates, 23 January 1788, *ibid.*

The *New Constitution* has still to undo her,
In front the sly CATO—in rear the ROUGH HEWER.[35]

In the absence of further evidence, it is impossible to be sure who "Cato" was, but Abraham Yates is not an improbable guess, and he is much more likely than George Clinton to have written the essays.

[35] "Parody of the Newsmongers Song," *Daily Advertiser*, 11 December 1788.

Appendix B[1]

The New York Instrument of Ratification

WE the Delegates of the People of the State of New York, duly elected and Met in Convention, having maturely considered the Constitution for the United States of America, agreed to on the seventeenth day of September, in the year One thousand Seven hundred and Eighty seven, by the Convention then assembled at Philadelphia in the Common-wealth of Pennsylvania (a Copy whereof precedes these presents) and having also seriously and deliberately considered the present situation of the United States, Do DECLARE AND MAKE KNOWN.

That all Power is originally vested in and consequently derived from the People, and that Government is instituted by them for their common Interest Protection and Security.

That the enjoyment of Life, Liberty and the pursuit of Happiness are essential rights which every Government ought to respect and preserve.

That the powers of Government may be reassumed by the People, whensoever it shall become necessary to their Happiness; that every Power, Jurisdiction and right, which is not by the said Constitution clearly delegated to the Congress of the United States,

[1] Record Group 11, The National Archives, Washington.

or the departments of the Government thereof, remains to the People of the several States, or to their respective State Governments to whom they may have granted the same; And that those Clauses in the said Constitution, which declare, that Congress shall not have or exercise certain Powers, do not imply that Congress is entitled to any Powers not given by the said Constitution; but such Clauses are to be construed either as exceptions to certain specified Powers, or as inserted merely for greater Caution.

That the People have an equal, natural and unalienable right, freely and peaceably to Exercise their Religion according to the dictates of Conscience, and that no Religious Sect or Society ought to be favoured or established by Law in preference of others.

That the People have a right to keep and bear Arms; that a well regulated Militia, including the body of the People *capable of bearing Arms*, is the proper, natural and safe defence of a free State;

That the Militia should not be subject to Martial Law, except in time of War, Rebellion or Insurrection.

That standing Armies in time of Peace are dangerous to Liberty, and ought not to be kept up, except in Cases of necessity; and that at all times, the Military should be under strict Subordination to the civil Power.

That in time of Peace no Soldier ought to be quartered in any House without the consent of the Owner, and in time of War only by the civil Magistrate in such manner as the Laws may direct.

That no Person ought to be taken imprisoned, or disseised of his freehold, or be exiled or deprived of his Privileges, Franchises, Life, Liberty or Property, but by due process of Law.

That no Person ought to be put twice in Jeopardy of Life or Limb for one and the same Offence, nor, unless in case of impeachment, be punished more than once for the same Offence.

That every Person restrained of his Liberty is entitled to an enquiry into the lawfulness of such restraint, and to a removal thereof if unlawful, and that such enquiry and removal ought not to be denied or delayed, except when on account of Public Danger the Congress shall suspend the privilege of the Writ of Habeas Corpus.

That excessive Bail ought not to be required; nor excessive Fines imposed; nor Cruel or unusual Punishments inflicted.

That (except in the Government of the Land and Naval Forces, and of the Militia when in actual Service, and in cases of Impeachment) a Presentment or Indictment by a Grand Jury ought to be observed as a necessary preliminary to the trial of all Crimes cognizable by the Judiciary of the United States, and such Trial should be speedy, public, and by an impartial Jury of the County where the Crime was committed; and that no person can be found Guilty without the unanimous consent of such Jury. But in cases of Crimes not committed within any County of any of the United States, and in Cases of Crimes committed within any County in which a general Insurrection may prevail, or which may be in the possession of a foreign Enemy, the enquiry and trial may be in such County as the Congress shall by Law direct; which County in the two Cases last mentioned should be as near as conveniently may be to that County in which the Crime may have been committed. And that in all Criminal Prosecutions, the Accused ought to be informed of the cause and nature of his Accusation, to be confronted with his accusers and the Witnesses against him, to have the means of producing his Witnesses, and the assistance of Council for his defense, and should not be compelled to give Evidence against himself.

That the trial by Jury in the extent that it obtains by the Common Law of England is one of the greatest securities to the rights of a free People, and ought to remain inviolate.

That every Freeman has a right to be secure from all unreasonable searches and seizures of his person his papers or his property, and therefore, that all Warrants to search suspected places or seize any Freeman his papers or property, without information upon Oath or Affirmation of sufficient cause, are grievous and oppressive; and that all general Warrants (or such in which the place or person suspected are not particularly designated) are dangerous and ought not to be granted.

That the People have a right peaceably to assemble together to consult for their common good, or to instruct their Representatives; and that every person has a right to Petition or apply to the Legislature for redress of Grievances.—That the Freedom of the Press ought not to be violated or restrained.

That there should be once in four years an Election of the President and Vice President, so that no Officer who may be appointed by the Congress to act as President in case of the removal, death, resignation or inability of the President and Vice President can in any case continue to act beyond the termination of the period for which the last President and Vice President were elected.

That nothing contained in the said Constitution is to be construed to prevent the Legislature of any State from passing Laws at its discretion from time to time to divide such State into convenient Districts, and to apportion its Representatives to and amongst such Districts.

That the Prohibition contained in the said Constitution against *ex post facto* Laws, extends only to Laws concerning Crimes.

That all Appeals in Causes determineable according to the course of the common Law, ought to be by Writ of Error and not otherwise.

That the Judicial Power of the United States in cases in which a State may be a party, does not extend to criminal Prosecutions, or to authorize any Suit by any Person against a State.

That the Judicial Power of the United States as to Controversies between Citizens of the same State claiming Lands under Grants of different States is not to be construed to extend to any other Controversies between them, except those which relate to such Lands, so claimed under Grants of different States.

That the Jurisdiction of the Supreme Court of the United States, or of any other Court to be instituted by the Congress, is not in any case to be encreased enlarged or extended by any Fiction Collusion or mere suggestion;—And That no Treaty is to be construed so to operate as to alter the Constitution of any State.

UNDER these impressions and declaring that the rights aforesaid cannot be abridged or violated, and that the Explanations aforesaid are consistent with the said Constitution, And in Confidence that the Amendments which shall have been proposed to the said Constitution will receive an early and mature Consideration: WE the said Delegates, in the Name and in the behalf of the People of the State of New York Do by these presents Assent to and Ratify the said Constitution. IN FULL CONFIDENCE NEVERTHELESS that until a Convention shall be called and convened for proposing Amendments to the said Constitution, the Militia of this State will not be continued in Service out of this State for a longer term than six weeks without the Consent of the Legislature thereof;—that the Congress will not make or alter any Regulation in this State respecting the times places and manner of holding Elections for Senators or Representatives unless the Legislature of this State shall neglect or refuse to make Laws or regulations for the purpose, or from any circumstance be incapable of making the same, and that in those cases such power will only be exercised until the Legislature of this State shall make provision in the Premises;—that no Excise will be imposed on any Article of the Growth production or Manufacture of the United States, or any of them within this State, Ardent Spirits excepted; And that the Congress will not lay direct Taxes within this State, but when the Monies arising from the Impost and Excise shall be insufficient for the public Exigencies, nor then, until Congress shall first have made a Requisition upon this State to assess levy and pay the Amount of such Requisition made agreably to the Census fixed in the said Constitution in such way and manner as the Legislature of this State shall judge best, but that in such case, if the State shall neglect or refuse to pay its proportion pursuant to such Requisition, then the Congress may assess and levy this States proportion together with Interest at the Rate of six per Centum per Annum from the time at which the same was required to be paid.

DONE in Convention at Poughkeepsie in the County of Dutchess in the State of New York and twenty sixth day of July in the year of our Lord One thousand Seven hundred and Eighty eight.

By Order of the Convention.
GEO: CLINTON President

Attested
JOHN MCKESSON
ABM B. BANCKER } Secretaries—

AND the Convention do in the Name and Behalf of the People of the State of New York enjoin it upon their Representatives in the Congress, to Exert all their Influence, and use all reasonable means to Obtain a Ratification of the following Amendments to the said Constitution in the manner prescribed therein; and in all Laws to be passed by the Congress in the meantime to conform to the spirit of the said Amendments as far as the Constitution will admit.

That there shall be one Representative for every thirty thousand

Inhabitants, according to the enumeration or Census mentioned in the Constitution, until the whole number of Representatives amounts to two hundred; after which that number shall be continued or encreased but not diminished, as Congress shall direct, and according to such ratio as the Congress shall fix, in conformity to the rule prescribed for the Apportionment of Representatives and direct Taxes.

That the Congress do not impose any Excise on any Article (except Ardent Spirits) of the Growth Production or Manufacture of the United States, or any of them.

That Congress do not lay direct Taxes but when the Monies arising from the Impost and Excise shall be insufficient for the Public Exigencies, nor then until Congress shall first have made a Requisition upon the States to assess levy and pay their respective proportions of such Requisition, agreably to the Census fixed in the said Constitution, in such way and manner as the Legislatures of the respective States shall judge best; and in such Case, if any State shall neglect or refuse to pay its proportion persuant to such Requisition, then Congress may assess and levy such States proportion, together with Interest at the rate of six per Centum per Annum, from the time of Payment prescribed in such Requisition.

That the Congress shall not make or alter any Regulation in any State respecting the times places and manner of holding Elections for Senators or Representatives, unless the Legislature of such State shall neglect or refuse to make Laws or Regulations for the purpose, or from any circumstance be incapable of making the same, and then only until the Legislature of such State shall make provision in the premises; provided that Congress may prescribe the time for the Election of Representatives.

That no Persons except natural born Citizens, or such as were Citizens on or before the fourth day of July one thousand seven hundred and seventy six, or such as held Commissions under the United States during the War, and have at any time since the fourth day of July one thousand seven hundred and seventy six become Citizens of one or other of the United States, and who shall be Freeholders, shall be eligible to the Places of President, Vice President, or Members of either House of the Congress of the United States.

That the Congress do not grant Monopolies or erect any Company with exclusive Advantages of Commerce.

That no standing Army or regular Troops shall be raised or kept up in time of peace, without the consent of two-thirds of the Senators and Representatives present in each House.

That no Money be borrowed on the Credit of the United States without the Assent of two-thirds of the Senators and Representatives present in each House.

That the Congress shall not declare War without the concurrence of two-thirds of the Senators and Representatives present in each House.

That the Privilege of the *Habeas Corpus* shall not by any Law be suspended for a longer term than six Months, or until twenty days after the Meeting of the Congress next following the passing of the Act for such suspension.

That the Right of the Congress to exercise exclusive Legislation over such District, not exceeding ten Miles square, as may be cession of a particular State, and the acceptance of Congress, become the Seat of the Government of the United States, shall not be so exercised, as to exempt the Inhabitants of such District from paying the like Taxes Imposts Duties and Excises, as shall be imposed on the other Inhabitants of the State in which such District may be; and that no person shall be privileged within the said Districts from Arrest for Crimes committed, or Debts contracted out of the said District.

That the Right of exclusive Legislation with respect to such places as may be purchased for the Erection of Forts, Magazines, Arsenals, Dockyards and other needful Buildings, shall not authorize the Congress to make any Law to prevent the Laws of the States respectively in which they may be, from extending to such places in all civil and Criminal Matters, except as to such Persons as shall be in the Service of the United States; nor to them with respect to Crimes committed without such Places.

That the Compensation for the Senators and Representatives be ascertained by standing Laws; and that no alteration of the existing rate of Compensation shall operate for the Benefit of the Representatives, until after a subsequent Election shall have been had.

That the Journals of the Congress shall be published at least once a year, with the exception of such parts relating to Treaties or Military operations, as in the Judgment of either House shall require Secrecy; and that both Houses of Congress shall always keep their Doors open during their Sessions, unless the Business may in their Opinion requires Secrecy. That the yeas & nays shall be entered on the Journals whenever two Members in either House may require it.

That no Capitation Tax shall ever be laid by the Congress.

That no Person be eligible as a Senator for more than six years in any term of twelve years; and that the Legislatures of the respective States may recal their Senators or either of them, and elect others in their stead, to serve the remainder of the time for which the Senators so recalled were appointed.

That no Senator or Representative shall during the time for which he was elected be appointed to any Office under the Authority of the United States.

That the Authority given to the Executives of the States to fill the vacancies of Senators be abolished, and that such vacancies be filled by the respective Legislatures.

That the Power of Congress to pass uniform Laws concerning Bankruptcy shall only extend to Merchants and other Traders; and that the States respectively may pass Laws for the relief of other Insolvent Debtors.

That no Person shall be eligible to the Office of President of the United States a third time.

That the Executive shall not grant Pardons for Treason, unless with the Consent of the Congress; but may at his discretion grant Reprieves to persons convicted of Treason, until their Cases, can be laid before the Congress.

That the President or person exercising his Powers for the time being, shall not command an Army in the Field in person, without the previous desire of the Congress.

That all Letters Patent, Commissions, Pardons, Writs and Process of the United States, shall run in the Name of *the People of the United States*, and be tested in the Name of the President of the United States, or the person exercising his powers for the time being, or the first Judge of the Court out of which the same shall issue, as the case may be.

That the Congress shall not constitute ordain or establish any Tribunals or Inferior Courts, with any other than Appellate Jurisdiction, except such as may be necessary for the Tryal of Causes of Admiralty and Maritime Jurisdiction, and for the Trial of Piracies and Felonies committed on the High Seas; and in all other Cases to which the Judicial Power of the United States extends, and in which the Supreme Court of the United States has not original Jurisdiction, the Causes shall be heard tried, and determined in some one of the State Courts, with the right of Appeal to the Supreme Court of the United States, or other proper Tribunal to be established for that purpose by the Congress, with such exceptions, and under such regulations as the Congress shall make.

That the Court for the Trial of Impeachments shall consist of the Senate, the Judges of the Supreme Court of the United States, and the first or Senior Judge for the time being, of the highest Court of general and ordinary common Law Jurisdiction in each State;—that the Congress shall by standing Laws designate the Courts in the respective States answering this Description, and in States having no Courts exactly answering this Description, shall designate some other Court, preferring such if any there be, whose Judge or Judges may hold their places during good Behaviour—Provided that no more than one Judge, other than Judges of the Supreme Court of the United States, shall come from one State—That the Congress be authorized to pass Laws for compensating the said Judges for such Services and for compelling their Attendance—and that a Majority at least of the said Judges shall be requisite to constitute the said Court—that no person impeached shall sit as a Member thereof. That each Member shall previous to the entering upon any Trial take an Oath or Affirmation, honestly and impartially to hear and determine the Cause—and that a Majority of the Members present shall be necessary to a Conviction.

That persons aggrieved by any Judgment, Sentence or Decree of the Supreme Court of the United States, in any Cause in which that Court has original Jurisdiction, with such exceptions and under such Regulations as the Congress shall make concerning the same, shall upon application, have a Commission to be issued by the President of the United States, to such Men learned in the Law as he shall nominate, and by and with the Advice and consent of the

Senate appoint, not less than seven, authorizing such Commissioners, or any seven or more of them, to correct the Errors in such Judgment or to review such Sentence and Decree, as the case may be, and to do Justice to the parties in the Premises.

That no Judge of the Supreme Court of the United States shall hold any other Office under the United States, or any of them.

That the Judicial Power of the United States shall extend to no Controversies respecting Land, unless it relate to Claims of Territory or Jurisdiction between States, or to Claims of Land between Individuals, or between States and Individuals under the Grants of different States.

That the Militia of any State shall not be compelled to serve without the limits of the State for a longer term than six weeks, without the Consent of the Legislature thereof.

That the words *without the Consent of the Congress* in the seventh Clause of the ninth Section of the first Article of the Constitution, be expunged.

That the Senators and Representatives and all Executive and Judicial Officers of the United States shall be bound by Oath or Affirmation not to infringe or violate the Constitutions or Rights of the respective States.

That the Legislatures of the respective States may make Provision by Law, that the Electors of the Election Districts to be by them appointed shall chuse a Citizen of the United States who shall have been an Inhabitant of such District for the Term of one year immediately preceeding the time of his Election, for one of the Representatives of such State.

DONE in Convention at Poughkeepsie in the County of Dutchess in the State of New York the twenty sixth day of July in the year of our Lord One thousand seven hundred and Eighty eight.

By Order of the Convention.
GEO: CLINTON President

Attested—

JOHN MCKESSON } Secretaries—
AB^M B. BANCKER }

Bibliography and Index

Bibliography

PRIMARY MATERIALS

Manuscript Collections

Abraham Bancker Papers, New-York Historical Society.
George Bancroft Transcripts of Livingston Letters, 1775–1799, New York Public Library.
De Witt Clinton Papers, Special Collections, Columbia University.
George Clinton Papers, New York Public Library.
James Duane Papers, New-York Historical Society.
William Duer Papers, New-York Historical Society.
Emmet Collection, New York Public Library.
John Jay Manuscripts, Columbia University.
John Lamb Papers, New-York Historical Society.
John Lansing, Jr., Papers, New-York Historical Society.
Gilbert Livingston Reports of the Poughkeepsie Convention, New York Public Library.
John McKesson Papers, New-York Historical Society.
Philip John Schuyler Papers, New York Public Library.
Abraham Yates, Jr., Papers, New York Public Library.

Newspapers

[Albany] *Federal Herald.*
Albany Gazette.

Albany Journal.
Hudson Weekly Gazette.
[Lansingburgh] *Northern Centinel.*
[New York] *Daily Advertiser.*
[New York] *Independent Journal.*
New-York Journal.
New-York Morning Post.
New-York Packet.
[Philadelphia] *Pennsylvania Gazette.*
[Philadelphia] *Pennsylvania Herald.*
[Poughkeepsie] *Country Journal.*

Broadsides and Pamphlets

Broadside Collection, New-York Historical Society.
Broadside Collection, New-York Public Library.
The Federalist. Jacob E. Cooke, ed. Cleveland, 1961.
The Federalist. John C. Hamilton, ed. Philadelphia, 1864.
Ford, Paul Leicester, ed. *Essays on the Constitution of the United States Published During its Discussion by the People, 1787–1788.* Brooklyn, 1892.
——, ed. *Pamphlets on the Constitution of the United States Published During its Discussion by the People, 1787–1788.* Brooklyn 1888.
Lee, Richard Henry. "Letters from the Federal Farmer," in *Empire and Nation.* Forrest McDonald, ed. Englewood Cliffs, N.J., 1962.
[Yates, Abraham]. *Political Papers, Addressed to the Advocates for a Congressional Revenue, in the State of New-York.* New York, 1786.

Published Correspondence, Writings, and Memoirs

Burnett, Edmund C., ed. *Letters of Members of the Continental Congress.* Washington, 1921–1936.
Campbell, William W. *Life and Writings of De Witt Clinton.* New York, 1844.
Clinton, George. *Public Papers of George Clinton, First Governor of New York, 1777–1795, 1801–1804.* Hugh Hastings, ed. New York, 1899–1914.
Duer, William Alexander. *New-York As it Was During the Latter Part of the Last Century.* New York, 1849.

——. *Reminiscences of an Old New Yorker.* New York, 1867.

Hamilton, Alexander. *The Papers of Alexander Hamilton.* Harold C. Syrett, ed., and Jacob E. Cooke, assoc. ed. New York 1961– .

——. *Works of Alexander Hamilton.* John C. Hamilton, ed. New York, 1891.

——. *The Works of Alexander Hamilton.* Henry Cabot Lodge, ed. New York, 1904.

Hamilton, James A. *Reminiscences.* New York, 1869.

Jay, John. *The Correspondence and Public Papers of John Jay.* H. P. Johnston, ed. New York, 1891.

Jefferson, Thomas. *The Writings of Thomas Jefferson.* Paul Leicester Ford, ed. New York, 1892.

Kent, James, *Memoirs and Letters of James Kent, Late Chancellor of the State of New York.* William Kent, ed. Boston, 1898.

King, Charles A. *Life and Correspondence of Rufus King.* New York, 1894.

Leake, Issac Q. *Memoir of the Life and Times of General John Lamb.* Albany, 1850.

Lee, Richard Henry. *The Letters of Richard Henry Lee.* James Curtis Ballagh, ed. New York, 1914.

Madison, James. *The Papers of James Madison.* Henry D. Gilpin, ed. New York, 1841.

Madison, James. *Writings of James Madison, Comprising His Public Papers and His Private Correspondence.* Gaillard Hunt, ed. New York, 1900–1910.

Sparks, Jared, ed. *Correspondence of the American Revolution; being Letters of Eminent Men to George Washington.* Boston, 1853.

Van Schaack, Henry. *Memoirs of Henry Van Schaack, Embracing Sections of his Correspondence.* Henry C. Van Schaack, ed., Chicago, 1892.

Van Schaack, Henry C. *The Life of Peter Van Schaack.* New York, 1842.

Washington, George. *The Writings of George Washington.* John C. Fitzpatrick, ed. Washington, 1931–1944.

Washington, George. *Writings of George Washington.* Jared Sparks, ed. Boston, 1834.

Webb, Samuel Blanchley. *Correspondence and Journals of Samuel Blanchley Webb.* W. C. Ford, ed. New York, 1893–1894.

Other Printed Sources

Bancroft, George. "A Hartford Convention in 1780," *Magazine of American History*, VIII, pt. 2 (1882), 688–698.

Commonwealth of Massachusetts. *Debates and Proceedings in the Convention of The Commonwealth of Massachusetts, 1788.* Boston, 1856.

Elliot, Jonathan, ed. *The Debates in the Several State Conventions on the Adoption of the Federal Constitution.* Philadelphia, 1876.

Farrand, Max, ed. *The Records of the Federal Convention of 1787.* New Haven, 1911.

Ford, Worthington C., and Gaillard Hunt, eds. *Journals of the Continental Congress, 1774–1789.* Washington, 1904–1937.

Freemen of New York. New-York Historical Society Collections, 1885. New York, 1886.

Hough, Franklin B., ed. *The New-York Civil List from 1777 to 1855.* Albany, 1855.

Lynd, Staughton. "Abraham Yates's History of the Movement for the United States Constitution," *William and Mary Quarterly*, third series, XX (1963), 223–245.

Munsell, Joel, ed. *The Annals of Albany.* Albany, 1850–1859.

New York State. *Debates and Proceedings of the Convention of the State of New-York.* New York, 1788.

New York State. *Journal of the Assembly of the State of New York.* New York and Albany, 1777–1790.

New York State. *Journal of the Senate of the State of New York.* New York and Albany, 1777–1790.

New York State. *Journal of the Convention of the State of New York.* Poughkeepsie, 1788.

New York State. *Laws of the State of New York Passed at the Sessions of the Legislature.* Albany, 1886–1888.

New York State. *Messages from the Governors.* Charles Z. Lincoln, ed. Albany, 1909.

O'Callaghan, Edmund Burke, ed. *Documentary History of the State of New York.* Albany, 1849–1851.

Prescott, Arthur Taylor. *Drafting the Federal Constitution.* Pineville, La., 1941.

Stokes, I. N. Phelps. *The Iconography of Manhattan Island, 1492–1909.* New York, 1915–1928.

Strayer, Joseph Reese, ed. *The Delegate from New York, or Proceedings of the Federal Convention from the Notes of John Lansing, Jr.* Princeton, 1939.

United States. *American State Papers: Documents, Legislative and Executive, 1789–1924.* Washington, 1832–1861.

United States. [Annals of Congress] *Debates and Proceedings in the Congress of the United States, 1789–1824.* Joseph Gales, compiler. Washington, 1834–1856.

United States. *Journal of the First Session of the Senate of the United States of America.* Washington, 1820.

United States Bureau of the Census. *Heads of Families at the First Census of the United States Taken in the Year 1790: New York.* Washington, 1908.

United States Bureau of the Census. *Historical Statistics of the United States: Colonial Times to 1957.* Washington, 1960.

United States Bureau of Rolls and Library. *Documentary History of the Constitution of the United States.* Washington, 1894–1903.

Webster, Noah. *New York Directory of 1786.* New York, 1906.

SECONDARY MATERIALS

New York State

Alexander, DeAlva Stanwood. *A Political History of the State of New York.* New York, 1906.

Barck, O. T. *New York City During the War for Independence.* New York, 1931.

Bayles, Richard Mather. *Historical and Descriptive Sketches of Suffolk County.* Port Feggerson, N.Y., 1874.

Becker, Carl Lotus. *The History of Political Parties in the Province of New York, 1760–1776.* Madison, Wis., 1909.

——. "Nominations in Colonial New York," *American Historical Review,* VI (1901), 260–275.

Boyd, Julian P. "Attempt to Form New States in New York and Pennsylvania in 1786–1796," New York State Historical Association *Quarterly Journal,* XXIX (1931), 257–270.

Clason, A. W. "Convention of New York, 1788," *Magazine of American History*, XVI (1880), 148–158.
Clearwater, Alphonso T., ed. *The History of Ulster County, New York.* Kingston, N.Y., 1907.
Cochran, Thomas. *New York in the Confederation: An Economic Study*. Philadelphia, 1932.
DeLancey, Edward Floyd. *Origin and History of Manors in the Province of New York and in the County of Westchester.* New York, 1886.
Dunlap, William. *A History of the New Netherlands, Province of New York and the State of New York.* New York, 1840.
Ellis, David. " 'Upstate Hicks' versus 'City Slickers' " *The New-York Historical Society Quarterly*, XLIII (1959), 203–219.
Ellis, David M., James A. Frost, Harold C. Syrett, and Henry J. Carman. *A Short History of New York State.* Ithaca, N.Y., 1957.
[Ellis, Franklin]. *History of Columbia County, New York.* Philadelphia, 1878.
Flick, Alexander C., ed. *History of the State of New York.* New York, 1933–1937.
——. *Loyalism in New York During the American Revolution.* New York, 1901.
Flick, Hugh M. "The Council of Appointment in New York State, The First Attempt to Regulate Political Patronage: 1777–1822," *New York History*, XV (1934), 253–280.
Fox, Dixon Ryan. *The Decline of Aristocracy in the Politics of New York.* New York, 1919.
——. *Yankees and Yorkers.* New York, 1940.
Gitterman, J. M. "The Council of Appointment in New York," *Political Science Quarterly*, VII (1892), 80–115.
Hamilton, Milton W. *The Country Printer, New York State, 1785–1830.* New York, 1936.
Hammond, Jabez Delano. *History of Political Parties in the State of New York.* Cooperstown, N.Y., 1846.
Hasbrouck, Frank. *The History of Dutchess County, New York.* Poughkeepsie, N.Y., 1909.
Heslin, James J. "Amendments Are Necessary," *The New-York Historical Society Quarterly*, XLIII (1959), 425–439.
Higgins, Ruth L. *Expansion in New York.* Columbus, 1931.

Howell, [George R.] and [T. J.] Tenney. *History of the County of Albany, New York, 1609–1886.* New York, 1886.

Hurd, Duane H. *History of Clinton and Franklin Counties, New York.* Philadelphia, 1880.

Jenkins, John Stillwell. *History of Political Parties in the State of New York.* Auburn, N.Y., 1846.

Johnston, Henry P. "New York After the Revolution, 1783–1789," *Magazine of American History*, XXIX (1893), 305–331.

Jones, Thomas. *A History of New York During the Revolutionary War.* New York, 1879.

Klein, Milton M. "Democracy and Politics in Colonial New York," *New York History*, XL (1959), 221–246.

Lamb, Martha J., and Mrs. Burton Harrison. *History of the City of New York.* New York, 1877.

Lossing, Benson John. *Empire State, a Compendious History of the Commonwealth of New York.* Hartford, Conn., 1888.

Lynd, Staughton. *Anti-Federalism in Dutchess County, New York.* Chicago, 1962.

——. "The Mechanics in New York Politics, 1774–1788," *Labor History*, V (1964), 225–246.

——. "Who Should Rule at Home? Dutchess County, New York, in the American Revolution," *William and Mary Quarterly*, third series, XVIII (1961), 330–359.

Macaulay, James. *The Natural, Statistical, and Civil History of the State of New York.* New York, 1829.

McCoy, Samuel D. "The Port of New York (1783–1789): Lost Island of Sailing Ships," *New York History*, XVII (1936), 379–390.

MacCracken, Henry Noble. *Old Dutchess Forever! The Story of an American County.* New York, 1956.

Mark, Irving. *Agrarian Conflicts in Colonial New York, 1711–1775.* New York, 1940.

Mau, Clayton C. *The Development of Central and Western New York.* Dansville, N.Y., 1958.

Miner, Clarence E. *The Ratification of the Federal Constitution by the State of New York.* New York, 1921.

Onderdonk, Henry. *Queens County in Olden Times.* Jamaica, N.Y., 1865.

Petrie, Robert C. "Sectionalism and Self-Interest in the Struggle for the Constitution in New York State." Unpublished M.A. thesis, Columbia University, 1954.

Platt, Edmund. *The Eagle's History of Poughkeepsie.* Poughkeepsie, N.Y., 1905.

Pomerantz, Sidney I. *New York: An American City.* New York, 1938.

Reynolds, Helen W. "The Court House of Dutchess County," *Dutchess County Historical Society Year Book for 1938*, pp. 74–98.

Ruttenber, E. M., and L. H. Clark. *History of Orange County, New York.* Philadelphia, 1881.

Scharf, John Thomas. *History of Westchester County, New York.* Philadelphia, 1886.

Simpson, Sarah H. J. "The Federal Procession in the City of New York," New-York Historical Society *Bulletin*, IX (1925), 39–56.

Smith, Thomas E. V. *The City of New York in the Year of Washington's Inauguration, 1789.* New York, 1889.

Spaulding, E. Wilder. *New York in the Critical Period, 1783–1789.* New York, 1932.

Spencer, Charles W. "Sectional Aspects of New York Provincial Politics," *Political Science Quarterly*, XXX (1915), 397–424.

Stevens, J. A. "New York and the Federal Constitution," *Magazine of American History*, II (1878), 404–406.

Street, Alfred B. *The Council of Revision of the State of New York.* Albany, 1859.

Sylvester, N. B. *History of Ulster County, New York.* Philadelphia, 1880.

Varga, Nicholas. "Election Procedures and Practices in Colonial New York," *New York History*, XLI (1960), 249–277.

Wilson, James Grant, ed. *The Memorial History of the City of New York.* New York, 1892–1893.

Yoshpe, Harry. "The DeLancey Estate: Did the Revolution Democratize Landholding in New York?," *New York History*, XLII (1936), 167.

——. *The Disposition of Loyalist Estates in the Southern District of the State of New York.* New York, 1939.

Young, Alfred Fabian. "The Democratic-Republican Movement in

New York State, 1788–1797." Unpublished Ph.D. dissertation, Northwestern University, 1958.

Zeichner, Oscar. "The Loyalist Problem in New York after the Revolution," *New York History*, XXI (1940), 284–302.

The Constitution

Bancroft, George. *History of the Formation of the Constitution of the United States of America.* New York, 1882.

Beard, Charles A. *An Economic Interpretation of the Constitution of the United States.* New York, 1913.

Benson, Lee. *Turner and Beard: American Historical Writing Reconsidered.* Glencoe, Ill., 1960.

Bishop, Hillman Metcalf. "Why Rhode Island Opposed the Federal Constitution," *Rhode Island History*, VIII (1949), 1–10, 33–44, 85–95, 115–126.

Brown, Robert E. *Charles Beard and the Constitution; a Critical Analysis of "An Economic Interpretation of the Constitution."* Princeton, 1956.

——. *Reinterpretation of the Formation of the American Constitution.* Boston, 1963.

Bruchey, Stuart, and E. James Ferguson. "The Forces behind the Constitution: A Critical Review of the Framework of E. James Ferguson's *The Power of the Purse*," *William and Mary Quarterly*, third series, XIX (1962), 429–438.

Crowl, Philip A. "Anti-Federalism in Maryland, 1787–1788," *William and Mary Quarterly*, third series, IV (1947), 446–469.

Curtis, George Ticknor. *Constitutional History of the United States from their Declaration of Independence to the Close of their Civil War.* New York, 1889–1896.

Farrand, Max. *The Fathers of the Constitution.* New Haven, Conn., 1921.

——. "The Federal Constitution and the Defects of the Confederation," *American Political Science Review*, II (1908), 532–544.

——. *The Framing of the Constitution of the United States.* New Haven, Conn., 1913.

Ford, Paul Leicester. *Bibliography and Reference List of the History and Literature Relating to the Adoption of the Constitution of the United States, 1787–1788.* Brooklyn, 1888.

Grigsby, Hugh Blair. *History of the Virginia Federal Convention.* Richmond, 1890–1891.

Harding, Samuel Bannister. *The Contest over Ratification of the Federal Constitution in the State of Massachusetts.* New York, 1896.

Hockett, Homer C. *Constitutional History of the United States.* New York, 1939.

Kelly, A. H., and W. A. Harbison. *The American Constitution, Its Origins and Development,* rev. ed. New York, 1948.

Kenyon, Cecilia M. "Men of Little Faith; the Anti-Federalists on the Nature of Representative Government," *William and Mary Quarterly,* third series, XII (1955), 3–43.

King, John Alsop. *Framing of the Federal Constitution and the Causes Leading Thereto.* New York, 1888.

Libby, Orin Grant. *Geographical Distribution of the Vote of the Thirteen States on the Federal Constitution, 1787–1788.* Madison, Wis., 1897.

McDonald, Forrest. "The Anti-Federalists, 1781–1789," *Wisconsin Magazine of History,* XLVI (1963), 206–214.

——. *We the People: The Economic Origins of the Constitution.* Chicago, 1958.

McMaster, John Bach, and Frederick D. Stone, eds. *Pennsylvania and the Federal Constitution, 1787–1788.* Lancaster, Pa., 1888.

Main, Jackson Turner. *The Antifederalists, Critics of the Constitution, 1781–1788.* Chapel Hill, N.C., 1961.

—— and Forrest McDonald. "Charles A. Beard and the Constitution: A Critical Review of Forrest McDonald's *We the People,*" *William and Mary Quarterly,* third series, XVII (1960), 86–110.

Nettels, Curtis P. "The American Merchant and the Constitution," Colonial Society of Massachusetts *Publications,* XXXIX (1943), 26–37.

Schechter, Frank I. "The Early History of the Tradition of the Constitution," *The American Political Science Review,* IX (1915), 707–734.

Schuyler, Robert Livingston. *The Constitution of the United States.* New York, 1923.

Thomas, Robert E. "The Virginia Convention of 1788: A Criticism of Beard's *An Economic Interpretation of the Constitution,*" *Journal of Southern History,* XIX (1953), 63–72.

Thorpe, Francis N. *Constitutional History of the United States.* Chicago, 1901.

Trenholme, Louise Irby. *The Ratification of the Federal Constitution in North Carolina.* New York, 1932.

Van Doren, Carl. *The Great Rehearsal.* New York, 1948.

Walker, Joseph B. *A History of the New Hampshire Convention.* Boston, 1888.

Warren, Charles. *The Making of the Constitution.* Boston, 1928.

Biography

Alexander, Edward P. *A Revolutionary Conservative: James Duane of New York.* New York, 1938.

Beveridge, Albert J. *The Life of John Marshall.* Boston, 1919.

Brant, Irving. *James Madison: The Nationalist, 1780–1787.* Indianapolis, 1948.

——. *James Madison: Father of the Constitution, 1787–1800.* Indianapolis, 1950.

Caldwell, Lynton K. "George Clinton—Democratic Administrator," *New York History,* XLIX (1951), 134–156.

Conway, Moncure Daniel. *Omitted Chapters of History Disclosed in the Life and Papers of Edmund Randolph.* New York, 1889.

Dangerfield, George. *Chancellor Robert R. Livingston of New York, 1746–1813.* New York, 1960.

Davis, Matthew L. *Memoirs of Aaron Burr with Miscellaneous Selections from his Correspondence.* New York, 1836.

Fitch, Charles E. *Encyclopaedia of Biography of New York.* New York, 1916–1925.

Hamilton, John C. *Life of Alexander Hamilton.* New York, 1834.

Hasbrouck, Gilbert D. B. "Governor George Clinton," New York State Historical Association *Quarterly Journal,* XVIII (1920), 143–164.

Horton, John Theodore. *James Kent: A Study in Conservatism, 1763–1847.* New York, 1939.

Jay, William. *Life of John Jay.* New York, 1833.

Jenkins, John Stilwell. *Lives of the Governors of the State of New York.* Auburn, N.Y., 1851.

Jenks, Major B. "George Clinton and New York State Politics, 1775–1810." Unpublished Ph.D. dissertation, Cornell University, 1936.

Johnson, Allen, and Dumas Malone, eds. *Dictionary of American Biography*. New York, 1928–1937.
Koch, Adrienne. "Hamilton and Power," *The Yale Review*, XLVII (1958), 537–555.
Lodge, Henry Cabot. *Alexander Hamilton.* Boston, 1882.
Lossing, B. J. *Life and Times of Philip Schuyler.* New York, 1873.
Miller, John C. *Alexander Hamilton: Portrait in Paradox.* New York, 1959.
Mitchell, Broadus. *Alexander Hamilton.* Vol. I, *Alexander Hamilton: Youth to Maturity, 1755–1788.* New York, 1957. Vol. II, *Alexander Hamilton: The National Adventure, 1788–1804.* New York, 1962.
Monaghan, Frank. *John Jay.* New York, 1935.
Parton, James. *The Life and Times of Aaron Burr*, enlarged ed. Boston, 1881.
Pellew, George. *John Jay.* Boston, 1898.
Poucher, J. W. "Melanchthon Smith," *Dutchess County Historical Society Year Book for 1925*, pp. 39–48.
Pound, Arthur. *Native Stock: The Rise of the American Native Spirit Seen in Six Lives.* New York, 1931.
Rives, W. C. *History of the Life and Times of James Madison.* Boston, 1866.
Rossiter, Clinton. *Alexander Hamilton and the American Constitution.* New York, 1964.
Rowland, Kate Mason. *The Life of George Mason.* New York, 1892.
Schachner, Nathan. *Alexander Hamilton.* New York, 1946.
Schuyler, George W. *Colonial New York: Philip Schuyler and His Family.* New York, 1885.
Spaulding, E. Wilder. *His Excellency George Clinton, Critic of the Constitution.* New York, 1938.
Sumner, William Graham. *Life of Hamilton.* New York, 1890.
Swiggett, Howard. *The Extraordinary Mr. Morris.* Garden City, N.Y., 1952.
Tuckerman, Baynard. *Life of General Philip Schuyler, 1733–1804.* New York, 1903.
United States Congress. *Biographical Directory of the American Congress, 1774–1927.* Washington, 1928.

Ver Steeg, Clarence. *Robert Morris, Revolutionary Financier.* Philadelphia, 1954.

Other Secondary Material

Adair, Douglass. "The Authorship of the Disputed Federalist Papers," *William and Mary Quarterly*, third series, I (1944), 97–122, 235–264.

——. "The Federalist Papers: A Review Article," *William and Mary Quarterly*, third series, XXII (1965), 131–139.

Aly, Bower. *The Rhetoric of Alexander Hamilton.* New York, 1941.

Ames, Herman V. "Proposed Amendments to the Constitution," American Historical Association *Report* for 1896, II.

Bailyn, Bernard. "Political Experience and Enlightenment Ideas in Eighteenth-Century America," *American Historical Review*, LXVII (1962), 339–351.

Bell, Whitfield J., Jr. "The Federal Processions of 1788," *The New-York Historical Society Quarterly*, CLVI (1962), 5–39.

Bemis, Samuel Flagg. *Jay's Treaty: A Study in Commerce and Diplomacy*, rev. ed. New Haven, Conn., 1962.

Binkley, Wilfred E. *American Political Parties: Their Natural History.* New York, 1943.

Bolles, Albert Sidney. *Financial History of the United States from 1774 to 1789.* New York, 1896.

Bourne, Edward Gaylord. "The Authorship of the Federalist," *Essays in Historical Criticism.* New York, 1901.

Brigham, Clarence S. *History and Bibliography of American Newspapers, 1690–1820.* Worcester, Mass., 1947.

Bruchey, Stuart. "Success and Failure Factors—American Merchants in Foreign Trade in the Eighteenth and Early Nineteenth Centuries," *The Business History Review*, XXXII (1958), 272–292.

Bullock, Charles J. *Finances of the United States, 1775–1789.* Madison, Wis., 1895.

Burnett, Edmund C. *The Continental Congress.* New York, 1941.

Burt., A. L. *The United States, Great Britain, and British North America from the Revolution to the Etablishment of Peace after the War of 1812.* New Haven, Conn., 1940.

Callender, Guy Stevens. *Selections from the Economic History of the United States, 1765–1860.* Boston, 1909.

Chambers, William Nisbet. *Political Parties in a New Nation.* New York, 1963.

Channing, Edward. *A History of the United States.* New York, 1905–1925.

Charles, Joseph. *The Origins of the American Party System.* Williamsburg, Va., 1956.

Cooke, Jacob E. "Alexander Hamilton's Authorship of the 'Caesar' Letters," *William and Mary Quarterly*, third series, XVII (1960), 78–85.

Corbin, John. *Two Frontiers of Freedom.* New York, 1940.

Corwin, Edward S. "The Progress of Constitutional Theory between the Declaration of Independence and the Meeting of the Philadelphia Convention," *American Historical Review*, XXX (1925), 511–536.

Crane, Elaine F. "Publius in the Provinces: Where Was *The Federalist* Reprinted Outside New York City?", *William and Mary Quarterly*, third series, XXI (1964), 589–592.

Dewey, Davis Rich. *Financial History of the United States*, 8th ed. New York, 1922.

Dietze, Gottfried. *The Federalist.* Baltimore, 1960.

Dodd, W. F. "The First State Constitutional Conventions, 1776–1783," *American Political Science Review*, II (1908), 545–561.

Dorfman, Joseph. *The Economic Mind in American Civilization, 1606–1865.* New York, 1946.

Douglass, Elisha P. *Rebels and Democrats; the Struggle for Equal Political Rights and Majority Rule during the American Revolution.* Chapel Hill, N.C., 1955.

East, Robert A. *Business Enterprise in the American Revolutionary Era.* New York, 1938.

Elkins, Stanley, and Eric McKitrick. *The Founding Fathers; Young Men of the Revolution.* (Service Center for Teachers of History, Publication Number 44.) Washington, 1962.

Ferguson, E. James. *The Power of the Purse.* Chapel Hill, N.C., 1961.

Fiske, John. *The Critical Period of American History.* Boston, 1888.

Ford, Paul Leicester, and Edward Gaylord Bourne. *The Authorship of the Federalist.* (Reprinted from *American Historical Review,* II [1897].) Brooklyn, 1897.

Garver, Frank H. "The Transition from the Continental Congress to the Congress of the Confederation," *Pacific Historical Review,* I (1932), 221–234.

Giesecke, Albert A. *American Commercial Legislation before 1789.* Philadelphia, 1910.

Greene, Evarts B. *The Revolutionary Generation, 1763–1790.* New York, 1943.

—— and Virginia Huntington. *American Population before the Federal Census of 1790.* New York, 1932.

Hamilton, John C. *History of the Republic of the United States as Traced in the Writings of Alexander Hamilton and his Contemporaries.* Philadelphia, 1864.

Hammond, Bray. *Banks and Politics in America, from the Revolution to the Civil War.* Princeton, 1957.

Harmon, George D. "The Proposed Amendments to the Articles of Confederation," *South Atlantic Quarterly,* XXIV (1925), 298–315, 411–436.

Hartz, Louis. *The Liberal Tradition in America.* New York, 1955.

Hatch, Louis C. *The Administration of the American Revolutionary Army.* New York, 1904.

Holmes, Oliver W. "Shall Stagecoaches Carry the Mail?—A Debate of the Confederation Period," *William and Mary Quarterly,* third series, XX (1963), 555–573.

Hudson, Frederick. *History of Journalism in the United States from 1690 to 1872.* New York, 1873.

Jameson, J. Franklin. *The American Revolution Considered as a Social Movement.* Princeton, 1926.

Jameson, John Alexander. *A Treatise on Constitutional Conventions,* 4th ed. Chicago, 1887.

Jensen, Merrill. *The Articles of Confederation; an Interpretation of the Socio-Constitutional History of the American Revolution, 1774–1781.* Madison, Wis., 1940.

——. "The Idea of a National Government During the American Revolution," *Political Science Quarterly,* LVIII (1943), 356–379.

Jensen, Merrill. *The New Nation: A History of the United States During the Confederation, 1781–1789.* New York, 1950.
Johnson, Allen. *Union and Democracy.* New York, 1915.
Kenyon, Cecelia M. "Republicanism and Radicalism in the American Revolution," *William and Mary Quarterly*, third series, XIX (1962), 153–182.
Key, V. O., Jr. *Politics, Parties, and Pressure Groups*, 4th ed. New York, 1958.
Labaree, Leonard Woods. *Conservatism in Early American History.* New York, 1948.
Lee, J. M. *History of American Journalism.* Boston, 1917.
Lobinger, Charles Sumner. *The People's Law.* New York, 1909.
Luetscher, George D. *Early Political Machinery in the United States.* Philadelphia, 1903.
McBain, Howard Lee. *De Witt Clinton and the Origin of the Spoils System in New York.* New York, 1907.
McCormick, Richard P. *Experiment in Independence: New Jersey in the Critical Period, 1781–1789.* New Brunswick, N.J.. 1950.
McKinley, Albert Edward. *The Suffrage Franchise in the Thirteen English Colonies in America.* Philadelphia, 1902.
McLaughlin, Andrew Cunningham. *The Confederation and the Constitution.* New York, 1905.
McMaster, John Bach. *A History of the People of the United States from the Revolution to the Civil War.* New York, 1885.
Mason, Alpheus T. "The Federalist—A Split Personality," *American Historical Review*, LVII (1952), 625–643.
Miner, Louie M.. *Our Rude Forefathers: American Political Verse, 1783–1788.* Cedar Rapids, Iowa, 1937.
Morgan, Edmund S. *The Birth of the Republic, 1763—1789.* Chicago, 1956.
Morris, Richard B. "The Confederation Period and the American Historian," *William and Mary Quarterly*, third series, XIII (1956), 139–156.
Mosteller, Frederick, and David L. Wallace. *Inference and Disputed Authorship: The Federalist.* Reading, Mass., 1964.
Mott, Frank Luther. *American Journalism.* New York, 1942.
Nettels, Curtis P. *The Emergence of a National Economy, 1775–1815.* New York, 1961.

Nevins, Allan. *The American States During and After the Revolution, 1775–1789.* New York, 1924.

Parrington, Vernon Louis. *Main Currents in American Thought.* New York, 1927.

Payne, George Henry. *History of Journalism in the United States.* New York, 1920.

Ramsay, David. *History of the American Revolution.* London, 1791.

Rodick, Burleigh Cushing. *American Constitutional Custom.* New York, 1953.

Rowland, Kate Mason. "The Mount Vernon Convention," *Pennsylvania Magazine of History and Biography,* XI (1887), 410–425.

Rutland, Robert Allen. *The Birth of the Bill of Rights, 1776–1791.* Chapel Hill, N.C., 1955.

Scanlon, James B. "The Federalist and Human Nature," *Review of Politics,* XXI (1959), 657–677.

Schouler, James. *History of the United States under the Constitution.* Washington, 1880.

Smith, Edward P. "The Movement for a Second Convention in 1788," in J. Franklin Jameson, ed., *Essays in the Constitutional History of the United States in the Formative Period, 1775–1789.* Boston, 1889.

Stephens, Frank Fletcher. *The Transitional Period, 1788–1789.* Columbia, Mo., 1909.

Stevens, Wayne Edson. *The Northwest Fur Trade, 1763–1800.* Urbana, Ill., 1928.

Swindler, William F. "The Letters of Publius," *American Heritage,* XII (1961), 4–7, 92–97.

Van Tyne, Claude H. *Loyalists in the American Revolution.* New York, 1902.

——. "Sovereignty in the American Revolution," *American Historical Review,* XII (1907), 529–545.

Warren, Charles. "New Light on the History of the Federal Judiciary Act of 1789," *Harvard Law Review,* XXXVII (1923), 49–132.

Warren, Joseph Parker. "The Confederation and Shays' Rebellion," *American Historical Review,* XI (1905), 42–67.

Warren, Mercy. *History of the Rise, Progress and Termination of the American Revolution.* Boston, 1805.

Williams, William Appleman. "The Age of Mercantilism: an Interpretation of the American Political Economy, 1763 to 1828," *William and Mary Quarterly*, third series, XV (1958), 419–457.

Williamson, Chilton. *American Suffrage from Property to Democracy*. Princeton, 1960.

——. *Vermont in Quandry: 1763–1825*. Montpelier, Vt., 1949.

Wright, Benjamin Fletcher. *Consensus and Continuity, 1776–1787*. Boston, 1958.

——. "*The Federalist* on the Nature of Political Man," *Ethics*, LIX (1949), no. 2, pt. 2.

Wright, Esmond. *Fabric of Freedom.* New York, 1961.

Index

Recent books published for the American Historical Association from the income of the Albert J. Beveridge Memorial Fund

AN AGRICULTURAL HISTORY OF THE GENESEE VALLEY, 1790–1860. *By Neil A. McNall.*

STEAM POWER ON THE AMERICAN FARM. *By Reynold M. Wik.*

ERA OF THE OATH: NORTHERN LOYALTY TESTS DURING THE CIVIL WAR AND RECONSTRUCTION. *By Harold M. Hyman.*

HISTORY OF MARSHALL FIELD & CO. *By Robert W. Twyman.*

ROBERT MORRIS: REVOLUTIONARY FINANCIER. *By Clarence L. Ver Steeg.*

THE FIRST RAPPROCHEMENT: ENGLAND AND THE UNITED STATES, 1795–1805. *By Bradford Perkins.*

MIDDLE-CLASS DEMOCRACY AND THE REVOLUTION IN MASSACHUSETTS, 1691–1780. *By Robert E. Brown.*

THE DEVELOPMENT OF AMERICAN PETROLEUM PIPELINES: A STUDY IN PRIVATE ENTERPRISE AND PUBLIC POLICY, 1862–1906. *By Arthur Menzies Johnson.*

COLONISTS FROM SCOTLAND: EMIGRATION TO NORTH AMERICA, 1707–1783. *By Ian Charles Cargill Graham.*

PROFESSORS & PUBLIC ETHICS: STUDIES OF NORTHERN MORAL PHILOSOPHERS BEFORE THE CIVIL WAR. *By Wilson Smith.*

THE AXIS ALLIANCE AND JAPANESE-AMERICAN RELATIONS, 1941. *By Paul W. Schroeder.*

A FRONTIER STATE AT WAR: KANSAS, 1861–1865. *By Albert Castel.*

BRITISH INVESTMENTS AND THE AMERICAN MINING FRONTIER, 1860–1901. *By Clark C. Spence.*

RAILS, MINES, AND PROGRESS: SEVEN AMERICAN PROMOTERS IN MEXICO, 1867–1911. *By David M. Pletcher.*

LaGuardia in Congress. *By Howard Zinn*

Tomorrow a New World: The New Deal Community Program. *By Paul K. Conkin.*

Conservative Crisis and the Rule of Law: Attitudes of Bar and Bench, 1887–1895. *By Arnold M. Paul.*

The United States and Pancho Villa: A Study in Unconventional Diplomacy. *By Clarence C. Clendenen.*

The Enterprise of a Free People: Aspects of Economic Development in New York State during the Canal Period, 1792–1838. *By Nathan Miller.*

The United States and the First Hague Peace Conference. *By Calvin DeArmond Davis.*

The New Empire: An Interpretation of American expansion, 1860–1898. *By Walter LaFeber.*

The Eleventh Pillar: New York State and the Federal Constitution. *By Linda Grant De Pauw.*